With Badges & Bullets

With Badges & Bullets

Lawmen & Outlaws in the Old West

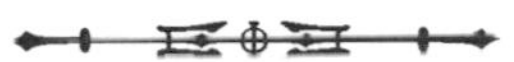

Edited by
Richard W. Etulain &
Glenda Riley

Fulcrum Publishing
Golden, Colorado

Library of Congress Cataloging-in-Publication Data
With badges & bullets : lawmen & outlaws in the Old West / edited by Richard W. Etulain and Glenda Riley.
p. cm. — (Notable westerners)
Includes bibliographical references and index.
ISBN 1-55591-433-0
1. Outlaws—West (U.S.) Biography 2. Peace officers—West (U.S.) Biography. 3. Frontier and pioneer life—West (U.S.) 4. West (U.S.) Biography. 5. West (U.S.)—History—1860–1890. I. Etulain, Richard W. II. Riley, Glenda, 1938– . III. Title: With badges and bullets. IV. Series.
F594.W76 1999
364.1'092'278—dc21
[B] 99-16315
CIP

Printed in the United States of America

0 9 8 7 6 5

Editor: Daniel Forrest-Bank
Designer: Bill Spahr
Cover art: Painting copyright © Thom Ross, *The Men from the Babocomari,* showing the McLaury brothers, the Clantons, and Billy Claiborne walking across Allen Street on their way to meet the Earp brothers and Doc Holliday at the OK Corral.

Fulcrum Publishing
4690 Table Mountain Drive, Suite 100
Golden, Colorado 80403
(800) 992-2908 • (303) 277-1623
www.fulcrumbooks.com

CONTENTS

SERIES FOREWORD

Along with the editors of *By Grit & Grace* and *With Badges & Bullets,* Fulcrum Publishing is proud to be the publisher of the first two volumes in the Notable Westerners series. The volumes in this series explore the real stories behind the personalities and events that continue to shape our national character.

The American West—land of myth, epitome of the independent American spirit. When we think of the men and women who shaped the West, we tend to think in terms of caricatures, of larger-than-life heroes and heroines. Notable men and women have always loomed large on the open and wide landscapes of the American West. From the earliest Native American leaders to more recent westerners, these influential people have attracted the attention of travelers, historians, and writers. Often, such visitors focus on how these heroes and heroines of the region were important in shaping and reshaping images of the West.

By Grit & Grace and *With Badges & Bullets,* as well as all forthcoming books in the Notable Westerners series, explore the personalities and influences of such outstanding western characters. Editors Richard W. Etulain and Glenda Riley draw on their long experience in western history and their wide associations with western historians of varied racial, ethnic, and social backgrounds, and gender. To these volumes, contributors bring expertise in their fields, knowledge of significant individuals, and lucid writing styles.

The result is a variety of essays providing insight into the movers and shakers of a unique region of the United States. The American West not only helped shape the American national character, but provides a continuing source of fascination for Americans and non-Americans alike.

Acknowledgments

The editors would like to thank several people and organizations for their help and support in preparing this book. First of all, we are much indebted to the contributors for taking the time from their full schedules to prepare essays for this collection. Their professionalism and insightful analyses are particularly appreciated.

Richard W. Etulain would like to thank the Center for the American West and the Research Allocations Fund at the University of New Mexico for supporting his research. He is also indebted to the University of New Mexico for a sabbatical leave, during which his essay and much of the work on this book were completed. He wishes to thank Frederick Nolan and Kathleen Chamberlain for reading and commenting on his essay on Billy the Kid. Jen Clark, Angela Thomas, Cindy Tyson, and David Key also helped in the preparation of this book.

Glenda Riley would like to express gratitude to Ball State University, especially to the Alexander M. Bracken Fund; to the Department of History at Ball State; and to research assistant Deborah L. Rogers.

In addition, the editors wish to indicate their appreciation to Bob Baron, Sam Scinta, and Daniel Forrest-Bank of Fulcrum Publishing for their encouragement and aid.

Richard W. Etulain
University of New Mexico

Glenda Riley
Ball State University

INTRODUCTION

RICHARD W. ETULAIN

Remember the dramatic conflicts in well-known novels like *The Virginian, Riders of the Purple Sage,* and *Shane*? Recall the clashes in familiar western movies like *Stagecoach, The Ox-Bow Incident,* and *The Unforgiven*? Who are the lawmen and who are the outlaws? Which characters live within the law, which live outside the law? Was there, in fact, always a clear distinction between officers of the law and lawbreakers in the Old West?

With Badges & Bullets focuses on these intriguing questions that have perplexed historians and biographers alike for decades. For example, in his sparkling new biography *Wyatt Earp: The Life Behind the Legend* (1997), journalist Casey Tefertiller writes that Wyatt Earp "became a vigilante, a marshal, and an outlaw all at the same time." Convinced that a faulty legal system no longer protected law-abiding citizens in Tombstone, Arizona Territory, Wyatt Earp took the law into his own hands, moving outside legal boundaries to bring what he considered order and justice to a chaotic situation.

The dilemmas Earp faced on the Arizona frontier in the 1880s were endemic to many frontier areas in the second half of the nineteenth century. Frank Richard Prassel notes this trend in his book *The Great American Outlaw: A Legacy of Fact and Fiction* (1993) when he states that stories of American outlaws span the "artificial boundaries and distinctions of race, education, and wealth." This being the case, when historians, biographers, and other students of American society and culture examine the so-called "law and order" of the frontier West, they continually run headlong into a troubling question: Where was the dividing line between lawmen and outlaws in this nascent region? Put another way, was the boundary between the roles of law officer and gunslinger so permeable as to become meaningless?

This collection of ten essays addresses these important, controversial questions by focusing on a clutch of significant western figures who epitomize frontier law and disorder. As the stories in this book make clear, some figures, such as Wyatt Earp, Wild Bill Hickok, Patrick Floyd Garrett, and Tom Horn, spent several years of their adult lives trying to uphold order—all at one time wore the badges of lawmen. Others, such as Doc Holliday, Belle Starr, and Pearl Hart, are more shadowy figures, occasionally breaking but usually living within the law. Still others, such as Joaquín Murrieta, Billy the Kid, and Jesse James, were clearly outlaws, devoting much of their lives to robbing, stealing, rustling, holding up banks and railroads, and sometimes even murdering opponents. Yet in most of the lives presented here, the line between legal and illegal actions was hazy, and frequently shifted.

The significance of these lively figures merits comment. Clearly, the emergence of lawman–outlaw characters in the nineteenth century reveals much about the continual waves of change that washed over the frontier West in the three generations following the 1820s. Pioneers moving down the major immigrant trails, the incorporation of large new spaces and peoples after the U.S.–Mexican War, the dramatic influx of newcomers to the West after the gold rush and the Civil War, and the later mushrooming hordes coming by railroad across the Mississippi River—these factors virtually transformed the West. As a result of these large and rapid sociocultural alterations, legal systems and community organizations were not solidly in place before another wave of change disrupted the earlier brave beginnings of permanence.

Furthermore, this constant barrage of change resulted in instability for many frontier places, such as mining camps, cowtowns, and other jerry-built settlements, in the latter half of the nineteenth century. California gold rush hamlets, mining camps like Deadwood and Tombstone, and cowtowns such as Wichita, Abilene, and Dodge City, as well as agricultural boomtowns and small commercial settlements such as Lincoln, New Mexico, exemplify these chaotic and violence-prone places between the 1850s and the 1880s. Such sites were especially numerous in the band of states and territories stretching from Montana and the Dakotas in the North to Texas, New Mexico, and Arizona in the South.

Businesspeople and other investors continually sought the services of strong and even violent men to keep the lid of disorder from flying off in these precarious frontier communities in the interior West. Thus, lawmen were sometimes well known for gunplay, fearlessness, and a willingness to take on any lawless opposition. Wyatt Earp, Wild Bill Hickok, Pat Garrett, and Tom Horn were notable among them. Unfortunately, under strong pressures of threatening circumstances or in heated conflicts arising from their own sense of right, these lawmen often transgressed the law to enforce order. Doc Holliday, for example, found little problem following the Earps when they crossed over the line to illegal actions. In fact, he sometimes urged them in that dangerous direction.

Other rebels believed that frontier legal guidelines were unjust and too often catered to the rich and powerful, so they became "social bandits," resisters to what they considered unfair systems. In gold rush California, for example, Joaquín Murrieta viewed these new legal organizations as prejudiced against foreigners, toward anyone not considered American. He fought back with what he deemed justified violence. Billy the Kid also rebelled against members of the notorious Santa Fe Ring and the Murphy-Dolan commercial "House" in Lincoln, New Mexico, whom he considered murderers of his friends, Englishman John Tunstall and lawyer Alex McSween. And when cattle baron John Chisum refused to pay the Kid wages he thought rightfully his, Billy rustled cattle and stole horses to compete with these powerful commercial and political forces. Meanwhile, Jesse James argued that banks and railroads mercilessly extracted the incomes of "honest" laborers like the James family. He also pointed to the Pinkerton Detective Agency as equally ruthless in its harassments and in gaining its information. Jesse and his gang violently combated the forces they judged as selfish and evil.

The situations of Belle Starr and Pearl Hart differed from those of most male outlaws as well as from one another. Belle frequently chose unwisely in her male companions, men who often resorted to unlawful deeds. Yet she was sometimes also a willing participant in these dangerous forays, occasionally leading rather than following. Pearl Hart also made poor choices. The men with whom she consorted became involved in wrongful actions, but in several events she too was as much leader as follower. Then, after 1899, when she and Joe Boot held up a stagecoach, Hart became widely known as a lady bandit, and she soon came to enjoy the notoriety surrounding her prison stay.

The ten essays in this volume serve to meet two major goals, both of which add to our understanding of the Old West. They deal with the gray areas between lawmen and outlaws and in doing so provide capsule biographies of interesting and notable westerners.

In the opening essay, a provocative and smoothly written story of Wyatt Earp, Gary Roberts deals clearly with the contradictions that surrounded Earp in the late nineteenth century and that still swirl around his life and legends. As Roberts points out, Earp epitomized the modernizing forces that swept through the United States and the American West during the Gilded Age. In reflecting his times, Roberts's Earp illustrates the contradictory pressures of order and disorder during the last quarter of the nineteenth century. In short, Roberts argues, Wyatt Earp "lived his life according to a code that seemed right to him, if not to those who judged him later."

Parallel contradictions mark the life of James Butler "Wild Bill" Hickok. As Joseph Rosa, the leading specialist on Wild Bill, notes, Hickok "remains enigmatic and controversial." Was he a valiant peace officer, a notorious gunfighter, or both? Some historians dismiss Hickok as a mere "mankiller," and others possibly place too much emphasis on Hickok as a "civilizer." But Rosa asserts that once these hasty generalizations are stripped away, we are left with "a man whose strength of character influenced others, and who would put himself out on a limb if he thought the cause was just."

Kathleen Chamberlain finds less to praise in her well-rounded essay on the career of lawman Patrick Floyd Garrett. Known primarily as "the man who shot Billy the Kid," Garrett ironically failed to excite the attention and admiration that his victim gained in the twentieth century. Much of the problem, Chamberlain maintains, was Garrett's personality and unwise actions. Grumpy and increasingly quarrelsome, Garrett failed in politics and several business ventures. He seemed unable to find himself, and his own life ended in a controversial violent death.

The abbreviated life of Tom Horn likewise exhibited a change in fortune. First, as a scout, packer, and Indian tracker, Horn gained a large reputation as a hardworking, resilient leader. But in his later career as a livestock detective and hired killer, as Larry D. Ball clearly shows, Horn hardened into a remorseless tracker of opponents. In these later activities he seemed convinced that his actions, though often outside the law, were justifiable in defending ranchers against rustlers. Horn's increasingly violent life also ended in controversy when he was declared guilty of shooting fourteen-year-old Willie Nickell and was hanged for the crime.

The illustrious Doc Holliday, as Gary Topping indicates in his lively essay, also played an ambiguous role in the late-nineteenth-century West. On occasion, especially in support of the Earp brothers, Doc sided with law officials attempting to quell frontier disorder. But on other occasions, moving with characteristic impunity, Holliday acted without concerning himself too much with legal niceties. In the end, Doc practiced what Topping calls "vigilante justice," a brand of action that seemed capricious at its worst and yet was a necessary tool in moving frontier societies from barbarism to civilization.

Joaquín Murrieta, as noted Chicano scholar Richard Griswold del Castillo demonstrates, acted out a more complicated role on the boundary between lawmen and outlaws. Although Murrieta's origins and deeds remain hazy, he represents a group that European westerners viewed as foreigners and opponents. Retaliating against numerous injustices he experienced, Murrieta violently fought back against Anglo-Americans, stealing, robbing, and even killing to protect himself and to uphold his group's interests. As Griswold del Castillo reveals, the dividing line between legal and illegal actions for minorities in the nineteenth century was usually fraught with even more complex difficulties than for nonminorities.

The brief life of the infamous Billy the Kid illustrates yet another path. Many forget that the Kid lived most of his short career on the side of frontier law. Not until his mother died in 1874 and his stepfather showed little interest in his rearing did the teenage Henry McCarty Antrim commit his first crime. For the next six years, as Richard W. Etulain points out in his brief overview, the Kid became increasingly active as a rustler of cattle and horses. Yet in his work for Englishman John Tunstall and lawyer Alex McSween, Billy sometimes seemed a law-abiding citizen. Even after the murderous Five-Day Battle in mid-July 1878, Billy declared he wanted no more fighting and wished to begin farming. In the final three years of his life, however, Billy lived well outside the law.

Meanwhile, Glenda Riley's well-written essay on Belle Starr provides a new feminist interpretation of the often-sensationalized life and dramatic career of this figure of the Old West. Here we see Starr's story from her varied roles as daughter, wife, and mother rather than primarily as the female sidekick of gunmen. Starr made many of her own choices, some of which took her outside the law and may have led to her violent death in 1889.

Next, in an intriguing essay, Elliott West finds the word "border" eminently useful in describing Jesse James's "life, reputation, and place in our popular culture." Growing up on a South–North border riven by the Civil War and living on shifting borders between the American South and West, James often claimed that he was a decent citizen unfairly blamed for misdeeds that he did not commit. Although James was obviously more guilty than innocent, as Elliott West persuasively shows, he remains a "border" figure among the legends surrounding him. Some agree with James that he fought against heartless institutions, whereas others see him as a criminal and a thug.

Finally, Shelley Armitage's essay on Pearl Hart provides a stimulating feminist reading of one of the West's most enigmatic characters. As Armitage asks in her subtitle, was Hart a desperate woman or a desperado? In answering that question, Armitage furnishes the most nuanced essay yet written on Hart, examining Hart's participation in establishing her own notoriety and her larger-than-life reputation.

This book provides provocative, illuminating, and balanced examinations of these ten important and mythic Wild West figures. These essays bring a new seriousness to a field sometimes too narrowly conceived and often trivialized. At the same time, the essays will delight and inform general readers and scholars alike because they focus on two questions essential to good historical writing: "What's going on here?" and "What's the significance of this story?" In the case of this collection, these questions are more than addressed, revealing with clarity and understanding the important life stories of some of the western frontier's most notable characters and securing their places in U.S. history as pioneers in the establishment of the American West.

1

WYATT EARP

The Search for Order on the Last Frontier

GARY L. ROBERTS

Of all the old-time lawmen of the boomtown West, Wyatt Earp remains perhaps the most controversial. In part this is because the Homeric themes of Wyatt Earp's legend have cut him loose from significant historical issues, thereby reducing the debate about him to a quarrel over the details of his life in order to prove him a hero or a villain. In the process, the substantial role he did play has been so obscured and trivialized that Wyatt Earp the man remains compelling, idolized, damned, and still strangely without substance.

Wyatt Earp, circa 1870. This photo is believed to have been made at Lamar, Missouri, at the time that the young Wyatt Earp was constable of Lamar Township. From the Charles W. Dearborn Collection, courtesy of C. Lee Simmons.

Biographer Stuart N. Lake described Wyatt Earp as an "epitomizing symbol of a powerful factor—an economic factor, if you will—all important in the history of the Western United States of America." And he was, although Earp represented not so much "the exact combination of breeding and human experience which laid the foundations of Western empire," to use Lake's phrase, as the forces of modernization in America's Age of Exploitation. Wyatt Earp was an instrument of change, a transition figure from the traditional frontier to the modern West, epitomizing the individualism, mobility, materialism, and violence that characterized the Gilded Age.

Wyatt Earp was a foot soldier in what historian Robert H. Weibe called "the search for order" in the late nineteenth century. Earp subscribed to the principles that dominated the time and served the forces of change for good and for ill. His world was one in which "survival of the fittest" was more than a social philosophy. Although not a complex man, he lived his life according to a code that seemed right to him, if not to those who judged him later. As a peace officer and an entrepreneur in the boomtown West, Earp threw his lot with conservative men of power. He embraced the Republicanism, capitalism, and Social Darwinism of railroad tycoons and industrial barons and served as their agent in the process of capitalist incorporation on the urban frontier.

When the West settled into the mundane realities of less troubled times, Wyatt Earp became an anachronism, a type of individual that some men were loath to remember. He represented much that Progressive reformers sought to change about America and as a result suffered a certain loss of respectability. Then he was swallowed up by the frontier myth and transformed into a "gunfighter," a man with no allegiances save for those that scribblers gave him. He found himself lost in the contradictions between what he was and what others said he was.

Earp's life began simply enough, but the seed of his personality and character were sown early. Wyatt Earp's father, Nicholas Porter Earp, was a strong-willed, opinionated, often profane, and sometimes belligerent man. Active in community affairs, he was generous to his neighbors but abrasive and often slow in paying his debts. The dominant force in Nicholas's life was his family. The rugged life of the frontier took from him one of his children and his first wife in 1839, leaving him with a son to rear alone. In 1840 he remarried, and his second wife, Virginia Ann Cooksey, a gentle, kindly woman, eventually bore eight children, six of whom survived to adulthood.

In 1845 Nicholas loaded his growing family into a wagon and left Kentucky for Illinois. The family settled at Monmouth in Warren County. Nicholas was never very happy there and was already planning to move on when the Mexican War erupted. He enlisted in the company of Captain Wyatt Berry Stapp, but his military career came to an abrupt and painful end when an uncooperative army mule kicked him in the groin and sent him home as a wounded veteran. However, the delicate nature of his disability did not deter him long, and on March 19, 1848, his fourth son was born. The child was named Wyatt Berry Stapp Earp.

Two years later, Nicholas moved his family again, this time to Pella, Iowa, a Dutch community where Wyatt Earp grew up. But Nicholas was still restless. In 1859 he purchased 240 acres of land in Barton County, Missouri, with the expectation of moving his family there. Life in western Missouri was dangerous, because of the depredations of Southern and Northern partisans in the struggle for control of "bleeding Kansas." The outbreak of the Civil War rendered any move to the border region foolhardy, and the Earps, like many other families with southern backgrounds, faced more important decisions. The three oldest boys—Newton, James, and Virgil—quickly enlisted in Union army regiments. Nicholas eventually served as Union provost marshal and raised three companies of troops for the Union cause. In 1861 he replaced O. H. Parish as marshal of Pella, serving in that post until mid-1863, when he was succeeded by H. Van Vliet. Nicholas soon resigned his various commissions and in 1864 organized a wagon train bound for California.

The trek west to San Bernardino, California, was a turning point in the life of young Wyatt. The journey took him into the new country where he would spend most of his life and tested his mettle in the face of hardship and real danger. By the time his family had rented a farm near the center of San Gorgonio Pass, Wyatt was already chafing at the idea of becoming a farmer. He took a temporary job as a driver for the Banning Stage Company and later worked as a teamster. When his older brother, Virgil, joined the family at San Bernardino in December 1865, Wyatt got his first real break. Virgil became assistant wagon master for a freighting firm, hauling goods to Prescott, Arizona, and Wyatt was hired as a driver. Later, Wyatt took a job with Chris Taylor of San Bernardino and drove freight wagons on a regular run to Salt Lake City.

According to Wyatt's "autobiography," a curious document written by his friend John Flood, a man named Charles Chrisman opened a competing line and hired Wyatt as a freighter. Then, Wyatt recalled, Chrisman and he set out for Julesburg, Colorado, where Chrisman won grading contracts with the Union Pacific Railroad. In the spring of 1868 Nicholas Earp decided to return to Illinois, and Virgil accompanied the family as far as Wyoming, where he joined Wyatt and Chrisman in their enterprise. Nicholas and the rest of his family took the Union Pacific Railroad east, while the two brothers spent their labors in the last push toward Promontory, Utah. In the "hell-on-wheels" towns that led the way west, the Earp brothers acquired skills as gamblers and learned to take care of themselves in a difficult environment. More importantly, they caught a glimpse of the capitalist dream that drove the rails west. By the spring of 1869, when the contract was completed, they had earned enough money to finance a trip home to Monmouth for a reunion with the family.

They arrived to find that Nicholas had moved again, this time to his property in Missouri. According to one unverified source, the Earp boys tarried in Illinois just long enough for Wyatt to get into a fracas with a man named Tom Piner at Walden's Hotel in Beardstown. Piner allegedly needled young Wyatt, calling him "California boy," whereupon Wyatt tossed him into the street. Then Piner fired a pistol at Earp, who, in turn, shot his assailant in the hip. If the incident did happen, it doubtlessly hastened the boys' departure. By the early fall of 1869 they had reached Lamar, Missouri, for a reunion with the rest of the Earp family.

Nicholas Earp was already well established at Lamar, active in community affairs as constable of the local township and the proprietor of a bakery. On November 17, 1869, he resigned his post as constable to become justice of the peace in Lamar. That same day, twenty-one-year-old Wyatt was appointed to replace him as constable. Wyatt moved into the home of his half brother, Newton, but on January 10, 1870, he married Urilla Sutherland, the daughter of William "Uncle Billy" Sutherland, who owned the Exchange Hotel. As justice of the peace, Nicholas performed the ceremony, and after the wedding Wyatt bought a house and dabbled in farming. When the town was incorporated on February 11, 1870, Wyatt became its first constable at a salary of $15 a month.

Lamar was no hell town. Although it had its share of saloons, Lamar's affairs had settled down considerably since the war. Undoubtedly, Wyatt Earp's inauspicious debut as a peace officer was more the result of the town's placid nature than of Earp's lack of ability to enforce the law. As the fall election approached, Wyatt announced his intentions to run again for the constable's post. Then, on September 20, in a somewhat surprising turn of events, Wyatt's half brother, Newton, entered the race against him. On November 8, 1870, Wyatt defeated Newton and two other challengers to retain his job.

Tragically, before the election could be held, Wyatt's young wife, Urilla, died—of typhus or typhoid, some accounts say; in childbirth with a stillborn child, according to others. Her death changed everything for Wyatt. On November 7, 1870, the day before he was reelected constable, Wyatt sold the house he and Urilla had shared. A short time later, he and his brothers, James, Virgil, and Morgan, got into a fight with Urilla's two brothers, Fred and Bert Sutherland, and the Brummett boys, Granville, Loyd, and Jordan, who bore a grudge against Wyatt and Nicholas, who had respectively arrested and tried them. The brawl ended with enough abrasions to satisfy both sides that they had won, but the incident marked the end of Wyatt Earp's sojourn in Lamar.

Wyatt worked several cases as constable in December, but on January 16, 1871, the Barton County Court ordered Earp "to be attached and safely kept" until he settled accounts owed the county in the conduct of his office. On January 25 the court ordered a suit against Wyatt, "former constable of Lamar Township," for recovery of money due to the county. In March two cases were filed against Earp for mishandling county funds. Wyatt never answered the charges, but by then he was gone.

Wyatt Earp, circa 1874. Wyatt Earp as he appeared in Wichita, Kansas. From the Charles W. Dearborn Collection, courtesy of C. Lee Simmons.

On April 6, 1871, Deputy U.S. Marshal J. G. Owens arrested Earp and two others, John Shown and Ed Kennedy, for stealing horses near Fort Gibson in the Cherokee Nation. The three accused men were arraigned in Van Buren, Arkansas, and when they could not post $500 bail, they were jailed. Later, Earp and Shown escaped from the Van Buren jail with five other prisoners. The following week, they were indicted at Fort Smith (the district court had just been transferred there from Van Buren), and Judge William Story issued bench warrants for them. Kennedy, the only one to actually stand trial, was acquitted in June. Perhaps that was why the matter was never pursued. At any rate, Wyatt had "gone west" on the run.

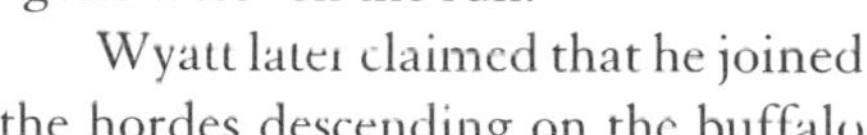

Wyatt later claimed that he joined the hordes descending on the buffalo range in Texas and Kansas. He probably did, although he may have spent some time at Fort Scott, where his second wife, Celia Ann "Mattie" Blaylock, apparently lived for a time. He wintered on the Salt Fork of the Arkansas in 1871–1872, where he met Bat and Ed Masterson, but he did not follow them to Dodge City when they quit the range for warmer climes. Instead, Wyatt probably joined his wandering father in Aullville, Missouri, or his brother Newton in Peace, Kansas. Some evidence further suggests that he worked as a freighter in business with Newton and Edward Sylvester Adam, Newton's brother-in-law.

In 1873 Wyatt drifted into Ellsworth, then the center of the Texas cattle trade. He was present the day that Billy Thompson shot Sheriff Chauncey B. Whitney and may have played a role in persuading Ben Thompson to surrender to authorities after Thompson held off the town while his brother escaped. By the fall of 1873 Wyatt's brother, James, had settled in Wichita, Kansas, where he tended bar and his wife apparently operated a brothel. Wyatt showed up there in 1874 after a season on the buffalo range and promptly got himself into a fight with a local citizen that landed him in jail on May 27, the same day that Charley Sanders, a black hod-carrier, was murdered by a Texan named Ramsey.

Wyatt said that Mayor Jim Hope put him on the police force that day, but records of the city of Wichita do not include a single reference to him that year. After the murder of Charley Sanders, Mayor Hope organized a secret police force, "sworn and armed," to be called out in case of trouble, which explains contemporary references to Earp as an officer, and his insistence that he was on the police force in 1874. Wyatt claimed other exploits for 1874, which were discounted by later writers because they were not reported in the Wichita press. But considered without the melodrama of John Flood or Stuart Lake, the incidents amounted to little more than conversations that did not lead to arrests, incidents unlikely to be reported by Wichita newspapers determined to play down violence and not report every incident, especially when Texas cattlemen were involved.

Occasionally, though, Wyatt did make the papers. In October 1874 he and John Behrens trailed a party of Texans seventy-five miles to collect a mass of unpaid bills. The Wichita *Eagle* observed that "those boys fear nothing and fear nobody" and recounted with obvious relish "how slick the boys did the work." Afterward, Earp and Behrens took jobs as drovers to protect a herd of cattle in the possession of Edward R. Ulrich, who was involved in a dispute over the ownership of the herd, known as the "Pole Cat War." Earp wintered with the Ulrich herd until the opposition enlisted the aid of the Summer County vigilantes and took possession of the herd at gunpoint the following spring.

On April 21, 1875, with a new marshal, Michael Meagher, in office, the Wichita town council named John Behrens assistant marshal and Wyatt Earp as a policeman. Only a few days after his appointment, Wyatt arrested a horse thief named W. W. Compton. Wyatt's restraint was notable when his prisoner tried to run away. He fired a shot in the air that brought the thief to a halt when he might have just as easily put a bullet into his back. There were also other occasions for which the local press praised the young officer. In December 1875 Earp arrested a drunk passed out near the bridge across the Arkansas River. Upon searching him, Wyatt found "in the neighborhood of $500 on his person." The *Beacon* reminded its citizens that "there are but few other places where that $500 roll would ever been heard from," adding, "the integrity of our police force has never been seriously questioned."

Wyatt was astute enough to understand the importance of the cattle trade to towns like Wichita. He was discreet when the occasion called for it, and he used his persuasive powers more than once to prevent arrests. At the same time, lawbreakers learned that Wyatt was a man of action and would not hesitate to perform his duties as a policeman. He had gained a reputation as a tough adversary, a man who would not compromise, and an effective officer who proved the maxim that good law enforcement is not newsworthy.

All was not rosy in Wichita for Wyatt Earp, however. On one humiliating evening in January 1876, as Wyatt sat in a card game, his revolver slid from its holster, fell to the floor, and fired, scattering the players. His family's reputation did not help much either. His sister-in-law, Bessie Earp, appeared routinely in the arrest records for prostitution, along with "Sally Earp," who may have been "Ceally" Blaylock, the woman who became Wyatt's second wife "Mattie."

In 1875 young Morgan Earp showed up in town and got into a small scrape that cost him $2 in police court. Once Wyatt became an officer, the Earp name abruptly dropped from police court records, which left some suspicion that Wyatt's new job gave him the unspoken leeway to make life easier for his relatives.

Earp's family also became an issue in the marshal's race of 1876, which led, indirectly, to Wyatt Earp's departure from Wichita. In a tight race, challenger Bill Smith charged that Mike Meagher had promised to add Wyatt's brothers to the force if he were reelected. Smith said that additional officers were not needed and implied that he did not want the Earps working for him if he became marshal. This comment enraged Wyatt, who attacked Smith on the eve of the election. Meagher stopped the fight and reluctantly fired Earp.

The *Beacon* observed that Earp had been an "excellent officer," but added that "the good order of the city was properly vindicated in the firing and dismissal of Erp [*sic*]." Wyatt's case subsequently came before the city council, which first refused to rehire him by a vote of six to two, then tied four to four in a second vote that left the matter tabled.

A few days later, on May 17, 1876, Wyatt Earp signed on as a deputy under Marshal Lawrence E. Deger in Dodge City. He served as a peace officer through the cattle season, and when the force was reduced in September, he alone was retained as a deputy under Marshal Deger. In the spring Wyatt headed north to Deadwood in the Dakota Territory with his brother Morgan. Unfortunately, the files of the Dodge City *Times* and most of the city records for 1876 were lost, along with the details of law enforcement in Dodge for a critical period in Wyatt's career. Still, enough evidence survived to show that Wyatt was a good officer.

When Earp returned to Dodge in July 1877, the *Times* reported:

> *Wyatt Earp, who was on our city police force last summer, is in town again. We hope he will accept a position on the force once more. He had a quiet way of taking the most desperate characters into custody which invariably gave one the impression that the city was able to enforce her mandates and preserve her dignity. It wasn't considered*

policy to draw a gun on Wyatt unless you got the drop and meant to burn powder without any preliminary talk.

Such praise was noteworthy. Yet just days after Wyatt's return to Dodge, he was arrested for slapping a prostitute named Frankie Bell, who "heaped epithets upon the offending head of Mr. Earp." The aggressive prostitute spent a night in jail and was fined $20, whereas Earp got off with a $1 fine. After the incident, Wyatt left Dodge for other climes without ever pinning on a badge. He struck the gambler's circuit in Texas, where he apparently met John H. "Doc" Holliday and worked for a time as a dealer at the Cattle Exchange, the Fort Worth saloon of R. J. Winders where his brother, Jim, tended bar. He also renewed his acquaintance with John Behrens, who was living in the area. In January Wyatt got into a fight with a cowboy named Russell at the Cattle Exchange and gave him "a first class pounding."

On April 9, 1878, Dodge City's popular marshal, Ed Masterson, was gunned down by two Texans. Charles Bassett succeeded Masterson. Bassett was a tough and courageous officer, but like Larry Deger in Dodge and Mike Meagher in Wichita, he preferred to be the administrator and leave the day-to-day operations to his officers. He needed an "enforcer," and on May 14 the *Ford County Globe* announced that "Wyatt Earp, one of the most efficient officers Dodge ever had, has just returned from Fort Worth, Texas. He was immediately appointed Asst. Marshal, by our City dads, much to their credit." Wyatt was just what Bassett needed. Working with Jim Masterson, Bat's brother as partner, the way he had with John Behrens and Jimmy Cairns in Wichita, Wyatt took charge. It proved to be a good arrangement. On June 18 the *Globe* remarked, "Wyatt Earp is doing his duty as Ass't Marshal in a very creditable manner.—Adding new laurels to his splendid record every day."

That summer, all of Dodge City's officers earned their pay. Early on the morning of July 25 the excitement got out of hand. A party of drovers was leaving town after a night of revelry, when one of them suddenly charged past the Comique Theatre firing his pistol. Inside, the patrons scrambled for cover. Wyatt Earp and Jim Masterson sent a volley of shots after the fleeing drovers. The cowboys fired back at them, and the "firing then became general." In the melee, a youth named George Hoy fell from his horse, seriously wounded by a gunshot to the arm. Hoy eventually died of complications on August 21.

A few days after Hoy's death, Texas "shootist" Clay Allison stopped in Dodge City, and although the newspaper's account of his arrival (*Ford County Globe,* August 6, 1878) was brief, the visit became the foundation of one of the enduring legends of early Dodge City. A persistent story evolved that

Allison made the Dodge City lawmen "hunt their holes." Writers like Stuart Lake have portrayed their meeting like a high-noon showdown, and skeptics have made much over the fact that no contemporary source has ever confirmed that the encounter took place.

Even so, it probably happened. Stripped of embellishments, the "showdown" was a brief conversation before Allison left town. Nothing occurred that made the papers, although gossip might have made the rounds among Dodge City's sporting men and the Texas drovers. Earp said that ten days later Allison returned to Dodge City and sent a messenger asking permission for him to visit the town and attend to business, which confirmed the basic chronology afforded by the *Globe*'s September 10 report that "Clay Allison came down from the west on the 5th." Although cowboy Charles Siringo later claimed that Allison, backed by twenty-five Texans, searched the saloons for Dodge City officers, Wyatt recalled that Allison "behaved like an exemplary citizen" during his second visit to Dodge City.

In the early morning hours of October 4, 1878, James "Spike" Kenedy, son of Texas rancher Mifflin Kenedy, fired two shots into a small frame dwelling owned by Mayor James "Dog" Kelly, with whom he had had two arguments. Unknown to Kenedy, Kelly was in the hospital at Fort Dodge and the house was occupied by two young women, Fannie Garretson and Dora Hand (alias Fannie Kennan). One of the bullets struck Dora Hand in the right side, killing her instantly.

Wyatt Earp and Jim Masterson immediately suspected Kenedy. A posse consisting of Sheriff Bat Masterson, Marshal Bassett, Assistant Marshal Earp, Deputy Sheriff Bill Duffy, and William Tilghman anticipated Kenedy's route, got ahead of him, and intercepted him in Meade City southwest of Dodge. Three times the officers demanded that Kenedy surrender, but when he tried to escape, they opened fire, one bullet striking Kenedy's shoulder and three taking down his mount. Unfortunately, then as now, "big shots" were treated differently than other folks. Despite Dora Hand's popularity, Mifflin Kenedy managed to get his son out of town without a formal hearing, much less a trial.

After the Dora Hand excitement, Dodge City settled down for the winter with periodic arrests for Earp and Masterson, who had their salaries cut back from $75 to $50 in December. Wyatt remained in Dodge that winter. He was a deacon in a local church and well thought of by most of the businessmen in town, although he apparently was cheating on Mattie with a local beauty named Lillie Beck. The winter lull ended on April 5, 1879, when "Cockeyed" Frank Loving killed Levi Richardson in the Long Branch Saloon. Four days later, on April 9, Earp's and Masterson's salaries were doubled in preparation for the cattle season, and the two were soon earning their pay.

Yet, all in all, it was a quiet summer, prompting the *Times* to brag, "Dodge City is hard 'to take.' . . . [T]he pistol brigands find it a 'warm berth.'"

In the absence of real trouble, the monotony was broken mainly by the "high old times" south of the tracks, which sometimes spilled over into the town's more respectable parts. At summer's end, the *Globe* opined that the townspeople "were extricating ourselves from that stupid lethargy which has fallen upon us of late, and were giving vent to our uncurbed hilarity—'getting to the booze joint,' as it were, in good shape, and 'making a ranika-boo play for ourselves.'" On September 5 the revelry broke loose in a free-for-all on Front Street, complete with flying vegetables, rotten eggs, and a few pistol balls. The *Globe* celebrated the "Day of Carnival" in good humor and observed that "The 'finest work' and neatest polishes were said to have been executed by Mr. Wyatt Earp, who has been our efficient assistant marshal for the past year."

The celebration proved to be a farewell party for Wyatt Earp. On September 4, 1879, he resigned as assistant marshal. He was already gone when Charles Bassett arrested A. H. Webb for clubbing B. Martin to death with a Winchester rifle on September 8. Bassett would soon resign from his job as well, but by then, Wyatt Earp and Mattie, along with Wyatt's brother, James, and his wife, were well on their way to Prescott, Arizona, to meet Virgil Earp. At Las Vegas, New Mexico, Doc Holliday joined their party. By November 1, 1879, the Earps had reached Prescott, and eight days later, the Prescott *Daily Miner* reported that Virgil was "about to pull out for Tombstone which is just now a great center of attraction." The Earps arrived in the new camp on December 1, without Doc Holliday, who decided to stay behind in Prescott.

Wyatt Earp and Bat Masterson, 1876. Looking determined and fit, two future legends of the Old West sport their badges as peace officers in cowtown Dodge City. Photograph no. 76637, courtesy of the Arizona Historical Society.

Wyatt Earp and his brothers clearly hoped that Tombstone would change their lives. They went there with the intention of going into business. They hoped to start a stage line, but when they learned that two lines were already operating out of Tombstone, Wyatt went to work as a shotgun guard for Wells Fargo. Virgil settled in with a fresh commission as a deputy U.S. marshal, and James took a job tending bar at a local saloon. Before long, Morgan and Warren Earp joined the other brothers, and the clan was together again. The Earps seem to have made a genuine effort to become legitimate businessmen, investing in mining properties, buying real estate, and courting prominent business leaders and leading Republicans. In March 1880 the Dodge City papers reported that Wyatt had heavy financial investments in the mines at Tombstone.

In fact, Wyatt and his brothers seemed to have found in Tombstone the best opportunity of their lives to put down substantive roots. Wyatt continued his interest in gambling to bankroll his investments and became a partner in the gambling concession at the Oriental Saloon, as well as other gambling operations. On July 28, 1880, the Tombstone *Nugget* reported that Sheriff Charles Shibell had appointed Wyatt as deputy sheriff for Pima County. Three days later, the Tombstone *Epitaph* endorsed the appointment as "an eminently proper one," observing that "Wyatt has filled various positions in which bravery and determination were requisites, and in every instance proved himself the right man in the right place." His brother, Morgan, succeeded him as shotgun guard for Wells Fargo.

As peace officers, the Earps naturally generated some resentment, but in June 1880 they acquired their first real enemy in Tombstone, in a farcical courtroom fracas in which Wyatt arrested both the presiding justice of the peace, James Reilly, and the defense attorney, Harry Jones. The incident led to a move to have Reilly recalled. The effort failed, but as a result Reilly nursed a grudge against Wyatt Earp.

Reilly was not the only enemy Wyatt made in Tombstone. Cochise County was home to a loose coalition of hard cases, drifters, and small ranchers used to having their own way in the brush, including rustling Mexican cattle across the line and making forays against larger ranchers in the region whenever they could. This coalition was disquieted by the Tombstone boom. Although it brought potential benefits to legitimate ranchers, the economic development of Tombstone created pressures and introduced changes that threatened the cowboys' cavalier approach toward the law. As peace officers, the Earps constituted that element of change, which clashed most directly with the rustlers.

The Democratic politicians who ran the county had natural allies among the Texas cowboys who populated the outlying areas and the shift miners who toiled in the Tombstone mines. They resented the Republican elite that dominated Tombstone. Within the town itself, economic interests competed to control the economic development through fair means and foul, especially through claim jumping and land-lot fraud. The Democrats and the land grabbers were potential Earp opponents, because the Earps affiliated with the Republican leadership and the stable business elite of Tombstone. Increasingly, the Earps were viewed as the "company men" of Tombstone's vested interests.

The Earps' first encounter with the cowboys came on July 25, 1880, just days before Wyatt's appointment as deputy sheriff, when Lieutenant J. H. Hurst enlisted the aid of Deputy U.S. Marshal Virgil Earp to recover six army mules stolen from Camp Rucker. With Wyatt and Morgan acting as posse men, Virgil accompanied Hurst to the Babocomari River ranch of Robert Findley "Frank" McLaury and Thomas McLaury, where the mules were known to have been corralled after they were stolen. The mules had been hidden by the time the officers arrived, but the incident engendered bitter feelings on the part of the McLaurys and their friends against the Earps.

The tension deepened on the evening of October 27, 1880, when Tombstone's Marshal Fred White was shot while attempting to disarm Curly Bill Brocius, one of a group of cowboys who were disturbing the peace. Deputy Sheriff Earp "buffaloed" Curly Bill on the spot. Virgil and Morgan helped round up others, and they were all deposited in the local jail. Before he died, White said the shooting was accidental. Later, at trial in Tucson, Wyatt testified on Curly's behalf.

For a time after the White shooting, the cowboys avoided Tombstone or remained on their best behavior when in town. Rows involving cowboys were not a problem in Tombstone. The Earps and the cowboys simply did not pay much attention to each other, and their incidental contact was congenial enough. Through 1880 and much of 1881, the cowboys, at least, were never overly concerned with that brood of black-suited Yankees by the name of Earp. The Earps simply were not that important to them.

In fact, linking the various groups—the cowboys, the Democratic politicos, and the town-lot manipulators—into a criminal combine as an explanation for the sanguinary conflict that eventually engulfed Tombstone is a postmortem conclusion based upon little real evidence. True enough, the opposition to the Earps did appear to be a set of concentric circles, but the connections were much more tenuous than the legend would later imply. What did exist in Cochise County were economic tensions and political rivalries more complicated than the normal boomtown high jinks. And the Earps were destined to be major players in events they could not forsee the night Fred White was killed.

The day after Marshal White died, Virgil Earp was named "assistant marshal for the village" until a special election could be held. Later, Virgil wrote that E. B. Gage and other prominent citizens urged him to run for the marshal's post. But the law-and-order crowd, including the *Epitaph,* instead backed Benjamin Sippy, a miner and ex-soldier, and on November

13, 1880, Sippy beat Virgil for the job by a vote of 311 to 259. Virgil officially resigned his post as assistant marshal two days later.

On November 12, the day before the special election, Wyatt Earp resigned as deputy sheriff to assist Bob Paul, who was contesting Shibell's reelection as sheriff of Pima County. Virgil did not run for marshal in the regular election in January 1881. Sippy, who had the backing of John P. Clum, editor of the Tombstone *Epitaph,* as well as most of the miners, won easily. These events left the Earps without official credentials in law enforcement save for Virgil's federal appointment and Wyatt's position as an investigator for Wells Fargo.

Nevertheless, the Earps kept a high profile in law enforcement circles. On January 14, 1881, Virgil and Wyatt took the initiative in protecting the life of Michael P. O'Rourke, an eighteen-year-old gambler called "Johnny-Behind-the-Deuce," from a mob bent on lynching him for killing a mining engineer in Charleston, a mining camp ten miles away. With Republican John Charles Fremont as governor, Wyatt hoped to be appointed as the first sheriff of Cochise County, a position that was created on January 31, 1881. Those hopes were dashed when Governor Fremont instead appointed John H. Behan, a Democrat, the former sheriff of Yavapai County, and the man who had succeeded Wyatt as deputy sheriff of Pima County.

In its article applauding the appointment of Behan, the Tombstone *Nugget* generously praised Wyatt's conduct as an officer. But the appointment of Behan infuriated John Clum, who openly criticized him in the *Epitaph.* Moreover, Behan's brazen disregard of his promise to appoint Wyatt as undersheriff engendered animosity between Behan and the Earps.

Wyatt learned hard lessons from the experience. Arizona was different from Kansas. In Kansas the Republicans dominated politics, and the town and county officials usually worked together. A spirit of cooperation between the sheriff's office and the town marshal's office had been the rule. Indeed, Wyatt probably agreed to take the post of chief deputy under Behan because he expected to be the chief enforcement officer as he had been under the marshals in Kansas. But Wyatt was not prepared for the partisan politics he encountered in Arizona.

By that time, southeastern Arizona had a reputation for lawlessness. As early as October 1880 the Pima County Republican Committee declared that, during the previous year, twenty-five homicides had been committed in Pima County (which included Tombstone at the time), fifteen persons had been arrested for murder, and only one man had been brought to trial. In early 1881 a Citizens' Safety Committee was organized in Tombstone, and by spring many substantial citizens of Tombstone were becoming disenchanted with both Sheriff Behan and Marshal Sippy.

On the night of March 15, 1881, bandits attempted to rob the Kinnear and Company stagecoach two miles west of Drew's Station en route to Benson. In the botched robbery, the outlaws killed the driver and a passenger. When the news reached Marshall Williams, the Wells Fargo agent in Tombstone, a posse including Williams, Wyatt as a "private man" for Wells Fargo, Virgil as federal deputy, Morgan Earp, Bat Masterson, and others immediately set out for the scene.

The following morning, Sheriff Behan, Buckskin Frank Leslie, and Deputy Sheriff Billy Breakenridge joined the party. Behan took command, and the posse pursued the still unknown fugitives for three days before arresting a small-time crook named Luther King at the ranch of Len Redfield. King confessed to a role in the holdup attempt and named Bill Leonard, Harry Head, and Jim Crane as his confederates in crime. At that point, Behan, Breakenridge, Williams, Leslie, and others quit the hunt and returned to Tombstone with the prisoner. The Earp brothers, Masterson, and Bob Paul continued the pursuit for another two weeks before returning to Tombstone exhausted and empty-handed. Wyatt and Bat reached Tombstone first. Wyatt met with Wells Fargo detective James Hume and the two of them urged Harry Woods, the undersheriff, to keep King in irons to prevent his escape. Moments later, the prisoner simply walked out of the jail and rode out of town.

The Earps were not pleased. They had hoped to capitalize on the arrest of King and the other criminals to secure their positions as defenders of law and order. Now, the only man arrested—and the key to the arrest of the others—had escaped, apparently with inside help. In an effort to salvage the situation, Wyatt met with Joseph Isaac "Ike" Clanton, a cowboy leader whose loyalties were thought to be malleable. Earp proposed to give Ike the Wells Fargo reward if Ike would betray Leonard, Head, and Crane to him. What he wanted out of the deal was the publicity of having arrested the murderers of Bud Philpot. Ike agreed to Wyatt's proposal, but before anything came from the plan, Leonard and Head were killed trying to rob a store in New Mexico.

Then, on July 5, 1881, Doc Holliday was arrested for attempting to rob the U.S. mail and murdering the driver and passenger, largely on the strength of an affidavit Sheriff Behan obtained from Kate Holliday, Doc's common-law wife. Five days later, the charges were dismissed by Justice Wells Spicer, who said "there was not the slightest evidence to show the guilt of the defendant." This was perhaps true, but Doc was already regarded as an unsavory character and had been a friend of Leonard's. At the very least, damage had been done to the image that the Earps wanted to convey.

Still, events turned in favor of the Earps that summer. First, the local authorities grew impatient with Chief of Police Ben Sippy, who was under a cloud of suspicion concerning debts both to the city and to private creditors as well as irregularities in the conduct of his office. On June 6, 1881, Sippy asked for a two-week leave of absence, and Virgil Earp was appointed to serve in his place as acting marshal while he was away. Sippy never returned.

Virgil made a difference as acting marshal. He immediately began to enforce the town's ordinances and to haul violators into court. On his first day in office, he prevented a shooting between Ike Clanton and a gambler named Denny McClain. The number of cases before justices' courts jumped so dramatically that both the *Epitaph* and the *Nugget* published approving reviews of the acting marshal and how he enforced the law. Indeed, Virgil even arrested Wyatt for disturbing the peace, for which his brother paid a $20 fine. Such fairness, the townsfolk hoped, meant that evenhanded justice finally had arrived inTombstone.

On June 22 a fire swept through the business district, causing great damage. Afterward, the *Epitaph* was effusive in its praise of Virgil. When claim jumpers squatted on town lots in the burned-out district, Virgil and Wyatt led a posse to remove the claim jumpers. Virgil Earp's forceful actions convinced the city fathers that he was the man to be town marshal, and on June 28 he was appointed to Sippy's post without a dissenting vote.

By midsummer 1881 the Earps were highly visible in Tombstone. At that point, no feud existed between the Earps and the Clanton-McLaury crowd. In fact, the Clantons clearly were outside the power struggle. Officially and unofficially, the Earps concerned themselves primarily with what happened within the city limits of Tombstone. The only exceptions were depredations that affected Wells Fargo or the mining and cattle interests of their backers. On the other hand, the Democratic politicos catered to the larger constituency of small ranchers and working men, which included the rustlers and those sympathetic to them, even if that meant ignoring cattle thefts and violent outbursts by their constituents.

But the situation was about to change. Since the spring of 1881 the cowboy brigands along the border had posed a serious threat not only to stage lines and honest ranchers, but also to peace with Mexico. Now the problem was so compelling that Arizona and New Mexico considered various options for the suppression of the cowboys, while diplomatic protests from Mexico prompted the U.S. State Department to demand action from the attorney general, who, in turn, ordered U.S. Marshal Crawley P. Dake to go after the outlaws. Throughout the summer, more and more incidents confirmed the threat. By midsummer John Clum had begun an editorial campaign against the "Cow-Boy Scourge." Most other papers in the region concurred, including the *Nugget* and the leading Tucson papers.

In August Mexicans killed several Americans at Guadalupe Canyon, including Newman Haynes "Old Man" Clanton, father of Ike, Fin, and Billy Clanton, and Jim Crane, the last of the Benson stagecoach robbers. The Guadalupe Canyon Massacre panicked Tombstone. Until then, Tombstone's population had felt secure. Virgil Earp had even reduced the size of the town's police force. Even so, the business community was nervous. Newspapers reported that legitimate ranchers had abandoned the San Simon Valley, timber was scarce for the mines because of horse thefts and fear among teamsters, and entrepreneurs were reluctant to invest in such a volatile business environment. Clearly, the threat was not on the streets of Tombstone but on the roads leading to Tombstone, and this potential danger to commerce and the security of the mines, however exaggerated, increased demands for action from businessmen and the big ranchers.

In September acting governor John J. Gosper personally investigated the situation in Tombstone and the town's environs. His report generally supported strong measures against lawlessness in the area, and he especially deplored the failure of local law enforcement officers to cooperate in the pursuit of criminals. He directly chastised both Sheriff Behan and Marshal Earp. When the Bisbee Stagecoach was robbed on September 9, 1881, as if to confirm Gosper's complaint, two posses were put in the saddle; Sheriff Behan led one and Deputy U.S. Marshal Earp led the other. Virgil's posse overtook the two suspects, who turned out to be Pete Spence, one of the cowboy crowd, and T. C. "Frank" Stilwell, who, embarrassingly, was one of Behan's deputies.

Still, the charges against both men were soon dropped. Later, Wyatt testified that, following the arrests, Frank McLaury, Ike Clanton, John Ringo, and two other cowboys accosted Morgan Earp for arresting Spence and Stilwell and threatened to kill him and his brothers if they ever came after them. Virgil claimed to have had a similar conversation with the elder McLaury. The cowboys seriously misunderstood the men they were dealing with. Cowboy depredations had intruded into the area of Virgil's responsibilities as a federal officer and Wyatt's work for Wells Fargo, and they would do their duty as they saw it.

In early October Virgil Earp again arrested Frank Stilwell and Pete Spence on federal charges for robbing the U.S. mail and hauled them off to Tucson for a hearing before the U.S. court commissioner. On October 22 Pete Spence was discharged, and Frank Stilwell was bound over for trial. Virgil returned to Tombstone on October 21 with Sheriff Behan.

In Virgil's absence a crisis was building in Tombstone. One evening, while drinking, Wells Fargo agent Marshall Williams let Ike Clanton know that he was aware of the deal Wyatt had made with him to betray Leonard,

Crane, and Head. Clanton then confronted Wyatt, accusing him of breaking faith and of telling Doc Holliday about the deal. Wyatt denied the accusation and told Ike he could ask Doc about it when he returned to town.

Wyatt Earp, 1885. Looking the part of a successful businessman, the dapper Mr. Earp was photographed in San Diego, California, for his most famous likeness. Courtesy of Craig A. Fouts.

By the time Virgil returned, the Citizens' Safety Committee was nervous and urged him to deputize his brothers. Wyatt had acted as Tombstone's chief of police while Virgil was in Tucson. A month earlier, Morgan had been appointed a "special policeman." Virgil now retained both men on the force. As a precaution, he also sent Morgan to Tucson to pick up Doc Holliday, who was there attending the San Augustin Festival. Doc returned to Tombstone on the afternoon of October 22, but by then Clanton had left town.

On October 24 four prisoners walked out of Sheriff Behan's jail. Virgil joined a posse in pursuit of the escapees, but he returned the next morning and went to bed. While he slept, Ike Clanton and Tom McLaury rode into Tombstone. Near one o'clock on the morning of October 26, 1881, Clanton accosted Doc Holliday in the Occidental Saloon. Doc denied knowing about any deal, and an argument ensued that lasted until Morgan Earp intervened and led Doc away. Clanton continued to berate them until Virgil stepped in and threatened to arrest them all. Later, Clanton met Wyatt and told him that he would be ready for Doc and the Earps the next morning.

Virgil, oddly, played poker with Clanton, Tom McLaury, and John Behan until the early morning hours, and apparently believed that Clanton's threats would evaporate when he sobered up. But the cowboy continued to drink and to denounce the Earps and Holliday to anyone who would listen.

The morning of October 26, 1881, rose clear and cold. Near nine o'clock, officer A. G. Bronk roused Virgil from bed and told him that Clanton was still on the prod. Collecting Wyatt and Morgan, Virgil set out to find him. Wyatt made a round of the saloons, but Virgil and Morgan found Clanton first on the street and promptly buffaloed him and hauled him into justice's court. Even there, Clanton kept up his tirade with such vitriol that Morgan offered to fight him on the spot. Cooler heads prevailed in the courtroom, while outside an angry Wyatt Earp knocked Tom McLaury senseless with the barrel of his revolver following a heated exchange of words.

Later that day, Billy Clanton and Frank McLaury arrived in town, unaware of what had happened. They entered the Grand Hotel and were about to have drinks when they learned about Wyatt's buffaloing Tom. Frank McLaury immediately went to look for his brother, determined to attend to the business that had brought him to Tombstone and then leave. But Ike's tirade never stopped, and after he caught up to the others at Spangenberg's Gunshop, they commiserated forcefully enough to send every good citizen who saw them scurrying away to tell the marshal. The Earps tried to keep track of their movements, and Wyatt almost caused a fight when he ordered Frank McLaury to get his horse off the sidewalk in front of Spangenberg's, where the Clantons and McLaurys appeared to be making purchases.

That confrontation might have ended the episode had not the good people of Tombstone kept up a steady barrage of reports. The Clanton bunch walked toward Dexter's Livery, apparently in preparation for leaving town. In the meantime, Sheriff Behan learned of the troubles and hurried off to find the Earps. After Virgil briefed him on what had happened, Behan promised that he would persuade the cowboys to leave town. Then, two of the leaders of the Safety Committee reported that the Clantons and McLaurys, now joined by at least two others, were next to W. A. Harwood's house behind the OK Corral on Fremont, near Third Street. They also reminded the chief of police that this was just the sort of behavior that he was hired to curtail. By then, Virgil had taken about all he could take from both the cowboys and the townsfolk. With his two brothers and Doc Holliday, he marched toward Fremont Street.

Behan caught up to Frank McLaury outside Bauer's butcher shop and walked with him to where the others, along with Bill Claiborne, were waiting between C. S. Fly's boardinghouse and Harwood's place. Behan was still talking to them when the Earps came into view. He ran to Virgil and told him that the boys were leaving town. Wes Fuller, a small-time gambler who hung out with the cowboys, had just joined the Clanton party. Seeing the Earps approach, he and Bill Claiborne fled the scene.

Virgil and the others never broke stride, even after Behan warned them they would be killed. Things had gone too far. Doubtlessly, the Earps were angry men, but when they turned into the narrow eighteen-foot-wide vacant lot between C. S. Fly's and Harwood's, Virgil and Wyatt were determined to arrest the cowboys. The Clantons and McLaurys were equally determined not to back down now that they were cornered. As the Tombstone *Nugget* later observed, "They were all of that class to whom any imputation of not possessing 'staying qualities' in a fight is sufficient to provoke one immediately."

With a cane in his gun hand, Virgil barked the order, "Throw up your hands!" And in that instant, the first shots were fired as the exposed chief of police screamed, "Wait! I don't mean that!" The fight became general, and in a matter of seconds, it was over. Tom and Frank McLaury were dead. Billy Clanton lay in a bloody heap screaming that he had been murdered. Ike Clanton had grappled with Wyatt for a moment before running away. He was spared by an amazingly restrained Wyatt Earp. Both Morgan and Virgil Earp were wounded in the fray. Doc Holliday had a scratch. Only Wyatt was untouched. Afterward, John Behan made a halfhearted attempt to arrest the Earps, but Wyatt bluntly told the sheriff that he would not be arrested by him.

The street fight disturbed the community. Although the McLaurys and Billy Clanton were buried with great fanfare under a banner that read "MURDERED IN THE STREETS OF TOMBSTONE," the *Epitaph* justified the incident as a tragic but necessary act and the *Nugget,* though it would later take a procowboy stance, provided a surprisingly balanced account of what had happened. On October 29 the city fathers took the precaution of relieving Virgil Earp of his duties as chief of police, pending the outcome of the affair. Ike Clanton swore out murder warrants for the Earps and Doc Holliday, who were quickly bailed out by several prominent businessmen.

So far, events had proceeded predictably. The shooting was a police matter, and the majority of the townsfolk seemed willing to leave it at that. Still, the violent deaths of three men caused many of those previously partial to the Earps to question Virgil's judgment in calling on his brothers and Doc Holliday to help him. Wyatt and Virgil Earp were the big losers. Neither of them wanted a shootout. Both men had worked very hard to establish themselves as businessmen and peace officers and to lay the groundwork for future political gains. Now Virgil's job was in jeopardy, and Wyatt's hopes of becoming sheriff of Cochise County were seriously damaged. Even if they were vindicated, they could not prevent some community backlash against their methods.

A coroner's jury returned an inconclusive report, declaring simply that the McLaurys and Billy Clanton had died of gunshot wounds inflicted by the Earps and Doc Holliday. That bit of news prompted the *Nugget* dryly to thank the jury for setting the record straight: "We might have thought they had been struck by lightning or stung to death by hornets." A preliminary hearing was set in the court of Justice of the Peace Wells Spicer on October 31, 1881. The hearing lasted throughout the month of November, and the outcome was far from certain.

On November 7 Wyatt and Doc were remanded to jail at the behest of Will R. McLaury, brother of Tom and Frank and a Fort Worth attorney, who was determined to see them hanged. However, following a habeas corpus hearing and new bail provided by E. B. Gage and J. M. Vizina, both prominent mining men, they were released on November 20. On December 1 Wells Spicer discharged the Earps, declaring that he did not believe the defendants could be convicted "of any offense whatever." Subsequently, a Cochise County grand jury refused to indict them.

The Fremont Street fiasco—later immortalized as the "Gunfight at the O.K. Corral"—quickly fouled the political climate. The Democrats saw an opportunity to use the Earps to discredit the Republicans. Wyatt's old enemy, James Reilly, wrote blistering letters to the *Nugget,* accusing Wells Fargo agents—and by implication the Earps—of masterminding stage robberies, attacking the Citizens' Safety Committee, and denouncing the Earps as "bad men."

In the street fight, however, Mayor Clum and the people he represented found both a confirmation of the cowboy menace and an opportunity to rid Tombstone of the thieves as well as the corrupt county machine. This theme was kept up by the *Epitaph,* and one business associate of Wyatt Earp described him by saying, "a more liberal and kind-hearted man I never met." Yet the townspeople at large agreed that the street fight was a dangerous act of violence that threatened the economic security of the town.

Still, the most serious short-term effect of the street fight was a frightening breakdown of order. For that, the friends and associates of the Clantons and McLaurys were largely to blame. The fight itself was the beginning of a blood feud, not the climax of some larger conflict. Both Ike Clanton and Will McLaury were determined to have vengeance. On the night of December 28, Virgil Earp was ambushed by a group of men armed with shotguns. With Virgil critically wounded, Wyatt Earp wired U.S. Marshal Crawley P. Dake, who immediately deputized Wyatt with the authority to appoint posse men and who left for Tombstone himself.

With the town still talking about the shooting, a city election was held on January 3, 1882. Acting chief James Flynn ran for the post of chief of police against David Neagle, a feisty Behan deputy with a reputation as a gunhand, who was on the People's Independent ticket. The *Nugget* warned that votes for Flynn would give a "new lease of power for the Earps" and told the voters that "the election to-day will decide whether Tombstone is to be dominated for another year by the Earps and their strikers." Neagle was elected chief of police, and John Carr was elected mayor, both on the People's Independent ticket.

Then, on January 6, 1882, the Bisbee Stagecoach was robbed again. Curly Bill Brocius and John Ringo were suspected, along with Spence and Stilwell, and, in fact, Ringo was arrested on the charge. He jumped bond—to "obstruct the execution" of warrants obtained by Wyatt Earp, according to his brother James Earp—but he returned to Tombstone and posted bail. On January 16 Doc Holliday and Ringo came close to gunplay on the street, but police officers intervened and arrested not only Holliday and Ringo but also Wyatt Earp. Later, Earp was released without charge.

A week later, Wyatt, Doc, young Warren Earp, and an assortment of Earp partisans departed Tombstone with warrants "for the arrest of diverse persons with criminal offenses." The posse descended on Charleston, the cowboy hangout, and patrolled its streets for two days, without any result other than antagonizing the local citizens.

In response to mounting criticism, Wyatt Earp did two remarkable things. First, he and Virgil resigned their commissions as deputy U.S. marshals to convince the public of their "sincere purpose to promote the public welfare, independent of any personal emolument or advantage." Second, Wyatt sent a message to Ike Clanton, asking for a meeting to end the feud between them. Crawley Dake refused to accept the Earps' resignations, and Ike Clanton refused to talk to Wyatt.

On February 11 Wyatt, Morgan, and Doc were arrested on warrants sworn out by Clanton in Contention, Arizona. Three days later the Earps went to Contention, surrounded by their supporters, to challenge one more effort to try them for murder. They were quickly released. Back in Tombstone, the rival groups watched each other publicly and warily. One local predicted, "Blood will surely come."

With a war chest provided by prominent businessmen and Wells Fargo, and with a coterie of deputies known to be skilled with firearms, Wyatt Earp made other sorties into the countryside. Then, on the night of March 17, 1882, Morgan Earp was assassinated as he shot pool in Campbell & Hatch's Billiard Parlor. A coroner's jury named Pete Spence, Frank Stilwell, Indian Charlie, and a man named "Fries" (later identified as Frederick Bode) as the killers.

Morgan's death fundamentally changed things for Wyatt Earp. So far he had worked within the limits of the law. He also had maintained business interests and political ambitions that indicated his intentions to stay in Tombstone. Now, one of his brothers was dead and another was permanently maimed by a band of cowardly backshooters. Moreover, some of the businessmen and politicos who had used the Earps for their purposes were waffling now that a frightening wave of violence had subverted legal processes. Privately, they encouraged the Earps' sixshooter justice; publicly, they worried about mounting criticism in the press.

Wyatt prepared for action. First, James departed Tombstone to escort the body of Morgan home to Colton. Then, Wyatt and an entourage of fighters escorted Virgil and his wife, Allie, to Tucson on March 20, 1881. That night as the train pulled out of Tucson, Wyatt, Doc, Warren, Sherman McMasters, and Turkey Creek Jack Johnson gunned down Frank Stilwell in the rail yard.

Wyatt and his associates returned to Tombstone and made final preparations for their war against the rustlers. John Behan made a fainthearted attempt to arrest Wyatt, but Wyatt and his men rode out of Tombstone in search of Morgan's killers. The effect of Earp's grim new strategy was electric. Pete Spence immediately surrendered to the sheriff. Deputy Sheriff William Bell arrested Hank Swilling, and Deputy Sheriff Frank Hereford arrested Bode. The arrests were fortuitous because Wyatt headed straight for Pete Spence's wood camp in the Dragoons, where they inquired about Spence and Indian Charlie and left Charlie dead in the brush.

The wives of Wyatt and Jim Earp left Tombstone on March 24 with the best wishes of the *Epitaph.* By then Behan had assembled a posse to pursue the Earp party. The group consisted mostly of the Clantons' friends, known outlaws, and hardcases such as John Ringo. Sheriff Bob Paul of Pima County, who had the duty of bringing in the Earps in the Stilwell case, was so disgusted by the makeup of the posse he would not join the group. He was certain that if the two groups met it would mean "bloodshed without any possibility of arrest." He hoped—in vain—that the Earps would surrender to the authorities in Tucson.

Instead, Wyatt's party stumbled headlong into a cowboy camp. In the melee that followed, the posse scattered in pell-mell flight while Wyatt Earp, apparently unaware that the others had left him, stood his ground, killing Curly Bill Brocius and mortally wounding Johnny Barnes. After that, the Earps crossed into New Mexico and eventually moved into Colorado. Behind the Earp party, Behan's posse found a cool reception among the big ranchers (most of whom applauded what the Earps had done).

Ironically, by the time President Chester A. Arthur threatened to declare martial law in Arizona to suppress the "Cow-Boy" problems, Wyatt Earp had already scattered the loose coalition that had been parties to the Earp-Clanton feud and had left Tombstone and environs in the grip of the corporate establishment whose agent he had been. Appropriately, the businessmen and social elite of Tombstone did not abandon him. While Arizona journals were rewriting the history recorded in their own back files, West Coast newspapers representing Republican and business constituencies continued to defend what Wyatt had done. Wells Fargo acknowledged his accomplishments in a remarkable public endorsement of his course of action, and the forces marshaled to prevent Doc Holliday's extradition back to Arizona were ample evidence of their gratitude.

Safe in Gunnison, Colorado, Wyatt spoke openly about returning to Arizona to face the charges against him and to run for sheriff of Cochise County. But he never did either. He was still in Gunnison when John Ringo perished, probably by his own hand. By then Clum had sold the *Epitaph* and left Tombstone as well. If Wyatt Earp's vendetta had been approved and supported privately by businessmen, Republican politicos, and prominent cattlemen, it also made Wyatt Earp a practical liability to them. Wyatt's campaign of vengeance killed his opportunities in Tombstone, and it was not in his interest or the interests of his supporters for him to return.

But the victory of mining interests and the forces of incorporation was short-lived. In the years that followed, plummeting silver prices, labor disputes, and the flooding of the mines destroyed the dream that had been Tombstone. As West Coast capitalists closed their offices and mining operations went bust, the story of the early days was left to the supporters of the cowboys and workingmen who had feared and hated the Earps. Telling the story of Tombstone was left to the vanquished.

In the summer of 1882 Wyatt traveled to San Francisco, where he renewed his relationship with Josephine Sarah Marcus, the actress "Sadie," whose affections he had stolen from John Behan in Tombstone. For a while, Mattie Earp, his second wife, waited dutifully for Wyatt at his parents' home in Colton. But when she learned of Wyatt's infidelity, she returned to Arizona, where she eventually committed suicide in 1888. Wyatt and Sadie remained together for the rest of Wyatt's life.

Tombstone ruined Wyatt Earp financially, but he managed to recover a modest prosperity in the years that followed. He took Sadie back with him to Gunnison late in 1882, where he gambled, worked as a saloon keeper, and occasionally helped out local police. In 1883 Bat Masterson called him to Dodge City to help their old friend Luke Short, who had been run out of town by his business rival, who also happened to be mayor. Wyatt descended on Dodge with a coterie of gunmen and helped Short reestablish himself there before heading back to Colorado.

In 1884 he joined the gold rush in Idaho's Coeur d'Alene country. He and his brother, Jim, opened a saloon at Eagle City, and he served as deputy sheriff of Kootenai County. The rush ended as quickly as it began, and in 1885 Wyatt traveled to El Paso, Texas, before opening a saloon in Aspen, Colorado. In 1886 Wyatt returned to California, where he enjoyed a more ordered life for a time, operating saloons in San Diego and running horses on California racetracks.

During those years, Wyatt often worked as an enforcer and investigator for corporations like the Santa Fe Railroad, the Southern Pacific Railroad, and Wells Fargo. He also dabbled in investments, prospected, gambled, and hobnobbed with wealthy and powerful men, but he never realized his dream of success—and he never escaped Tombstone. Controversy continued to follow him. In December 1896 he acted as referee in a boxing match between Ruby Bob Fitzsimmons and Tom Sharkey. He gave the fight to Sharkey on a foul, a decision that produced a major controversy, during which all the old stories about Tombstone were revived and Wyatt was subjected to a pounding by the press.

Wyatt escaped in 1897, when he and his wife followed the gold rush to Alaska. In 1899 he settled down in Nome and opened the Dexter Saloon. While there, his younger brother, Warren, was killed in Arizona. In 1905 Wyatt joined the rush to Goldfield, Nevada, along with Virgil, who died there on October 19, 1905. After that, Wyatt and Sadie Earp spent most of their last years in southern California, dividing their time between Los Angeles and the region around Parker, Arizona. Eventually they settled into a small cottage in Vidal, California, although they continued to spend extended periods in Los Angeles. He dabbled in prospecting and oil wells, eking out a bare existence through his last years.

Wyatt Earp was thirty-three years old when he rode out of Tombstone for the last time. He was nearly eighty-one when he died in Los Angeles of prostate cancer and chronic cystitis on January 13, 1929. In all those years he never stepped clear of the shadow of what had happened in Arizona. If his enemies had killed him on the streets of Tombstone or gunned him down in the Dragoons, he might well have been laid to rest honorably. But he did not fall with six-guns blazing. Instead, he lived through many years with the memory of what had happened and surrounded by people who would not forget but who told the story in grotesque parody.

The course Wyatt chose after Morgan's death ensured the controversy that followed, but he never doubted his choices. The men he killed were bad men who died only after he had exhausted all other options, or so he believed. He did not brood over what had happened in Tombstone, and he made every effort to find a life free of the memory of the events that happened there. He preferred new enterprises that promised success and respectability. More than anything else, Wyatt Earp wanted people to think highly of him.

Still, each time he became involved in even the most inconsequential incident, the stories flooded forth again. The press would not let the Tombstone story die, and the tales grew wilder and wilder with each telling. Wyatt Earp became entrapped in his own distorted past, and he did not know how to handle it. He remained oddly vulnerable and exploited for the rest of his life, so obviously unable to defend himself that people as diverse as Bat Masterson, John Clum, and Walter Noble Burns felt compelled to champion him in print.

In 1925 Wyatt Earp confided to his friend John Hays Hammond, "Notoriety has been the bane of my life. I detest it." At the same time, Wyatt craved vindication. By 1925 William S. Hart, John H. Flood Jr., and Sadie Earp had persuaded Wyatt to write an account of his life, and Wyatt spent much of his time during his last years in a vain attempt to publish his own version of what had happened in Tombstone. He dictated his memories to Flood, who took meticulous shorthand notes for months on end. Unfortunately, Flood was no writer and the resulting manuscript was hopelessly stilted and inept.

Despite the assistance of Hart, Wyatt's efforts to have the Flood manuscript published were futile. In 1926 Walter Noble Burns, fresh from the success of his biography of Billy the Kid, approached Earp. Wyatt's friends were impressed, but Wyatt himself balked. While Hart and Flood worked on Earp, Burns grew impatient and proceeded to write *Tombstone: An Iliad of the Southwest* (1927). Burns portrayed Earp as the "lion of Tombstone" and drew a striking and affectionate portrait of "an imperturbably calm man, not unkindly, not without humor and a certain geniality, magnanimous to his enemies, generous and loyal to his friends," until the attacks on his brothers transformed him into "an avenger, terrible, implacable, merciless." Then, Burns wrote, "There was no flinching in what he did, and no alibis or apologies afterward."

Indeed, Burns presented a compelling image of Wyatt, yet Wyatt tried to stop the book's publication. When it was released, Wyatt felt betrayed again. Burns's book had a fateful effect, however. A journalist named Stuart N. Lake read it and contacted Wyatt about writing his life story. Again, Wyatt was not enthusiastic, but in the summer of 1928 he and Lake began a brief collaboration. Wyatt was a reluctant participant in the project, fearful for his reputation and suspicious of Lake. The publication of William M. Breakenridge's *Helldorado* in the fall of 1928 was the final humiliation. Wyatt threatened to sue the former Cochise County deputy and his publisher and became even more protective of his reputation and more cautious with Lake. Then, abruptly, Wyatt Earp was dead.

Lake salvaged what he could from his brief association with a man he had come genuinely to admire. He penned an extraordinary story that made Wyatt Earp an American legend. If Wyatt had lived, the book might have been very different. But if he could have seen *Frontier Marshal* (1931) as it finally appeared, the old frontiersman probably would have approved of

Wyatt Earp, circa 1928. In this photograph of Wyatt taken near the end of his life, the old frontiersman looks the part of the respectable and successful man he aspired to be. Photograph no. 76624, Lincoln Ellsworth Collection, Arizona Historical Society.

what Lake had written and even sworn it was true. Ironically, the book that Wyatt had hoped would settle all the old questions and rescue his reputation merely assured his place as perhaps the most controversial peace officer in frontier history.

Wyatt Earp was a hard man who lived in troubled times. His values remained consistent with the modernizing forces that were changing America in the late nineteenth century. He even won the admiration of rich and powerful men like Horace Tabor, Lucky Baldwin, and William Randolph Hearst, who shared those values and called him friend. He never doubted his code, and he never sought absolution for his actions. He did what he thought was right, and, judged by the standards of justice at the time, he was right more often than not.

There were moments in Wyatt Earp's life when violating his standards compromised his reputation, but overall, like the age that spawned him, he was a mass of contradictions that ultimately yielded positive change. All nerve and self-confidence, Wyatt was determined to make a place for himself in the "root-hog-or-die" environment that was precursor to the modern West. In the end, he never realized his dreams of success, but he was not ashamed of his life. And for good reason.

2

Wild Bill Hickok

Living Legend, Dead Hero, Frontier Icon

Joseph G. Rosa

There is no Sunday west of Junction City, no law west of Hays City, and no God west of Carson City," declared James Butler Hickok in 1874, which prompted the editor of the Wichita, Kansas, *Weekly Beacon* on October 28 to add that "his remark bids fair to go into history as thoroughly representative of an epoch." If Hickok (or "Wild Bill" as he was generally called) did coin what has since become a much-used quote, he displayed a greater grasp of western social affairs than he is generally credited with, and he had the ability to describe graphically the difference between settled, civilized areas and the border or frontier.

Hickok's declaration received nationwide attention and was read avidly by a public besotted with the derring-do of "Wild West" heroes, of whom he was certainly the most famous at the time. It was the era of the western dime novel and, to a lesser extent, theatrical plays and exhibitions depicting life on the frontier as some imagined it and others experienced it. Hickok first received national attention via the February 1867 issue of *Harper's New Monthly Magazine.* In an article titled simply "Wild Bill" written by Colonel George Ward Nichols, an established writer and former aide-de-camp to General William T. Sherman in the Civil War, the colonel's description of "William Hitchcock's" marvelous adventures and miraculous escapes (aided by his wonderfully intelligent mare "Black Nell") enthralled or irritated some of those who knew Hickok personally. Many have concluded that Hickok himself was responsible for the tall tales, but truth and fiction seemed equally divided, and others besides Hickok talked to Nichols. Nevertheless, once the article was published, Wild Bill became a national celebrity and captivated readers in Europe, where the magazine enjoyed a limited circulation.

Like most plainsmen, Hickok was adept at leg-pulling. When Colonel Nichols interviewed Wild Bill in 1865, he was convinced that Hickok had

Wild Bill Hickok, circa 1864–1865. The original is a carte de viste *uncredited but believed to be the work of Charles W. Scholten of Springfield, Missouri, who photographed Hickok several times. This image typifies the legendary "Wild Bill." Courtesy of James Joplin.*

killed "hundreds of men." Nichols stated: "I believed then every word Wild Bill uttered, and I believe it to-day." Interviewed by Henry M. Stanley in 1867, who asked him how many men he had killed "to his certain knowledge," Hickok replied "considerably over a hundred, a long ways off." Such a large number of victims should have alerted both men to Hickok's sense of humor, but it did not. An inveterate gambler, Wild Bill remained poker-faced when confronted by greenhorns, and we can only guess at his mood when in August 1873 in Springfield, Missouri, he was approached by a cub reporter and asked for his views on "Caesarism." Apparently, there was some talk of upgrading Ulysses S. Grant from president to emperor. According to the *Weekly Patriot* of October 9, the young man sought out Wild Bill for an opinion because he was the "Great Statesman of the Plains." Between frequent "sips of something at the bar," he learned that if Grant was elevated to emperor, Hickok expected to be made U.S. marshal for the Oklahoma Territory, and if he was not, "I will get it or I'll take it. If anyone else gets it I'll go down there, and then there'll be hell. There will be Caesarism there for a certainty." Eventually tiring of both the subject and the interviewer, Hickok threatened to boot him out of the saloon!

Wild Bill's sense of humor and delight in practical jokes as a child and teenager were among his family's fondest memories. Indeed, they admitted that they had never really known him as an adult and regarded the "tall tales" he told various journalists and other gullibles as an extension of his youthful high spirits. Cyrus Edwards, who knew Wild Bill at Junction City in 1867 and later at Ellsworth, Kansas, recalled that Hickok was actually two people. He was outwardly cool, collected, and utterly fearless in a fight or in carrying out his duties as a peace officer. But away from the public, he was a man who loved to read books and who was extremely knowledgeable about the West and the events that took place in Missouri during the Civil War. Socially, Edwards said of Hickok, "I never saw a better behaved man in the presence of nice women."

This view was shared by Elizabeth Bacon Custer, who also admitted that she wished she could have accompanied him on a scout, simply because she was convinced that in his company she would have been perfectly safe.

The well-mannered side of Hickok, when he could be charm itself and impress people with his courtesy and knowledge of the West, was in direct contrast to the man of action who left no one in any doubt that he would resort to force if "put upon" or if his official status demanded it. As some learned to their cost, Wild Bill was a good friend in a crisis, but he was also an implacable enemy. Even Hickok's personal appearance was impressive. He was a man who stood out in a crowd. He had distinctive features: high cheekbones, broad forehead, large jawbones, an aquiline nose, and a firm chin. A straw colored moustache that varied in length or fashion adorned a sensuous mouth, and his blue-gray eyes, normally gentle and friendly, became icy cold when he was aroused. He stood over six feet tall, was broad shouldered and narrow waisted, and wore his auburn hair shoulder length, plainsman style, which many believed served as an incitement to Indians to try to "lift" it.

Hickok's reputation as an "Indian fighter" stems from his employment by the frontier army following the Civil War. In early 1867, in the wake of a number of Indian attacks on settlements, the U.S. government ordered General Winfield Scott Hancock to Kansas in command of an expedition designed to convince the Indian tribes that the United States wanted peace and, if necessary, would use force to preserve it. "Hancock's Indian War," as it was later called, achieved little but eventually led to a peace treaty in 1868. Hickok was among a number of frontiersmen hired as scouts, couriers, and guides. During the five months in which he was actively engaged with the Seventh Cavalry, Hickok received a lot of attention from the press and from the calvary's second in command, Major General George A. Custer. In 1872, writing in *The Galaxy* magazine, Custer recalled how impressed he was by Hickok's strength of character and his control over others and declared that Hickok was "a Plainsman in every sense of the word, yet unlike any other of his class . . . then as now the most famous scout on the Plains."

Like many of his contemporaries, Hickok was variously employed between military engagements. He also served as a deputy U.S. marshal and as a peace officer at Hays City and Abilene, reputed to be two of the "toughest" towns in Kansas. Once Hickok became involved in law enforcement, his reputation snowballed. Although he was not a professional peace officer, he took the job seriously. Generally regarded as a "terror to evil-doers," and as a "bad man to fool with" (bolstered by his exposure in *Harper's* magazine), Hickok became an object of public awe and admiration.

By 1872 Hickok had forsaken life on the plains and stints as a peace officer for more relaxing pursuits, notably gambling, which was an abiding passion. It was during that summer, while languishing in Kansas City, Missouri, that he was persuaded by Sidney Barnett, a Canadian promoter, to make his first theatrical public appearance by acting as master of ceremonies at a "Grand Buffalo Hunt" to be held at Niagara Falls. It proved to be a financial failure, but Hickok's fame as an Indian scout drew a large crowd. Later, in the summer of 1873, when Hickok lived in Springfield, Missouri, where he gambled for a living, he received a letter from his scouting companion and friend of many years Buffalo Bill Cody, asking Hickok if he would like to come east to New York and appear in his theatrical combination that toured eastern cities, staging western dramas, sometimes as many as three different plays a week.

Unlike Hickok, Bill Cody loved attention and was quickly put out if he thought that someone else was stealing his thunder. Such jealousy seems odd when one recalls that Cody was one of the truly great Indian scouts and trailers, as well as a renowned buffalo hunter. His theatrical aspirations sprang from a meeting with the redoubtable Ned Buntline (E.Z.C. Judson) at Fort McPherson in 1869. Ned's reputation as a dime novelist and alcoholic was legion, even though he was "out West" on a series of temperance lectures. According to Hiram Robbins, who managed Cody's theatrical troupe for some time and also wrote some of the plays, Ned was looking for Wild Bill. He was probably familiar with Hickok's appearance in two of *DeWitt's Ten Cent Romances* in 1867 ("Wild Bill the Indian Slayer" and "Wild Bill's First Trail"). Robbins claimed that when Ned approached Hickok, the frontiersman refused to speak to him. So Ned talked instead to Cody. Within months, his dime novel *Buffalo Bill, King of the Border Men* was serialized by the *New York Weekly* and other periodicals. Based largely upon Wild Bill's adventures, the yarn made Cody famous and Hickok angry. Ned had Wild Bill killed by a woman in revenge for her "lover" Dave Tutt, who in real life had been killed by Wild Bill in a shootout in Springfield in 1865.

In December 1872 Cody and his friend John B. Omohundro, better known as "Texas Jack," were persuaded by Ned Buntline to resign as army scouts and go east to Chicago, where they appeared in a series of stage dramas based upon the *Border Men* novel. When the season ended in early 1873 they parted ways from Buntline in a dispute over profits and decided to set up their own show. But they needed a replacement, and Hickok was the obvious choice. While Cody, Omohundro, and Buntline had been treading the boards in the East, Hickok was again the center of attention out West. In February 1873 it was widely reported that he had been murdered by some Texans at Fort Dodge. Several sympathetic "obituaries" were published bemoaning his loss before Hickok himself advised the press that reports of his death were premature. In the Springfield *Advertiser,* however, as a tongue-in-cheek gesture, he announced "I am dead!" for the benefit of the Kansas

City newspapers. Hickok could not resist a dig at Ned Buntline's abortive attempts to murder him with his pen, "having failed he is now, so I am told, trying to have it done by some Texans, but he has signally failed so far."

Confident that Hickok and Buntline would not meet face-to-face, Cody reasoned that Wild Bill would be a splendid draw. Cody's offer of a large financial reward eventually overcame Hickok's reluctance to appear on stage, so Wild Bill made his debut in a surprise appearance at the Bowery Theater, where he gave an "exhibition of rapid pistol-shooting and fancy shots." To an audience already captivated by the dime novel stories about Hickok and Cody, the sight of the real "Wild Bill" drawing and firing pistols with skill and rapidity (accompanied by a lot of noise and clouds of white powder smoke) must have been mind-boggling.

One can only assume that Hickok was in desperate need of cash for him to have agreed to appear with Cody and to play himself on stage. Such actions were totally out of character. But the public was delighted, and Hickok became the center of attention. One report noted that he was an excellent billiard player and that his cueing was as deadly as his sixshooter prowess. Hickok's acting ability, however, left much to be desired, although some thought that "the great plainsman, humble scout, and law-preserver, Wild Bill, created a decided sensation in the drama, and gave a realistic rendition of scenes in the Western wilds." One enthusiast described him as "one of the greatest scouts of modern times," whereas another declared that he was "said to be the only member of the combination who is a real Indian fighter." Cody, who in 1872 had been awarded the Medal of Honor for his actions when Indian fighting in Nebraska, must have been quite miffed, but he was professional enough to remain silent. Nevertheless, Hickok's presence was a distinct asset despite his infuriating habit of firing his black powder blanks too close to the legs of the Indian "supers" (whites dressed as Indians).

Hickok, however, never accepted himself as a "living legend." In fact, his reputation as a "mankiller," which he steadfastly denied, displeased him. In addition, he was not impressed by the press's inaccurate reports (forgetting, perhaps, his own leg-pulling contribution), some of which were a curious blend of fact and fiction. In the February 21, 1874, issue of the Springfield, Massachusetts, *Republican,* the editor claimed that in Hickok's capacity as the "United States Marshal for the state of Kansas," he had made arrests where no one else dared.

By March 1874, despite the adulation of an admiring public and his financial rewards, Hickok was bored and readily acknowledged that he was no actor. One evening he told Cody's wife, Louisa, that he thought the trio were simply "making fools of themselves." He hated performing for the crowds, living out of a suitcase, and traveling constantly. Finally, when the troupe reached Rochester, New York, Hickok quit. Both Cody and Omohundro implored him to finish the season, but once Hickok's mind was made up, Cody recalled, he could not be dissuaded. As parting gifts, the two scouts gave him $1,000 in cash and a pair of .44-caliber Smith & Wesson "American" revolvers. Hickok then headed back to the West.

By the summer of 1874 he was back in Kansas City. From there he moved on to Cheyenne, where he spent much of the next eighteen months between trips to Kansas City and St. Louis. His gunfighting days might have been well behind him, and gambling was now an abiding passion, interspersed with hunting and guiding tourists. But Hickok's legendary reputation kept him in the public eye. In Cheyenne on March 5, 1876, he married Agnes Lake Thatcher, the widow of Bill Lake Thatcher, a circus owner who had been murdered in 1869. She first met Hickok in Abilene in 1871, and they had conducted a postal romance for some years. The press welcomed his marital venture and wished them both well. After a short honeymoon in Cincinnati, Hickok left Agnes with her family and returned west to join the gold rush to the Black Hills, and his destiny at the hands of the assassin Jack McCall.

James Butler Hickok was among the mass of people who migrated west during the 1850s and post–Civil War era. It was a largely unknown region that attracted all kinds. Many of those who went west came from the more settled areas of the East or from long-established societies in Europe for whom the American West represented a new life and a challenge. But for Hickok, the frontier was familiar territory. Born on May 27, 1837, in Homer, Illinois (later renamed Troy Grove), he was the fifth of seven children born to William Alonzo and Polly Butler Hickok, one of whom died in infancy. The Hickoks' origins can be traced back to Stratford-upon-Avon, Warwickshire, England, where they were neighbors of William Shakespeare. The American branch of the family began with William Hickocks, who sailed for Boston in 1635. By the eighteenth century, the name was generally spelled Hickok. During the Revolutionary War and again from 1812 to 1815, the Hickoks fought on the side of the Americans, yet remained proud of their English heritage. On Hickok's mother's side, the Butlers claimed kinship to General Benjamin Butler of Civil War fame. Today's Butlers are proud to include one George Bush as a relative.

When Alonzo and Polly, who were married in 1827, had their first child, Oliver, in 1830, they decided to leave the civilized East and head west, a move the family did not welcome. Hickok's parents were determined to strike out on their own. By the time James was born, they were established in Homer, which was still considered a part of the Illinois frontier. For some time, William ran a local store. The 1837 financial panic all but ruined him, however, and he was forced to hire himself out to neighbors to support his growing family.

By 1850, when James was thirteen, William and others were actively involved in the "Underground," an abolitionist movement devoted to assisting black slaves in escaping their indenture. As family tradition has it, on one occasion James accompanied his father in the transference of former slaves to a new hiding place. Bounty hunters gave chase and opened fire, and James heard his first shot "fired in anger." Indeed, for some years the family employed a young black woman named Hannah, who had been rescued from slavery. She later moved to Maldern, Illinois, and married. James, like the rest of the family, treated her with kindness and in later years was more at ease with black troops than were some of his contemporaries. General Phillip Sheridan was aware of this affinity and personally asked Hickok to keep an eye on the "colored troops" when he served with Generals William H. Penrose and Eugene A. Carr in 1868–1869.

William Alonzo Hickok's death in 1852 left the family property in the hands of James, Lorenzo, and Horace (their elder brother Oliver had left for California in 1851), and two sisters, Celinda and Lydia. James, whose adventuresome spirit, on occasion, had brought him into conflict with his parents, was "all fired anxious" to head west, but was persuaded to bide his time. Although the children had been brought up to be God-fearing and were reasonably well educated for their time, only James evinced any signs of independence. Family sources hint that this individualism had much to do with his relationship with his mother, a very demanding and possessive woman who managed to exert her influence over everyone but James.

James Hickok's chance to leave home came with the Kansas-Nebraska Act in 1854, which opened up the Kansas Territory to settlement. In June 1856, following much soul-searching and discussion over the pro- and anti-slavery disputes that were disrupting settlement, James and Lorenzo decided to go to Kansas to seek suitable farming land. If their search was successful, the family would join them. The pair had hardly reached the territory, however, when they received a letter advising them that their mother was ill. Lorenzo decided to return, leaving James to complete the search on his own.

James Hickok spent several months in the Leavenworth area, hiring himself out as a plowman or for odd jobs, before joining the expedition of Englishman Robert Williams that founded the village of Monticello in Johnson County. Here James (by now called "William" or "Bill" for an indeterminate reason) was accepted as a member of the community and acquired sixty acres of land. When elections were held in early 1858, he was one of four constables elected to support local magistrates. In his letters home he spoke of serving subpoenas, of working on his land, and of his particular passion—Mary Owen, the part-Shawnee daughter of John Owen, who had married into the tribe.

The Hickoks were appalled to learn about Mary and her background. Lorenzo was swiftly dispatched to talk James out of any ideas of marriage. James, however, had other plans. When he learned that his land had been preempted by a Wyandot Indian who had prior claim, he left Monticello and moved to Olathe to join his cousin Guy Butler. From there he went to Leavenworth and hired on as a teamster with Jones & Cartwright, for whom he worked for nearly two years. Here he met the Cody family and became a welcome guest. His brother, Horace, came out to visit him in 1859 and soon found himself divested of his best shirts, which James took with him on one of his trips to Denver City. Polly was very critical when she heard of her independent son's defection. She wrote to Horace and said she was "sorry to hear that James had gone to Pike's Peak[.] I do not know what he means by doing [so,] as he has in [not] writing to us [, for] we have had but one letter from him since you went away." She also expressed her concern over James's demeanor—was he cold toward his brother, and did he owe anyone money?

In May 1861 the family was alarmed to receive a letter from Guy Butler advising them that he had heard that James had died from "newmonia." Guy also said that Jones & Cartwright owed James money. Horace wrote immediately to the company at Leavenworth, which replied that James had been alive and well when he left them in late April, and that they had paid him off.

On July 12 Hickok was involved in an incident in Rock Creek, Nebraska Territory, which became immortalized as the "McCanles Massacre" and remains one of the most controversial incidents in his career. A row over money owed by Russell, Majors & Waddell to one David McCanles in payment for a building to be used as a relay station on their Pony Express route led to a shootout in which McCanles and two others were killed. James is alleged to have shot McCanles, but some think the real culprit was Horace Wellman, the station keeper, who had no liking for McCanles. Hickok, whose presence at the station has never been explained satisfactorily, Wellman, and J. W. ("Doc") Brink, a Pony Express rider, were arrested and given a hearing before a justice of the peace. The justice accepted their plea that they had been defending company property and they were released. In 1867 Colonel Nichols, in his *Harper's* story, increased the number of men involved to ten, and described, in Hickok's own words, how Wild Bill had fought and killed all of them!

During the Civil War, James Hickok served first as a teamster and then as a wagon master before joining the provost marshal's staff. His duties were varied. Recently, it has been discovered that on one occasion he was ordered into Springfield to prowl around the saloons during the day to see how many soldiers were drinking when they should have been on duty elsewhere. He was rescued from this and other mundane tasks (for some of which he was not paid) by General John B. Sanborn, who commanded the District of South-West Missouri. Hired as a scout and spy and paid $5 a day (a horse and equipment were also supplied), Hickok soon proved his worth. In later years, Sanborn described him as the coolest and best man he had. By the war's end, he was generally called "Wild Bill," a title some thought he was given because of his actions against rebel guerrillas.

The publication of the *Harper's* article in late January 1867 aroused a lot of anger in Springfield, Missouri, much of it directed toward Nichols. In the January 31 issue of the *Missouri Weekly Patriot,* the editor, although critical of Nichols, decided that Wild Bill was the innocent party and declared, tongue-in-cheek:

> *James B. Hickok . . . is a remarkable man. . . . No finer physique, no greater strength, no more personal courage, no steadier nerves, no superior skill with the pistol, no better horsemanship than his could any man of the million Federal soldiers of the war, boast of; and few did better or more loyal service as a soldier throughout the war.*

Hickok's growing reputation as a fighting man was further enhanced by Henry M. Stanley, who would later track down the missing explorer and missionary Dr. David Livingston in Africa. Stanley interviewed Hickok at Fort Zarah in early April 1867. Stanley had heard much of "Wild Bill" and was

> *agreeably disappointed when, on being introduced to him, we looked on a person who was the very reverse of all we had imagined. He was dressed in a black-sacque coat, brown pants, fancy shirt, leather leggings, and had on his head a beaver cap. Tall, straight, broad compact shoulders, herculean chest, narrow waist, and well-formed muscular limbs. A fine handsome face, free from any blemish, a light moustach* [sic], *a thin pointed nose, bluish-grey eyes, with a calm, quiet, benignant look, yet seemingly possessing some mysterious latent power, a magnificent forehead, hair parted from the center of the forehead and hanging down behind the ears in long, wavy, silk curls. He is brave, there can be no doubt; that fact is impressed on you at once before he utters a syllable. He is neither as coarse and illiterate as* Harper's Monthly *portrays him.*

Back in Troy Grove, the Hickoks were bemused by the conflicting reports of James coming back from the West. Writing from California, Oliver also expressed his own doubts about the *Harper's* yarn and added, "I would like to try him a shot or two with a rifle." Polly, still the domineering matriarch, refrained from comment on James's exploits in her known and limited correspondence. In a letter to her brother in 1868, however, she told him that Oliver was still living in California, while Lorenzo and James were out West—Lorenzo in New Mexico, and James in Kansas. Both had been in "government employ ever since the war."

Some sources claim that James spent a short time in Troy Grove in 1859 helping with the harvest, but the only authenticated visit was in 1869. He stopped off en route at Mendota, Illinois, and had his photograph taken dressed in the buckskin suit he had worn in the late Indian campaign. The family was delighted to see him, and local children later recalled being treated to an exhibition of his marksmanship. No reference to that visit has been found in family correspondence, but James's niece, Ethel, told this writer that he brought expensive gifts for his mother and sisters. They appreciated the gifts but would have preferred financial assistance. Nevertheless, Ethel hastened to add that her father, Horace, had assured her no one complained. Rather, they were all pleased to see him after his absence of so many years.

It is curious why the border scriveners elevated James Butler Hickok into a demigod and the foremost "mankiller" on the plains. Even if we disregard Hickok's leg-pulling, if one were to believe even half the alleged killings credited to "Wild Bill," he would indeed deserve such a reputation. Yet a number of discrepancies are revealed on examination. David C. McCanles, who may or may not have fallen victim to Hickok, was killed in 1861. It was 1865 before he fell out with his friend, Davis K. Tutt, over a card game debt in Springfield, and they fought a duel in the public square, which neither one wanted. Not until 1869 did Hickok again resort to his pistols. This time it was in his capacity as acting sheriff of Ellis County, Kansas. He killed one Bill Mulvey in August and Samuel Strawhun a month later. He next fired in anger in July 1870, when attacked by two soldiers at Hays City, killing one and wounding the other. Finally, on October 5, 1871, he shot gambler Phil Coe and also his own friend and former city jailer Michael Williams, who ran into the line of fire when Hickok and Coe exchanged shots. These killings total seven known individuals—a far cry from the "considerably over a hundred" men with which Hickok jokingly credited himself.

On the few occasions that Hickok indulged in fisticuffs, the press showed little interest. Stanley recalled the occasion when someone insulted him in a saloon, and Hickok picked up the miscreant and threw him across a billiard table. Later, during the period he was with Generals Carr and Penrose in 1868–1869, Hickok had a dispute with Mexican scout Mariano Autobees and ended up thrashing him. Next, in Wyoming, according to Luther North (the younger brother of Major Frank North, leader of the famous Pawnee

Battalion of Indian scouts), Hickok and a brawny mule skinner had a fistfight from which Hickok emerged the victor. Evidently, editors cared more for gory encounters—presumably in the belief that their readers shared their preferences. In truth, many journalists failed to understand the motivations of so-called "mankillers" or "shootists," as Hickok and his contemporaries were sometimes called. Although the word "gunfighter" can be traced back to 1874, it did not come into use until the 1890s, when it replaced the more explicit "mankiller." Today, of course, the term is generic and covers both the "good" and the "bad" men for whom the pistol was either a necessary tool for survival or the means by which one could gain wealth or prestige by force and fear.

This photograph of Wild Bill in buckskins is credited to Wilbur Blakeslee of Mendota, Illinois. Various dates have been suggested, but it is now thought that it was made by Blakeslee in March 1869, when Hickok passed through on his way to visit his mother. Within a year Hickok had discarded the center parting, which lends credence to the dating. Courtesy of the Kansas State Historical Society.

The gunfighter and the old-time duelist differed in many ways. Dueling required a certain discipline and was conducted under strict rules. In continental Europe the preference was for the sword, while Great Britain favored the pistol. England banned dueling early in the nineteenth century, but not so Ireland, whose "Code Duello" with its strict rules for duelists and their seconds was adopted in the United States, particularly in the South. When "revolving pistols" (as Sam Colt described his revolvers) appeared on the scene in the 1830s, the code was soon discarded in the West; being able to beat an opponent into action or to "get the drop" counted far more than protocol.

The revolver influenced social attitudes and proved a great asset in the hands of the military—in 1844 the Texas Rangers used it to great effect when outnumbered by Comanche Indians. It also encouraged men who avoided or feared hand-to-hand conflict to acquire a revolver or "equalizer." The bully and petty criminal's reliance on the revolver prompted some Californians in 1854 to condemn the "universal and cowardly practise of carrying revolvers." By the Civil War, however, the weapon was much in demand.

Cavalry regiments and guerrilla bands on both sides found the revolver indispensable. Some of these men were armed with as many as eight of them or carried spare loaded cylinders in belt pouches or in saddlebags. By the close of the war, a revolver was as much a part of a man's attire as a necktie.

The immediate postwar period set the stage for the legendary gunfighter, and he appeared in various guises. Hickok, regarded by many as the archetypal gunfighter, earned a reputation as one who always "has got his man." On November 15, 1881, the Kansas City *Journal of Commerce* explained to its readers that the "gentleman who has 'killed his man' is by no means a rara avis and could be found in church, on the street, driving a cab or indeed in almost any occupation, and if his homicidal talents had been employed in the enforcement of law and order, he would be ranked as a 'great Western civilizer.'" Many have since dubbed Wild Bill a "civilizer" in the belief that his employment as a peace officer in such places as Hays City and Abilene had led to a decline in crime and immorality. In reality, Wild Bill and other noted individuals who were hired to enforce and preserve law and order in the cowtowns were not concerned with morals unless they contravened city ordinances or state laws. As long as they could curb violence and prevent anarchy among the transient Texas cowboys, according to the townsfolk, they were doing their jobs.

To the press and public, however, Wild Bill was a larger-than-life individual, a two-gun Galahad, who, in a biblical sense, single-handedly tamed the likes of Hays City and Abilene, wreaking vengeance upon those who transgressed moral and state laws. Such an image is ridiculous and misleading, and it annoyed Hickok. There was little he could do, however, and he must have bitterly regretted some of his teasing exaggerations.

The old-time gunfighter, therefore, was a complex character who bore little resemblance to today's conception of him. Television and the movies portray him as a man apart, a loner, a man with a purpose who epitomizes good in the fight to save communities or individuals from evil. The gunfighter then rides off into the sunset to face a new challenge. He is a man without responsibilities and little or no physical contact or personal commitment. He remains a remote and shadowy character.

To suggest that Hickok was a loner, a man without friends, and in mortal fear of his life is a mistake. Wary he may have been of unprovoked attack or a bullet in the back, but he was very much a social animal. Gambling might have been compulsive for Hickok, but his passion was women. Throughout his career, as evidence shows, Hickok had many female companions. His first "love" was Mary Owen, the part-Shawnee girl he met in Kansas. Later, he was alleged to have had an affair with Dave McCanles's mistress, Sarah Shull, in Rock Creek. She denied it, but admitted that she had been attracted to him. During the Civil War, Hickok consorted with various women who worked in the saloon and gambling dens in Springfield or Rolla. There was also Susannah Moore, said to have been a Union spy, whom Hickok had met in the Ozarks.

According to the Leavenworth, Kansas, *Daily Bulletin* of February 13, 1867, "Wild Bill" arrived from the Far West accompanied by his "wife" and $20,000 worth of furs. We suspect that this valuation was inaccurate, and the reference to a "wife" an error. However, it might have been "Indian Annie," an Ellsworth laundress, who was described in later years as "Mrs. Wild Bill Hickok." She had had two children, a boy and a girl. Some claim that the boy was Hickok's son, but there is no concrete evidence to support this claim. As the city marshal of Abilene in 1871, Hickok shared his cabin with a succession of unnamed women. In more recent years the discovery of a tintype photograph of Wild Bill accompanied by a poem written in pencil by a young lady named Sadia or Sadie (and based upon a poem by John Saxe) suggests that he had an affair while at Springfield in 1872–1873. It is also a part of Hickok's mythology that he married Calamity Jane (Martha Jane Canary) and that they had a daughter. Recent research, however, has confirmed a long-held belief that this story was an elaborate hoax.

Agnes Lake's relationship with Hickok was another matter. When she and her circus appeared in Abilene in 1871, she fell for him "clear to the basement," according to Charles Gross, who added that she "tried her best to get him to marry her & run the Circus[.] Bill told me all about it. I said why don't you do it[?] He said 'I know she has a good show, but when she is done with the West, she will go East & I don't want any paper collar on[,] its me for the West. I would be lost back in the States.'"

But, as previously noted, following several years of correspondence, the pair were married in Cheyenne five months before Hickok's death. Agnes wrote to his mother and said, "I loved James for three years before I married him." Following his death, she declared: "It is impossible for a human being to love any better than what I did him. I can see him day and night before me. The longer he is dead the worse I feel." Yet within a year she was in the Black Hills visiting his grave, accompanied by her new husband-to-be, George Carson, who soon disappeared. Until Agnes's death in 1907, she retained the Hickok name.

The bedrock of Hickok's legend, to some historians, was his mankilling reputation and his marksmanship. Although research has lowered his victim "tally," and despite expert analysis and practical tests, many still accept his status as a "pistoleer extraordinary." As early as July 1, 1879, the editor of the Cheyenne *Daily Leader,* when citing an erroneous report that Hickok's ivory-handled pistols had been stolen from his coffin, claimed that they were "made expressly for him and were finished in a manner unequalled by any ever before manufactured in this or any other country. It is said that a bullet from them never missed its mark." The article went on, "Remarkable stories are told of the dead shootist's skill with these guns. He could keep two fruit cans rolling, one in front and one behind him, with bullets fired from these firearms. This is only a sample story of the hundreds which are related of his incredible dexterity with these revolvers."

Few would doubt that Hickok was a good pistol shot, but whether he (and others) could really shoot as well as some believe is a moot point. The recent discovery of the coroner's report and witness statements taken following Hickok's duel with Dave Tutt in 1865 has revealed that when he shot Tutt, who faced him sideways (dueling fashion), they were seventy-five yards apart! Nevertheless, a study of some of the better-known marksmen and markswomen of Hickok's day reveals how good he might have been had better records been kept of his shooting. Indeed, the skill displayed by the likes of Doc Carver, Adam Bogardus, Walter Winans, Lillian Smith, and Annie Oakley is impressive. Carver and Bogardus appeared at one time with Buffalo Bill's Wild West Exhibition, as did Smith and Oakley. Many thought that Lillian was the better shot of the two, but she lacked Annie's presence and eventually left the company. Winans, who performed truly remarkable pistol feats at Britain's famous Bisley range, did not have much time for target shooting. Rather, he believed that a man should be taught to shoot accurately and with speed (no more than three seconds to aim and fire) in order that he could survive a life-or-death situation. He tried to interest the British government in his theory but met with little success.

Shortly before his death in January 1917, Buffalo Bill gave an interview to journalist and gun enthusiast Chauncey Thomas, which appeared in *Outdoor Life* (in later years he claimed to own some of Hickok's targets, the whereabouts of which are unknown today). According to Thomas, Cody told him that Hickok's marksmanship was good, but others were better. Wild Bill's secret lay in his keeping cool under fire and never getting rattled. Most men, when they pulled their pistols, cocked them after they cleared the holster. Hickok, however, cocked his pistol as he drew and fired as it came level. "Bill Hickok was not a bad man, as is so often pictured," Cody said. "But he was a bad man to tackle. Always kinda cheerful, almost about it. And he never killed a man unless that man was trying to kill him. That's fair."

Cody's comments might conflict with the recollections of others, but we cannot fault him when he described how Hickok cocked his pistol as he drew it—which is what would have happened when using the butt forward reverse or plains draw. The palm of the hand faced outward and went around the inside of the butt. At the same time the index finger was pushed through the trigger guard and the thumb locked around the hammer spur. As the pistol was pulled up and spun forward, it was also cocked and lined up on its target. Like anyone who relied upon a firearm, Hickok constantly checked his weapons. Each chamber was carefully loaded, and before placing the copper percussion caps on the cones or nipples set in the rear of the chambers, they were checked to ensure that they contained their fulminate of mercury. When the hammer struck the cap, it exploded the fulminate, which flashed a flame into the powder in the chamber and discharged the pistol. On one occasion when questioned by Charles Gross at Abilene, concerning his habit of reloading his pistols daily, paying special attention to the powder and caps, Hickok remarked that he was not ready to go yet and "when I pull I must be sure."

Hickok's concern over the reliability of his ammunition was reflected in his firearms. His role as a fictional "two-gun Galahad" stemmed from his habit of carrying two pistols ("he was never seen without them," Custer recalled), which led some to accuse him of "grandstanding." This criticism is nonsense. Hickok (and others) carried two pistols simply because black powder was subject to dampness that caused misfires, and sometimes caps failed, or spent caps jammed the action. A second or "reserve" pistol was a necessity.

Nevertheless, despite their shortcomings, "cap-and-ball" revolvers were remarkably accurate. The ability to hit two-foot-high letter "Os" in saloon signs at distances ranging from 50 to 100 yards, as well as other seemingly difficult targets, is among the many feats credited to Hickok. Perhaps he could. But like most frontiersmen faced with a potential killing situation, he was more concerned with accuracy at thirty paces. And the classic feat of pushing a cork through the neck of a whiskey bottle with a bullet without breaking the neck would depend on the caliber—a .36 would be better suited than a .45.

In 1854 the British government ordered trials of Colt's Dragoon and Navy pistols. The .44-caliber Dragoon was accurate at 450 yards and the .36-caliber Navy from 50 to 200 yards. Later, in the 1870s, U.S. government trials of Colt's .45-caliber "Peacemaker" confirmed its accuracy and reliability. Like the British government, however, the U.S. government decided that revolvers were basically short-range weapons. What really counted was the ability of those armed with them.

A spectacular feature of the gunfighter myth, of which Hickok was said to be its chief exponent, was the so-called "lightning draw." The modern term "fast draw" meant nothing to the old-timers. Their word was "quick," and the expression "quick as thought" described a mental reaction rather than physical speed. When Hickok drew a pistol, he had already made up his mind to use it, whereas lesser individuals, who grabbed for a weapon in haste or in anger and then hesitated, perished or suffered serious wounds.

Hickok's reputation by the late 1860s ensured attention wherever he went. Elizabeth Bacon Custer recalled that once Hickok became aware of such attention he would disappear into the nearest saloon. One brave tourist even sent him flowers and an invitation. Hickok declined both, and it was only through the intercession of General George Custer that he was persuaded to emerge. One tourist, a young Ohio girl, was reported to have rendered Hickok speechless when she confronted him with the remark that her "papa" had told her to "come out here and marry some great man like you." Those fortunate individuals who managed to converse with Hickok were impressed. W. E. Webb, who met Wild Bill at Hays City in 1869, later recalled that he and his companions tried to persuade Hickok to forsake the pistol for some less dangerous pursuit, but to no avail. Hickok was determined to remain on the frontier.

Wild Bill's appointment as a deputy U.S. marshal in August 1867 involved him in federal offenses, but during his period as a peace officer in Hays City and Abilene he was faced with civil crimes and politics. Hickok was no stranger to politics. A year earlier, in March 1868, when moves were afoot in Congress to impeach President Andrew Johnson, Hickok was a member of a political group called the "Republicans of Ellis County," which met at Lawrence in support of the motion. Wild Bill was elected vice president and spoke at some length. These ventures did not endear him to the Ellis County Democrats.

Founded in September 1867, Hays City was, for some time, an end-of-track railroad town, mostly populated by gangers, graders, and others. This population was followed by an influx of gamblers, prostitutes, and troops from nearby Fort Hays. Much of the violence was racially inspired. Early in 1869, when black troops from the fort created a near riot, Lieutenant Colonel Anderson D. Nelson, the post commander, threatened to place Hays City under martial law. Furious, the governor demanded an explanation. Nelson assured him that it was only a threat. By July, when the elected sheriff of Ellis County was no longer in office (for unexplained reasons), the citizens organized a petition to the governor, asking him to appoint one R. A. Eccles as sheriff. The petition was promptly ignored. In August the county commissioners and the vigilance committee held a special election for the sheriff post and other officers. Wild Bill was elected acting sheriff. Although the governor promptly declared Hickok's election to be illegal, the commissioners announced that they were guided by state statutes. Later, the governor realized that they had a point. In 1870 the governor asked the state legislature to change the rules so that only the governor could appoint a midterm sheriff in the absence of an undersheriff.

During Hickok's brief but hectic term in office, he killed two men in the line of duty. A few days after an election, Wild Bill was confronted by an armed drunk, Bill Mulvey, a St. Louis "tough." He and several other drunken "roughs" or "wolves" were shooting up the town. When Mulvey decided to include citizens in his target practice (fortunately without hitting anyone), Hickok arrived and ordered Mulvey to disarm. When Mulvey's response was to aim his pistol at Wild Bill, Hickok opened fire. Shot through the neck and the lungs, Mulvey died a few hours later.

Mulvey's death did not concern many of the townsfolk. There had been trouble with the rowdy element for some months. It came to a head shortly before the citizens' petition was sent to the governor, when several troublemakers were singled out and ordered to leave town. Among these were Joseph Weiss, a former inmate of the state penitentiary (and now a deputy U.S. marshal), and Samuel Strawhun, a teamster and occasional army courier. Alonzo B. Webster, the postmaster, who later became the mayor of Dodge City, was given the unenviable task of ordering them out of town. Weiss and Strawhun invaded his post office and attacked him. Webster shot Weiss dead, and Strawhun fled when Hickok appeared and offered to take over the fight.

Late on the night of September 27 Strawhun reappeared with some cronies and got drunk in John Bittles's saloon. They removed beer glasses to a vacant lot with threats to "send up" (kill) anyone who attempted to retrieve them. The place was like bedlam when Hickok arrived. He retrieved some of the glasses and placed them on the bar. When Strawhun threatened Wild Bill, Hickok shot him. Some claimed that Strawhun smashed a beer glass and, grasping it by the handle, jabbed it at Hickok, a move that could have blinded or scarred Hickok for life. Others said that Strawhun pulled a pistol. The following morning, the coroner's jury decided that Hickok had shot in self-defense. "Too much credit cannot be given to Wild Bill for his endeavour to rid this town of such dangerous characters as this Stranhan [*sic*] was," wrote an eyewitness.

The next month, Hickok prevented a saloon lynching, which won him the gratitude of Major George Gibson, the new post commander at Fort Hays. Soon afterward, however, Gibson questioned Wild Bill's authority to act as sheriff when Hickok tried to remove one Bob Connors (charged with a murder at Pond Creek) from the post guardhouse. Hickok admitted that he did not have a commission signed by the governor, who reiterated his belief that Hickok had "no legal authority whatsoever to act as Sheriff of Ellis County, nor under the circumstances through which the vacancy occurred can any Sheriff be chosen until the regular election in November."

Interspersed with his duties as acting sheriff was Hickok's active role as a deputy U.S. marshal. The discovery of subpoenas and other documents hidden for more than a century indicate that Hickok's duties were varied. Employed originally by U.S. Marshal Charles C. Whiting in 1867, he was then commissioned by Whiting's successor, Dana Houston, and remained active until early 1871. The majority of Hickok's cases concerned the theft of government property (horses and mules), desertion from the army, illegal selling of tobacco and whiskey, and theft of timber from government land for use as railroad ties and cordage. Hickok was also involved in cases related to counterfeit money. One individual, who made the mistake of passing Hickok a fake bill, was hotly pursued to Abilene and arrested.

Adolph Roenigk recalled in 1927 that on one occasion when Wild Bill arrived at Fossil Creek (since renamed Russell) in his capacity as a deputy U.S. marshal, he was dressed in a buckskin suit, complete with fringes on the sleeves and the seams of his trousers. Around his waist was a belt containing a pair of sixshooters. This image is identical to the photograph of Hickok made at Mendota early in 1869. Roenigk, however, thought he presented "such a picture as could be seen on a dime novel."

Hickok had been ordered to check reports that a number of men were cutting railroad ties and cordage at Paradise Creek, about twenty-four miles from Fossil Creek Station. At that time locomotives burned wood in Kansas, but by the time the railroad reached Colorado, coal became the principal fuel. Because Paradise Creek was sited on what was still government land, and cutting wood there was illegal, Hickok hired a horse and set out. Lieutenant L. W. Cooke of the Third Infantry advised him that he had seen one of the men, John Hobbs, who claimed to have a contract, cutting ties. Hickok questioned Hobbs and his companions, but was not satisfied with their explanation and placed Charles Hamilton, Charles Vernon, and Hobbs under arrest.

Back at Hays City, Hickok and Cooke gave evidence before Commissioner Hill P. Wilson. Wilson decided that there was a case to answer and ordered Hickok to take the men to Topeka, Kansas, for trial. The men were later discharged, however, presumably for want of evidence. Hickok, meanwhile, having lost the election for sheriff to his Democrat deputy, Peter Lanniahan, spent some of his time in Topeka. In early 1870 he began a tour of Missouri, visiting friends from the war. In Jefferson City he was introduced to the members of the state legislature, which caused something of a sensation on the floor of the House. Back in Kansas, he headquartered at Junction City, where he became a familiar figure, occasionally demonstrating his marksmanship by shooting stable rats or quail.

In July 1870 Hickok returned to Hays City. Whether this trip was to visit friends or related to his work as a deputy U.S. marshal is uncertain. Late on the night of July 17 he was involved in a shootout with two Seventh Cavalry troopers, Jeremiah Lonergan and John Kile, a conflict described by some as a "drunken row," and by others as a deliberate attack on Hickok. Grabbed from behind by Lonergan and pulled to the ground, which prevented him from drawing his pistols, Hickok was then attacked by Kile. In Kile's attempt to shoot him, his Remington pistol misfired. By this time Hickok had managed to draw one of his own pistols. He shot Kile twice and then Lonergan through the knee, forcing his opponent to release him. Afterward, Hickok escaped the wrath of his attackers' companions and hid out on Boot Hill, which gave him a good vantage point. Kile died the next day in the post hospital. It was claimed later that Custer issued a "dead or alive" order for Hickok, but the general was in New York at the time. Official post returns, however, confirm that no military action was taken because Kile's death was the result of a drunken row and was not in the line of duty. Ten years later, J. W. Buel, in his *Heroes of the Plains* (1882), claimed that Hickok had battled with fifteen troopers.

Wild Bill's press-inspired reputation as a "terror to evil-doers" continued to anger him. Yet, try as he might, he was never able to dispel the more ridiculous and sometimes malicious tales. His appointment as marshal of Abilene was, in part, due to his reputation and because he was the kind of individual who would "fight fire with fire," according to Mayor Joseph G. McCoy, who hired him.

Abilene was the first of Kansas's famous cowtowns. When Joseph G. McCoy first saw Abilene in early 1867, it consisted of a post office and several saloons and had been a remote stagecoach stop until the Union Pacific Railway Company (Eastern Division) put it on the map. A cattle buyer from Illinois, McCoy was anxious to find a place from which to transport Texas longhorn cattle to eastern markets by rail. State legislation barred such cattle because of the Texas Fever endemic to them, which was life-threatening to domestic stock. But following lengthy debate, the Kansas state legislature agreed finally to the movement of Texas cattle through Kansas to a railhead, provided they were kept well away from domesticated areas and drovers kept to predetermined routes. Abilene then sold McCoy sufficient land to build shipping pens, alongside which the U.P.E.D (Union Pacific Railway Company, Eastern Division) constructed a switch that permitted the loading of one hundred cars at a time. Flyers were dispatched to Texas and soon herds of cattle were being driven along a trail established between Texas, via Indian Territory (present-day Oklahoma) and Kansas, by an Indian trader named Jesse Chisholm. The Chisholm Trail stopped at Wichita. From there to Abilene the route was the "Abilene Trail" or "McCoy's Extension." On September 5, 1867, the first cattle train left Abilene for the East.

By 1869, however, the citizens of Abilene, fed up with the antics of the Texas cowboys, gamblers, pimps, and prostitutes, applied for incorporation

Wild Bill's most famous portrait, one of four made by Gurney & Son in New York, circa 1873–1874. Courtesy of Joseph G. Rosa.

and were granted third-class city status. This recognition enabled them to hold local elections and pass ordinances to control gambling and prostitution. The first marshal was Thomas James "Bear River" Smith, appointed in early May 1870 by acting mayor T. C. Henry. Tom Smith proved to be an excellent marshal because of exper-ience he gained as a troubleshooter a year or so before on the main Union Pacific route across Wyoming Territory. In November 1870, though, he was killed by a couple of homesteaders, who were subsequently given long jail sentences. Most of Abilene's citizens would have preferred they receive the rope.

Several stopgap marshals were employed during the winter of 1870–1871, but with a new cattle season about to start, the council realized that they needed another strong man like Smith. Newly elected mayor Joseph G. McCoy recommended Hickok, and on April 15, by a majority vote, the city council approved the mayor's choice of Hickok as the new marshal.

Hickok's brief but hectic period as marshal of Abilene during its greatest and last season as a cowtown greatly contributed to his legendary status. Since the town's incorporation, Abilene had expanded. During the cattle season (May to October), its population mushroomed by an estimated five thousand Texas cowboys (spread across the season) and several hundred "undesirables" involved in gambling and prostitution. Despite the income from fines and license fees imposed by the council and enforced by the police, the presence of the Texans and the gambling elite was a constant irritation to the more God-fearing folk. In July the "respectable ladies" of Abilene persuaded the mayor and council to move most of the saloons, gambling dens, and bordellos from Texas Street to a new location a quarter mile south. This "Devil's Addition" pleased the Texans. An omnibus ran a regular service from the city to the addition for the benefit of visitors, an arrangement that worked well until late September, when the council ordered Hickok and his deputies to close the place down.

Hickok took his job seriously. On May 8, when a councilman absented himself during a meeting, Hickok was ordered to bring him back. When

"How to get a quorum in a council meeting in Abilene, 1871. Courtesy of the Kansas State Historical Society.

the man refused, Wild Bill picked him up, threw him over his shoulder, and carried him back into the room. To prevent any further attempts to escape, Hickok remained outside the door. Many people found the incident amusing, and a cartoon was produced and widely circulated. Others, however, were furious. On May 18 the Abilene *Chronicle* accepted that Hickok was only obeying orders but thought that the council's treatment of its reluctant member made it a laughingstock.

By July 1871 Hickok had posted anti-firearm notices all over town, but he was well aware that no amount of legislation would disarm the Texans. This problem was noted by a correspondent for the Kansas City *Journal of Commerce,* who remarked on Hickok's habit of visiting the railroad depot to keep an eye on new arrivals, and his strict and efficient enforcement of police regulations. On August 13 the paper reported that Hickok had struck a Texas drover on the head with the butt of his revolver and then booted him in the face. No explanation was offered, and it was claimed that friends of the injured man had advised Hickok to leave town, "but they mistook their man, as 'Wild Bill' is the last man to be driven away by such threats. At last accounts he was still there and unharmed."

One prominent Texan who claimed to be unafraid of Hickok or his awesome reputation was John Wesley Hardin. He came up the Chisholm Trail with the Columbus Carrol herd early in cattle-shipping season and was reported to have killed several Mexican herders en route. While in Abilene, Hardin murdered a man by shooting him through the wall of his hotel room, and he also chased another Mexican to Sumner City and shot him for the murder of fellow Texan William Cohron. Hardin's meeting with Hickok, however, was never reported in the contemporary press, and its only source is in Hardin's autobiography, published a year after his death in 1895. According to Hardin, he fooled Hickok with the "Border Roll": when ordered to disarm, one pulled one's pistols from their holsters, reversed them, and offered them butts forward. As the unsuspecting lawman reached for them, it was a simple matter to spin them back into the hand. Understandably, like his predecessor, Tom Smith, Hickok did not trust the Texans, who had a disturbing reputation for ambushing one another or those who had offended them. Few Texans, however, cared to tangle with Hickok. The cry "Wild Bill is on the street!" usually served to keep things peaceful.

In September, when Hickok and his policemen were ordered to close down the "Devil's Addition," those who left created a mass exodus to Kansas City, St. Louis, and other places east and west. The place was almost deserted, and the remaining cattlemen returned to the few saloons on Texas Street. On the evening of October 5 some Texans who had stayed behind for the Dickinson County Fair (but were deterred by heavy rain) meandered around town, where they amused themselves by "persuading" citizens to buy rounds of drinks. At around nine o'clock, approximately fifty carousers, led by Texas gambler Phil Coe, reached the Alamo saloon, drunk and ready for a fight. A shot was fired, and Hickok appeared at the front of the saloon. He had warned the Texans earlier against carrying firearms within city limits and angrily demanded to know who had fired the shot. There is some confusion over what happened next. In the October 14 issue of the *Chronicle,* the editor provides what is considered to be the most graphic account. Wild Bill, aware that the crowd was determined to "fight," confronted Coe, who said that he had shot a dog:

> *Coe had his revolver in his hand, as had also other parties in the crowd. As quick as thought, the Marshal drew two revolvers and both men fired almost simultaneously. Several shots were fired during which Mike Williams, a policeman, came around the corner for the purpose of assisting the Marshal, and rushing between him and Coe received two of the shots intended for Coe. . . . The Marshal, surrounded by the crowd, and standing in the light, did not recognize Williams, whose death he deeply regrets. Coe was shot through the stomach, the ball coming out through his back; he lived in great agony until Sunday evening. . . . It is said that he had a spite at Wild Bill and had threatened to kill him—which Bill believed he would do if he gave him the opportunity. One of Coe's shots went through Bill's coat and another passed between his legs striking the floor behind him. The fact is Wild Bill's escape was truly marvellous.*

The two men were about eight feet apart when they opened fire. Coe must either have been drunk or a poor shot to have missed Hickok at that distance. The *Chronicle* concluded that any more attempts to kill police officers would mean further loss of life on the part of the violators. Other local papers, in their own reports of the shootout, agreed that in those circumstances Hickok's actions were justifiable. Predictably, in Texas, editors called for Hickok to be hanged or jailed.

Many of Abilene's citizens sympathized with Hickok and shared his grief over Williams's death. Some recalled later that when Hickok carried Williams into the Alamo saloon and laid him down on a billiard table, tears ran down his cheeks. Hickok recovered swiftly and then began the task of driving the Texans out of town and back to their camps. Within an hour, Abilene was like a ghost town.

The October 10 issue of the Kansas City *Journal of Commerce* reported that Williams had been trying to stop two fighting Texans when he was shot, having reached them "simultaneously with the discharge of 'Wild Bill's' pistol. The latter did not observe the former at the time." It was agreed that the shooting was an accident. Hickok paid for Williams's funeral, which was well attended, and the McGee Hook and Ladder Company escorted the coffin to the burial ground on Jefferson Street. Hickok is said to have visited Mike's young widow and given her his version of events.

Late in November Hickok was en route to Topeka by train when a woman warned him that she had heard five Texans planning to ambush him. He was then able to "circumvent" the parties, forcing them at pistol point to remain on board the train when he left it at Topeka. This "bloodless coup" was applauded by the press, and the Topeka *Daily Commonwealth* of November 25 declared that "we think he is entitled to the thanks of law-abiding citizens throughout the State for the safety of life and property at Abilene, which has been secured, more through his daring, than any other agency."

In December 1871 the Abilene city council drastically reconsidered the Texas cattle trade, arguing that its evils far outweighed its economic advantages. During the discussions it was decided that the town no longer needed the expensive services of a marshal of Hickok's caliber (he was paid $150 per month with a percentage of court fines and fifty cents a head for shooting stray dogs!). On December 13 Hickok and his police force were discharged. Pending negotiations for his last month's salary, Hickok went to Kansas City, which was to become his headquarters for the next eight months.

Socially, James Butler Hickok was now either a "notorious character" or a "famous" individual, depending upon one's viewpoint, but he remained in the public eye. In the summer, as has been noted, he appeared in Niagara Falls as master of ceremonies for Barnett's "Grand Buffalo Hunt." Barnett had not been very successful with its organization. The Quaker Indian agent blocked Barnett's attempt to hire Pawnee Indians from their Nebraska reservation, and the Indian Bureau refused to let them cross the border into Canada. Texas Jack Omohundro, who had been hired originally to take charge of the Pawnees, also backed out. Fortunately for Barnett, he was able to secure Sac & Fox Indians from their Canadian reservation. Wild Bill's appearance at the Falls on August 28 and 30, 1872, delighted the audience, especially those who had read newspaper or dime novel accounts of "Wild Bill" and now had an opportunity to see him in person.

Back in Kansas City, Hickok caused a stir during the Exposition Fair. On September 27, before an audience of approximately thirty thousand people, he stepped up and stopped the band from playing "Dixie," much to the annoyance of about fifty Texans who had requested it. Some of them pulled their pistols, but he "came away unscathed."

Hickok soon tired of Kansas City, or perhaps he was among a number of gamblers forced to move on by the city council. At any rate, by early October 1872 Hickok had settled in Springfield, Missouri, where he remained until August 1873, when Buffalo Bill Cody persuaded him to join his theatrical troupe. Soon after Hickok's arrival in 1872, it was reported that a "Wild Bill's Outfit" had killed Chief Whistler and two other members of the Cut-Off band of Sioux living in the Nebraska Republican River country. Some believed it was Hickok, but the real culprit was later identified as Mortimer N. Kress, known locally as "Wild Bill of the Blue River" to distinguish him from his better-known namesake.

When Hickok left Cody in March 1874, he returned to Kansas City, stopping off in North Topeka, where it was reported that he was suffering from eye trouble induced by the bright lights used in Cody's dramas. Others remarked upon his eyesight and treatment for "opthalmia." The late Mari Sandoz, in her book *The Buffalo Hunters,* claimed to have seen a report prepared by the surgeon at Camp Carlin in Wyoming Territory, which said that Hickok had advanced glaucoma. Camp Carlin never had a surgeon. It was simply a remount depot attached to Fort D. A. Russell. No such report was found amongst its records. Professional opinion, however, suggests that Hickok's eye trouble was probably trachoma, a common complaint on the Plains.

Hickok did not remain long in Kansas City and soon moved to Cheyenne, Wyoming Territory, where his presence was noted and welcomed in some quarters, especially among those who expressed concern at the lawless characters flooding into the city en route for the Black Hills. Surely the man who had tamed Abilene could do the same for Cheyenne? Hickok, however, had no intention of joining the police force. Instead, he pursued his love of gambling.

During the winter of 1874–1875 Hickok's sojourn in Cheyenne attracted little attention. In June 1875 he was among a number of individuals charged with vagrancy, for having no "visible means of support." His friends were outraged, and his case was continued—as it was several times—until his death led to a dismissal of the charge. Soon thereafter, Hickok disappeared from Cheyenne for some months. Some reports say that he may have ventured into the Black Hills. Annie Tallent, the first white woman into the Hills, recalled that in the summer of 1875 she had met Hickok in Cheyenne and that he had questioned her at some length about the Hills.

By April 1876, following his marriage to Agnes Lake in March, Hickok was in St. Louis, where it was reported that he had just returned from the Hills and would be happy to talk about it. He also organized an expedition that was later abandoned. Instead, he joined "Colorado" Charlie Utter's wagon train, which left Cheyenne for the Hills in late June.

Utter's party reached Deadwood, Dakota Territory, around July 12. Five days later, Hickok wrote to Agnes, advising her that he had been prospecting and that they would eventually have a home and be happy. Back in Cincinnati, Agnes was content. She had earlier advised Polly Hickok that James would send for her when he was settled. The night before his death on August 2, Hickok penned a letter to Agnes that contained this prophetic statement: "If such should be we never meet again, while firing my last shot, I will gently breathe the name of my wife—Agnes—and with wishes even for my enemies I will make the plunge and try to swim to the other shore."

It is a part of Hickok's mythology that he prophesied his own death. In fact, several people came forward later and recounted his comments on the subject. In 1881 J. W. Buel issued a pamphlet advertising his upcoming book *Heroes of the Plains* in which he credited Hickok with the following statement: "When I die it will be just as you see me now, and sickness will not be the cause. For more than ten years I have been constantly expecting to be killed, and it is certain to come before a great while longer."

Shortly after noon on Wednesday, August 2, 1876, Hickok sat in on a poker game with Captain R. W. Massie, Carl Mann, and Charles Rich in Nuttall & Mann's Saloon No. 10. Hickok, the last to arrive, complained that Rich had taken his customary wall seat, but he was persuaded to sit with his back to the room. For several years Hickok had made it habit to avoid such risk. At approximately four o'clock, Jack McCall entered the place, wandered around until he came up behind Hickok, and, thrusting a Colt Navy revolver within two inches of Wild Bill's head, fired. Hickok died instantly.

Jack McCall's motive for killing Hickok has never been established. The evening before, he had lost money to Hickok, and although he had been unable to meet his debt, Hickok had given him enough money to buy breakfast. Rumors were rife that Jack was bribed to kill Hickok because the gambling elite feared him and there was a possibility that he might be persuaded to become city marshal. After the shooting, McCall was arrested and tried by an illegal-miner's court (Deadwood was founded on what was still an Indian reservation), found "not guilty," and released, which caused an uproar. He fled the Hills when threatened by California Joe (Moses E. Milner) and was rearrested by a deputy U.S. marshal. Put on trial in Yankton in December, McCall was found guilty of murder and hanged on March 1, 1877.

Richard B. Hughes, who was in Deadwood at the time of Hickok's murder, recalled that Hickok was mourned only by those of his "own kind." Nevertheless, Hughes paid tribute to Hickok's reputation as a mankiller and a pistol shot ("no man living could draw and shoot as quickly and accurately"), whose name was "a familiar one from the Rio Grande to the British possessions." Others, however, were genuinely saddened by Hickok's death, particularly in Kansas and Missouri, where he had earned much of his reputation.

The Hickok family was devastated by the news of James's death. Hickok's sister, Lydia, writing from her home in Kansas, wished that her brother had died with Custer. Polly Hickok, prostrate with grief, died two years later still mourning the death of her youngest son.

By the early years of the twentieth century, the legendary Wild Bill Hickok had become a folk hero, and once film Westerns became popular, he was featured in a number of them. As late as the 1930s Wild Bill remained the public's most popular Wild West character, and during World War II he was honored when one of the famous Liberty ships, launched in 1943, was named *James B. Hickok* and saw action in the Atlantic convoys. Today, and despite New West "revisionism," Hickok's real and imaginary exploits continue to enthrall succeeding generations of Wild West fans.

Historically, of course, the life of the real Wild Bill remains enigmatic and controversial. If we strip away Wild Bill Hickok's mantle as a "mankiller" or a "civilizer" and ignore his "pistoliferous prowess," we are still left with a character who stood far above many of his contemporaries, a man whose strength of character influenced others and who put himself out on a limb whenever he thought the cause was just. Debate over what might have happened to Hickok had he survived McCall's assassination attempt is academic. What is important is that Hickok, who had never backed off from a face-to-face encounter, should die in a manner that further immortalized the man and the myth that was Wild Bill Hickok.

3

PATRICK FLOYD GARRETT

"The Man Who Shot Billy the Kid"

KATHLEEN P. CHAMBERLAIN

"¿Quien es?" Garrett heard the voice as he sat in near total darkness. "¿Quien es? ¿Quien es?," the speaker repeated when he received no reply.

Patrick Floyd Garrett in the early 1880s, probably in Tascosa, Texas. Courtesy of the Center for Southwest Research, University of New Mexico.

In the split second that followed, Patrick Floyd Garrett, sheriff of Lincoln County, New Mexico, fired a bullet into Billy the Kid, striking just above the young man's heart, killing him, and forever linking the two men inextricably in history books, legend, literature, song, and film.

Besides hunting down the Kid and firing one of the best-known bullets in history, Garrett also experienced the Civil War, Reconstruction era Louisiana, and frontier New Mexico. He punched, sometimes rustled cattle, hunted buffalo, and trailed outlaws in that lawless region dubbed "West of the Pecos." Like other men known primarily for peacekeeping in the Old West, Garrett occasionally straddled the line between lawman and outlaw. He was fired from at least one job for stealing cattle and elected sheriff precisely because he and Billy were friends. Moreover, Garrett investigated one of the most controversial murder cases in New Mexico history. When he died mysteriously a decade later, Garrett had as many enemies as friends.

Yet ironically, most know Garrett only as "the man who shot Billy the Kid," no doubt because it is this single distinction that dime novels played

repeatedly to eager American audiences. Later, biographer Walter Noble Burns and filmmakers re-created Billy the Kid, and Garrett became the necessary, but bland, face of law and order. In addition, after that hot night on July 14, 1881, Billy the Kid, not Pat Garrett, intrigued the nation and the world. In that year, for example, seven cities jockeyed for the "honor" of being known as Billy's birthplace. Rumors circulated that the Kid's trigger finger was sliced off before burial and that a doctor exhumed the body for experimentation. Teenage girls cried, while Garrett fought bureaucracy merely to collect his $500 reward. In short, Billy the Kid became pop culture's darling; Pat Garrett, his killer, did not.

Another reason why the remainder of Garrett's life never became the subject of novels or movies is Pat Garrett himself. He did not successfully capitalize on his reputation. Ranching bored him, and he was too cantankerous for politics. Even his friends thought him grumpy, some calling him "one of the meanest sons-of-bitches around." Garrett drank heavily. He amassed gambling debts, and, at the very least, he neglected his family. Since Garrett's death, writers have described him as mercenary, cowardly, and generally disliked. In essence, Garrett shot Billy the Kid through the heart, then spent the rest of his life shooting himself in the foot.

Garrett's turbulent life began on June 5, 1850, in Chambers County, Alabama. At age six he and his family moved to Claiborne Parish, Louisiana, where his father, John L. Garrett, purchased two cotton plantations. The Civil War did not bankrupt the Garretts, but their fortune suffered during Reconstruction. In January 1869 young Pat threatened to kill a brother-in-law, who reportedly cooperated with carpetbaggers, but ran away instead to avoid shooting his sister's husband. Garrett lodged with relatives in Dallas County, Texas, and worked on the J. B. Lowery Ranch. He even may have driven cattle north to Kansas; noted lawman Wyatt Earp recalled housing Pat in the Dodge City lockup for drunken and disorderly conduct.

In 1875 Garrett hunted buffalo, but by February 1878 the twenty-eight-year-old had drifted into eastern New Mexico in search of a settled life. Pete Maxwell of Fort Sumner hired Garrett to herd cattle but fired him six months later, allegedly for rustling. Garrett then purchased a local restaurant, and when that failed, he tended bar in Fort Sumner.

That same year, Garrett met two men who would change his life. One was Barney Mason, a local tough and rustling companion. The other was young William Antrim, alias William H. Bonney or the Kid, whom Pat encountered when the conflict between factions in nearby Lincoln County, known as the Lincoln County War, was reaching a climax. Later, Paulita Maxwell, Pete's sister, said, "When we saw Pat and Billy together we used to call them the long and the short of it." Others dubbed them "Big Casino and Little Casino": Pat stood six feet, five inches tall, and Billy was of average height, about five feet, seven inches. Even Billy occasionally called his friend a "long-legged son-of-a-bitch." In fact, Garrett's legs did not match the store-bought trouser sizes of his day, and he usually was forced to sew pieces onto the pant legs to make them long enough.

Patrick Floyd Garrett, sheriff of Lincoln County. Courtesy of Lincoln Heritage Trust, Lincoln, New Mexico.

In 1878 Bonney, Garrett, and Mason rustled cattle together. It is entirely possible that, given different circumstances, Pat might have crossed the line into outlawry, perhaps as one of Billy's gang members. By 1879, however, Garrett had changed. He married Juanita Martínez, who died three weeks later. Then, on January 14, 1880, he married Apolinaria Gutiérrez in a church ceremony in Anton Chico, even though Garrett disliked religion and remained agnostic all his life. Mason also married on January 14 in Anton Chico, in what was probably a double wedding because sources say the officiating priest and witnesses were identical. Now, Garrett sought stability and respectability and made it known that he welcomed a job as stock detective. Leading Lincoln County cattlemen, such as John Chisum and Joseph C. Lea, had something more important in mind, and Garrett's friendship with Billy made him the ideal candidate.

After the Lincoln County War ended in 1878, Billy rustled for a livelihood and targeted Chisum, whom he believed owed him $500 for his loyalty and fast gun during the conflict. According to Billy, Chisum reneged, so the Kid took his payment in cattle. Billy even threatened the rancher's life, driving Chisum into an alliance with James J. Dolan, a bitter opponent during the "war." When Billy Wilson—one of the Kid's gang—passed a counterfeit $100 bill to Dolan, perhaps as a joke, Dolan joined Lea and Chisum in endorsing Garrett for sheriff of Lincoln County. Wilson's "joke" also alerted the U.S. Treasury Department. Thus, during the search for Billy, Garrett obtained assistance from Special Agent Azariah F. Wild and federal law enforcement funds.

In his campaign for sheriff, Garrett advertised his "quick gun" and freely dispensed liquor and cigars. On November 2, 1880, Garrett won, with his term slated to begin on January 1, 1881. During the interregnum, the territorial sheriff-elect was busy selecting deputies and posting bond, because he would also collect county taxes and keep property records—tasks Garrett despised. Neither Chisum nor Dolan intended to wait that long, and so Garrett was immediately appointed deputy. Thus, from November 2 to December 31, 1880, Garrett was particularly active in his mission to end Billy the Kid's reign of terror.

Before Garrett could organize a posse, Agent Wild devised a multipronged assault on the Kid's known hangouts, but when Billy intercepted the U.S. mail and read Wild's confidential reports to Washington, the plan was aborted. With the lawmen temporarily stymied, Billy raided a White Oaks ranch about November 20. Nervous locals demanded action, and Deputy Sheriff Will Hudgens raised a posse, which included among others a young blacksmith named Jim Carlyle. The posse stumbled upon Billy's gang almost immediately, but when the White Oaks men failed to capitalize on the encounter, chaos resulted and the outlaws escaped.

As an arctic front swept across New Mexico, Billy and his men inched through ice and snow to the nearby Greathouse and Kuch Ranch, the posse hot on their trail. When the ranch cook ventured outside the next morning, posse members nabbed him and discovered that Billy, Wilson, and Dave Rudabaugh, a ruthless killer, were inside. Carlyle shouted for the gang to surrender, but Billy stalled for time. He invited Carlyle inside to talk, and Jim Greathouse agreed to serve as exchange hostage.

Inside, Carlyle presumably tried to reason with the outlaws while Greathouse shuttled messages back and forth. Yet as time dragged on, the posse worried, especially after Greathouse announced that the blacksmith acted like he was drinking. Finally, Hudgens ordered Carlyle released and threatened to shoot Greathouse if Billy refused. A shot was fired, by whom and for what reason is unknown. Carlyle apparently panicked. He dived out a window, and bullets struck him. He crawled on hands and knees to reach safety, but a bullet in the back finished the young blacksmith. Again, the desperadoes fled. The posse and press later blamed Billy for Carlyle's death, but it is as likely that he was cut down by his own men. Two nights later, an angry White Oaks mob burned the Greathouse and Kuch Ranch to the ground.

In the meantime, Garrett had assembled a posse that included Wild, Mason, Deputy U.S. Marshal Bob Olinger—whose own mother called him a born killer—and cattle detectives from the Texas Panhandle. Garrett's strategy was to haunt the outlaws' known hideouts and pursue them relentlessly. On November 30 he captured several of Billy's men.

At the same time, Lea tried the more benign tactic of offering leniency to gang members who agreed to defect. Garrett probably discussed leniency with Billy, but the Kid guessed his old friend lacked authority to offer complete clemency. Still, Pat had high hopes for thirty-year-old Charlie Bowdre, who was married and most likely to rehabilitate. The two spoke in mid-December. Bowdre was tired and frightened, but indecisive. He needed a murder indictment dropped, he said, but even then, Bowdre feared Billy. He could never deny shelter, food, or weapons to the Kid. Nevertheless, Bowdre agreed to seriously consider the offer.

As Bowdre pondered the offer, Texans Frank Stewart and Charles Siringo scouted the Las Vegas, New Mexico, region, while Garrett and his men questioned ranchers around Fort Sumner. They nabbed Juan Gallegos, a friend of Billy's, and interrogated him relentlessly. After Gallegos finally admitted that Billy was holed up at a nearby ranch, Garrett coerced local Juan Roibal into "leaking" the news to Billy that the posse had given up the search and departed. Thus, on December 19, as Garrett's posse hid inside an old army hospital in Fort Sumner, Billy arrived to celebrate. Caught in an ambush, the Kid escaped, but his friend, Tom O'Folliard, died in agony with a bullet in his stomach.

Garrett used the newly fallen snow, full moon, and his knowledge of the Kid's habits to follow the trail. He was not surprised when it led straight to an old forage station called Stinking Springs. The posse arrived around two o'clock in the morning, spotted horses tied outside, and cold-camped on that frigid plain. When the sun rose white over a frozen horizon, one man stepped outside carrying a feedbag for his horse. "Drop your weapons!" Garrett shouted, thinking it was Billy. Instead, Bowdre spun around, shocked. He foolishly pulled his pistols, and the young man who had debated going straight died an outlaw.

A standoff ensued. Billy's horse was inside the rock house, but Rudabaugh, Wilson, and Tom Pickett needed one more to make a break for freedom. By afternoon, Pat noticed the men trying slowly to ease a second horse inside. He shot the animal in its tracks, and it fell, barricading the door. Billy realized that his own horse would bolt rather than step over the carcass of another animal.

Still, Garrett needed a second ploy. So posse members lit a blazing fire and grilled meat. Sure enough, hungry, cold, and arguing among themselves, the outlaws tossed out their weapons in exchange for food. Billy later told reporters he had opposed surrendering, but was outvoted. Curiously, the rock house held an arsenal; the gang could certainly have waited out a posse exposed to cold, snow, and wind, but apparently Billy and his cohorts opted for full bellies. Moreover, it is strange that for all their weapons, the young men had apparently stockpiled no food.

Garrett escorted his prisoners to a nearby ranch and hearty Christmas dinner. Then, at Fort Sumner, Billy bid farewell to Paulita Maxwell. The next day, Garrett lodged the outlaws in Las Vegas, where Sheriff Desiderio Romero and deputies regarded the prisoners and Garrett alike with such low esteem that they threatened to seize Rudabaugh, a former Las Vegas policeman, who eight months earlier had killed a local jailer. Fortunately, Garrett produced federal warrants for Rudabaugh.

Nevertheless, when Garrett tried to move his prisoners to Santa Fe for safekeeping, a mob led by Romero stormed the train depot. Garrett and Deputy U.S. Marshal Frank Stewart guarded the railroad car, even threatening to arm the prisoners, while Deputy Marshal J. F. Morley located the chief engineer and demanded a crew brave enough to move the train. When that failed, Morley reportedly guessed which levers to pull and moved the train out of Las Vegas himself.

In Santa Fe Garrett accepted the thanks of the territory, but discovered that praise did not include payment of the $500 reward. Instead, acting governor William G. Ritch said he lacked authority, then declared Garrett's claim not legal because it stipulated delivery of the Kid to "the sheriff of Lincoln County"; Pat was not sheriff until January 1, 1881, and he had not delivered Billy to the current sheriff. Governor Lew Wallace was in the East, and having completed his novel *Ben Hur,* his primary goal was to secure a post as far as possible from territorial New Mexico. On the other hand, grateful citizens, such as Chisum and Dolan, were not hesitant. While territorial leaders balked, they raised more than $1,000 for Garrett and his men.

After two months in Santa Fe, Garrett escorted the Kid south to Mesilla on March 28, 1881. Billy stood trial, was convicted of murder, and was sentenced to hang. On April 21 the Kid returned to the town of Lincoln to await a May 13 execution. Garrett dismissed all deputies except J. W. Bell, a former member of the Carlyle posse, and Olinger, and lodged Billy upstairs in the Murphy and Dolan store, which was now a public building. On April 28, while Garrett was in White Oaks, Billy made a dramatic escape.

Garrett had repeatedly warned Bell and Olinger to keep up their guard, but on April 28, after Olinger took five other prisoners across the street to the Wortley Hotel for lunch, Billy asked Bell to take him to the privy. There, some believe, Billy found a gun hidden for him, and on the way back, the Kid suddenly drew on Bell, and when Bell turned and tried to flee, Billy shot him. The other possibility is that Billy climbed the interior staircase well ahead of Bell and had managed to loosen and remove one handcuff. Billy swung the loose cuff, gashing Bell's scalp, and in the tussle that followed, Billy seized Bell's pistol. When Bell ran, Billy shot the deputy in the back.

Although there are conflicting stories surrounding Bell's death, there are none regarding Olinger's. Olinger heard the gunshot as he ate at the

Wortley and raced across the street. Billy retrieved a loaded shotgun from Garrett's office, then waited in the upstairs east window, where he could survey the street between the courthouse and Wortley. As Olinger approached, someone shouted to him, "Bob, the Kid has killed Bell!" Olinger reportedly looked up at that very moment to find Billy grinning and a shotgun pointed directly down at him, and replied, "Yes, and he has killed me, too." Soon after, Billy rode out of Lincoln, leaving, according to Garrett, a shocked and terrified citizenry. Strangely, Garrett made few moves to hunt Billy, and New Mexicans began to wonder. Could Garrett recapture the Kid? Did he want to? After all, hanging the condemned was among a sheriff's most hated tasks. In this case, Billy was well liked and the two were friends.

Patrick Floyd Garrett, James Brent, and John Poe, circa 1884. Courtesy of the Center for Southwest Research, University of New Mexico.

John Poe, a deputy U.S. marshal and deputy sheriff sent from the Texas Panhandle to curb rustling, said that Garrett quietly sought information. Yet Garrett was ambivalent. Sometimes the sheriff insisted that Billy was still in New Mexico; often he argued that the Kid had left the territory. When Poe discovered that Billy was hiding out near Fort Sumner, Garrett visibly hesitated. Only under pressure did he follow up, taking Poe and Roswell lawman Thomas C. "Kip" McKinney with him. Poe scouted Fort Sumner, but as an Anglo stranger among several hundred Hispanics, he learned little. Nevertheless, after questioning a local rancher, Poe became convinced that Billy indeed lurked close by.

Even so, Garrett wanted to end the search. He agreed, however, to talk with Pete Maxwell. Near midnight on July 14, 1881, as Poe and McKinney waited on Maxwell's porch, Garrett tiptoed inside Maxwell's darkened bedroom and sat on the edge of Maxwell's bed, where the two spoke in whispers. Perhaps one or two minutes later, Billy stepped onto the porch. Hatless, shoeless, and armed only with a butcher knife, Billy spotted two shadows on the porch. Unnerved, the young outlaw asked in Spanish, "¿Quien es?" (Who is it?). He received no answer. Then Billy

Ash Upson, journalist and close friend of Pat Garrett, who authored Garrett's The Authentic Life of Billy the Kid. *Courtesy of the Center for Southwest Research, University of New Mexico.*

entered Maxwell's bedroom still inquiring, "¿Quien es? ¿Quien es?"

Garrett sat motionless. If he stood, his height would give him away. "That's him," Maxwell whispered, and Garrett later claimed, "I knew the Kid's voice too well to be mistaken." Garrett fired, then raced Maxwell out the door, shouting for Poe and McKinney to hold their fire. Did Billy fire once as Garrett claimed? The bullet was never found. In fact, Garrett and Poe may have conspired to say Billy carried a six-gun inside Maxwell's home. Otherwise, Garrett killed an unarmed man, even though Billy was under a death sentence and never would have surrendered. With Poe and McKinney outside, Garrett could not have simply let Billy go free even if he wanted to, which he probably did not.

In the ensuing years, historians and Billy the Kid enthusiasts have dissected these final moments of Billy's life. Those unwilling to allow the Kid his untimely death have developed theories that kept Billy alive. In the long run, one must ask why Garrett, Poe, McKinney, and Maxwell would conspire to save Billy. That the Kid was evidently unwilling to leave New Mexico eliminated all other options. Had Garrett allowed the young outlaw to flee, and then had Billy returned to the territory in a year or so, Garrett would have looked like a fool and his reputation as a lawman would have been destroyed forever.

Nevertheless, Garrett soon discovered that having a reputation as the man who shot Billy the Kid brought him fame, but no financial rewards. He had to petition the territorial legislature for his reward. Although dime novel authors enhanced Garrett's fame, their works brought him no fortune. Finally, Garrett decided to write his own account and accepted a $1,000 offer from publisher Charles Greene of Santa Fe. Garrett asked his friend, Ashmun "Ash" Upson, to write the book. Upson, an alcoholic journalist who lived with the Garretts from 1880 until his death in 1894, wrote *The Authentic Life of Billy the Kid, the Noted Desperado of the Southwest, Whose Deeds of Daring and Blood Made His Name a Terror in New Mexico, Arizona, and Northern Mexico* in 1882. It was a literary and publishing gaffe. Inaccurate and based in part on Upson's claim that he boarded with Billy's mother in Silver City and thereby had known Billy as a boy, the book was a marketing disaster, as Greene lacked the expertise to promote the book and sold few copies.

Despite the fact that Garrett was at the peak of his career as lawman, he declined to run again for sheriff in 1882 and instead made a bid for councilman. He ran on the Democratic ticket with Albert Fountain, an ambitious politician who had arrived in New Mexico in 1862 with the California Infantry and served as one of Billy the Kid's defense lawyers during his 1881 trial. But Garrett proved a poor politician. Republican opponents John A. Miller and David G. Easton had supported Garrett for sheriff in 1879, and when the *Rio Grande Republican*—with typical campaign bravado—dubbed Garrett ungrateful and egotistic, he bristled. When the *Republican* ran an anti-Garrett letter signed only "X," he confronted the suspected author and smashed a six-gun across the man's skull. The election was close, but ended in a bitter defeat for Garrett.

Disgusted, Garrett turned to ranching but was soon bored and unable to earn enough money to cover his growing gambling debts. At this point, he and his old friend, Barney Mason, answered a call from the Texas Panhandle, where striking cowboys and small ranchers plagued large ranchers. Governor John Ireland authorized a group to protect the wealthy ranchers and asked Garrett to lead them. It is noteworthy that Garrett usually favored frontier nobility—not small ranchers—even though he never attained the status for himself. Even so, Garrett discovered that the large ranchers were far more interested in getting rid of the small ranchers than in seeing justice done. Far too many of the men Garrett captured were "shot trying to escape" or lynched.

By 1884 Garrett had returned to New Mexico, accompanied by Brandon Kirby, former captain in the British army and partner with Charles Cree of Scotland. Kirby sought large chunks of ranch property for himself and the Cree family. Garrett sold some of his own holdings and persuaded Poe, Lea, and others to sell land too. In 1885 Garrett was hired as manager of the new V. V. Ranch. The Crees irked their Lincoln County neighbors by their snooty attitude, and Kirby's dictatorial treatment of hired hands—he called them "cow servants"—guaranteed failure. The Crees sold out after the brutal winter of 1886–1887, and Garrett returned to his Roswell ranch and experimented with peach and apple orchards, pecan trees, and grapes. He planted roses and Kentucky bluegrass and surrounded his adobe house with oak groves.

Then Garrett had a vision—an irrigated Pecos Valley. In 1887 he and fellow rancher and friend, William L. Holloman, created the Holloman and Garrett Ditch Company to divert North Spring River water. But the firm lacked capital. Thus, Garrett bought an interest in the Pioneer Ditch

Company, which made him partners with businessman and rancher Charles B. Eddy and with Charles Greene, his former publisher. Greene soon went broke, and in 1889 Eddy convinced railroad financier James J. Hagerman of Colorado to buy in. A financial wizard, Hagerman exhibited open disdain for the poorly educated Garrett. He reorganized and renamed the company, squeezing out both Garrett and Eddy in the process.

Garrett tried his hand at politics again, this time in Chavez County, where political power lay in the hands of Republicans, not Democrats, as it did in Lincoln County. After losing a run for the sheriff's seat, an embittered Garrett sold his property and moved to Uvalde, Texas, where he bought land and began to raise and race horses. He was also appointed county commissioner.

This was a peaceful period in Garrett's life. He spent time with his family, especially daughter Elizabeth, who was born blind in 1885. In all, Pat and Apolinaria had eight children—those born before Uvalde were jokingly called the "first crop" and those who came after were the "second crop." Elizabeth said the children adored their father. Despite his own lack of schooling, Pat insisted that his children obtain an education, especially Elizabeth, who became an accomplished musician in her adulthood.

Also during the Uvalde years, Garrett became friends with John Nance Garner, future vice president of the United States. Later, on an excursion to the Texas-Mexican border, Garrett spotted Billy Wilson, now a customs guard, who, shaken by the encounter, confided that he had received a twenty-five-year sentence in federal court for passing counterfeit money and escaped from Leavenworth Prison. Wilson was now married, had a child, and held a respectable job. He had long feared recognition and recapture. Eager to help, Garrett wrote to George Curry, a friend and rising political star in New Mexico, who, in turn, contacted Governor William Thornton and arranged a special presidential pardon for Billy the Kid's former gang member.

But again Garrett was bored. On February 29, 1896, Albert Fountain and his nine-year-old son were murdered. Fountain had secured grand jury indictments in the town of Lincoln against Oliver Lee, James Gililland, and William McNew for rustling. As he drove the long, lonely road from Lincoln to Mesilla that wound across desolate White Sands, Fountain and his young son simply disappeared. Investigators found the buckboard and bloody items, but neither the bodies nor the court papers. Governor Thornton offered a $2,000 reward and promised Garrett $150 per month to act as private detective in the case.

Garrett sold his Uvalde property to Garner and returned to New Mexico. The Fountain case proved frustrating, however. To legitimize his investigation, Garrett pressed to be named sheriff, but even with his new title, he collected evidence slowly and methodically. After two years of painstaking work, evidence implicated Lee, Gililland, and McNew. On April 1, 1898, Garrett gathered the evidence and took it to the grand jury in Tularosa. On the way, he engaged in a controversial—albeit typical—three-day, high-stakes poker game in Tobe Tipton's Saloon, with opponents Oliver Lee and his lawyer Albert B. Fall, among others. Afterward, Garrett allegedly told Lee he might return with indictments for his arrest. Forewarned, Lee fled.

Warrants in hand, Garrett arrested McNew and held him without bail in Las Cruces. Lee and Gililland eluded the law until July 13, 1898, when Garrett led deputies Kent Kearney, Jose Espalin, Ben Williams, and Clint Llewellyn to Wildey Well on Lee's Dog Canyon Ranch and cornered the fugitives. Despite the advantage, Garrett was forced to withdraw after a heated gun battle. Kearney was killed—Garrett could not even retrieve the body—and two others were slightly wounded. One deputy was drenched after Lee and Gililland shot holes in the water tank under which he had taken cover.

For six months, Lee and Gililland dodged Garrett, frequently claiming that the sheriff was a dangerous man. The duo migrated from one friendly ranch to another, often stopping at Charles Graham's ranch in the Caballo Range. Their primary contact with the outside world was through Eugene Manlove Rhodes, a young cowhand on the Graham Ranch and a budding writer. It was also Rhodes who helped devise a solution to the standoff. On January 30, 1899, the territorial legislature created Otero County from parts of Lincoln, Doña Ana, and Socorro Counties. Otero included the region where Fountain and his son had disappeared. George Curry was appointed sheriff, and the fugitives agreed to surrender if Curry, not Garrett, took custody. Judge Frank Parker agreed, but first the pair had to surrender to him in Las Cruces.

On March 13, 1899, Lee, Gililland, and Rhodes boarded the train at Aleman, New Mexico, knowing that until Curry took charge, they were in Garrett's jurisdiction. Despite Garrett's badge, the pair said they feared for their lives, maybe sensing they would receive the same chance from Garrett as they had reportedly given Fountain and his son or that Garrett had once given Billy the Kid.

The accused killers were well disguised. During their months on the run both had grown heavy beards and long hair. Rhodes had also given Lee a pair of blue glasses and Gililland an old derby hat to complete the masquerade. At Rincon, Garrett and Texas Ranger John R. Hughes boarded the train and strolled to the smoking car where Lee, Gililland, and Rhodes sat. According to Lee, Garrett stared hard at him, then walked on. The two were eventually jailed in Alamogordo and tried on May 29, 1899, in Hillsboro, both locations outside of Garrett's jurisdiction. Fall's defense maintained that without bodies, the prosecution could not prove murder.

After a three-week trial, the jury deliberated for ten minutes and found the two not guilty. The case remains officially unsolved. It is noteworthy that during the investigation Garrett tried to enlist in the Rough Riders but was denied a commission.

By 1899, however, he was fifty years old, a heavy drinker, and in debt. Three years earlier, the Albuquerque Bank of Commerce had filed suit for repayment of a $1,000 loan pending since 1890, and the court had ordered Garrett to repay it plus $733 in interest. Because Garrett could not pay, the probate clerk was directed to take possession of Garrett's property, but his land was already mortgaged to rancher W. W. Cox and businessman Martin Lohman.

Garrett also got into trouble with Doña Ana County, which owed him $4,000 in expenses but neglected to pay. Following Fall's advice, Garrett kept a portion of the taxes collected and allowed the court to charge him with misappropriation of funds. Garrett was permitted to keep the money, but the charge stayed on his record.

This period proved especially difficult for Garrett, and from about 1899 on he sank rapidly into financial misfortune and mental depression. Garrett declined to run for sheriff. Nearly destitute, he continued to bet on horses and cards. With most of his land mortgaged, Garrett homesteaded and acquired title to 160 acres in Bear Canyon, located in the San Andres Mountains, about thirty miles from Las Cruces. The quality of the land, however, was poor.

By 1901 Garrett was desperate for money. On December 16, 1901, at the request of influential New Mexicans and Texans, President Theodore Roosevelt named Garrett customs collector at El Paso. The president even praised the former lawman's past glory as the man who shot Billy the Kid. A lucrative job, the nomination provoked envy from Republicans, who correctly accused Garrett of switching parties for political advantage. Despite numerous protests, including reminders of the misappropriation charge, the Senate Committee on Finance confirmed the appointment on December 20.

Within six months of the appointment, Garrett was in trouble. Rancher J. D. Campbell shipped more than three thousand head of cattle from Mexico to El Paso in four separate shipments and declared them calves—the duty was $2 for calves under one year of age and $3.75 for older cattle. Garrett argued that at least half were not calves. Campbell appealed, and the New York Board of Appraisers—the final authority—compromised, placing the higher duty on 587 head. Campbell accepted the decision. Garrett appealed, but the case was eventually dismissed.

Still, the confrontation elicited more complaints. Opponents called Garrett "unfit" and "contentious," and Garrett sported an increasingly short temper made worse by age and alcohol. In February 1903 I. A. Barnes, a

Texas importer, circulated a petition for Garrett's removal from his post as customs collector and proposed his own appointment. Few took Barnes's protest seriously, but the petition prompted the secretary of the treasury to reprimand Garrett and to send a special agent to investigate.

The agent, Joseph Evans, ordered Garrett to appoint George M. Gaither as cattle inspector. Garrett claimed that Gaither was unfit, but appointed him for a thirty-day trial period. At the conclusion of that time, Garrett fired Gaither and told Washington that "he had tried." In reality, Garrett hated the implication that he was incompetent and resented Gaither. Nevertheless, Gaither demanded reinstatement. Garrett simply shrugged and mumbled that he had no authority to hire the man full time.

On May 8 the argument erupted on a downtown street in El Paso. A verbal confrontation became a fistfight, and both Garrett and Gaither were arrested. By this time, too, the U.S. Treasury Department was tired of Garrett and wanted him removed. Thus, following the fight, the department hired Barnes—the same man who circulated the petition—as special investigator. It seems that Barnes did little more than to compile complaints and submit them to Secretary of the Treasury Leslie M. Shaw. When Shaw asked Garrett for a report of his fight with Gaither, the former lawman replied with resignation that despite extenuating circumstances, he accepted full responsibility and expected no special consideration.

Meanwhile, local Republicans maneuvered to get Garrett removed. They repeatedly denounced Garrett's failure to participate in party affairs and criticized his appointments. The Republican Old Guard made sure the pillars of Christian society knew that Garrett drank, shunned churches, neglected his wife, and befriended Tom Powers, disreputable owner of the Coney Island Saloon. In 1905 the opposition reached frenzied proportions after Garrett took Powers to what has been called a Rough Riders meeting in San Antonio, Texas. Powers, it seems, wanted to meet President Roosevelt, and Garrett not only accommodated but introduced the shady saloon owner as a Texas rancher. Locals discovered the deception and informed the president. Worse, photographs taken during the gathering revealed Roosevelt posing with Garrett and Powers.

Even so, Roosevelt might have overlooked the indiscretion. Secretary Shaw, however, had already deluged the president with complaints, and by 1905 Roosevelt had no doubt already decided to remove Garrett. When the New Mexican traveled to Washington to apologize—with Powers again in tow—the impropriety merely confirmed Roosevelt's suspicions that Garrett was inefficient and immoral. Roosevelt later told writer and Garrett supporter Emerson Hough that Garrett had been a personal choice that simply proved wrong.

Following his removal, Garrett struggled economically. He prospected briefly, then paid a fee to become a practicing attorney in Mexico. Unfortunately, his single client, an accused murderer, was convicted and sent to prison. In 1906 New Mexico politician Thomas Catron sued Garrett for repayment of a $500 loan, and the Albuquerque bank filed suit again. This time, Garrett transferred his cattle to rancher and neighbor William Webb Cox—ironically, brother-in-law to Oliver Lee—to avoid repossession. Garrett managed to repay the original $1,000 loan, but not the interest. Somehow, he obtained a loan to pay his mortgage, but gambled it away, prompting a frustrated Martin Lohman to discount the mortgage to $2,000 and sell it to his partner, Cox. In another 1906 blow, Doña Ana County ordered Garrett to pay $922.72 in back taxes and would have auctioned his stock on September 4 had Garrett not transferred it to Cox.

Next, Garrett turned to Hough for assistance. Hough had initially approached Garrett to rewrite his 1882 book, but when problems arose, Hough wrote his own account, *The Story of the Outlaw,* with assistance from the man who had shot Billy the Kid. Garrett wanted royalties, but Hough could not comply.

Garrett implored Cox to return his cattle, but Cox wanted a mortgage payment. Finally, Garrett asked Curry—now territorial governor—for a job as prison warden. Curry ignored the request, and Garrett finally found meager employment in an El Paso real estate firm. But Garrett's life spun out of control. For several months he lived with "Mrs. Brown," a known prostitute, seemingly having abandoned his wife and children, although daughter Elizabeth vehemently denied such a claim. Impoverished, Apolinaria worked as a practical nurse and Pat's daughter, Anne, started a catering business. Meanwhile, the once-respected lawman drank heavily, gambled, and brawled in public in El Paso. People in El Paso who knew him remarked that his temper combined with alcohol made Garrett a widely feared man. They claimed he could be mean and unpredictable.

By March 1907, with the Garrett family frantic for cash, Pat's son Dudley Poe leased the Bear Canyon property to local cowboy Jesse Wayne Brazel. The five-year lease, negotiated in secret, also included A. P. "Print" Rhode, Cox's brother-in-law. Unknown to Dudley, Brazel and Rhode planned to experiment with raising goats.

Unfortunately, Garrett hated Rhode. Worse, he despised goats. One can only imagine the fireworks when he visited Bear Canyon one day and found both residing on his land. Garrett lashed out at his son. In turn, Dudley Poe and Brazel argued. By December 1907 Garrett tried to break the lease in court, using an archaic law that made it illegal to herd livestock near a dwelling, in this case a rock house that was virtually uninhabitable. Justice of the Peace Charles M. Anthony could not locate an impartial jury and recessed until spring, hoping that things would cool off.

Alas, in January 1908 James P. Miller arrived. A killer who had presumably murdered a brother-in-law, Miller hoped to graze one thousand head of Mexican cattle in Bear Canyon, an answer to Garrett's prayers if only he could remove those pesky goats. Despite pleas and threats, Brazel refused to cancel the lease unless he could sell all twelve hundred goats at $3.50 per head. Reluctantly, Miller signed a contract with Brazel to purchase the goats, then offered Garrett $3,000 for the land, plus an additional sum if Garrett would help drive the cattle up from Mexico.

By February 20 Garrett believed his money problems were over. Suddenly, Brazel notified Garrett that he had inadvertently miscounted his goats. He owned eighteen hundred, not twelve hundred, and refused to cancel the lease unless Miller purchased them all. Miller hedged and told Garrett that it might be easier to find other property. At this point, Garrett wrote to his old friend Curry: "I am in a hell of a fix. I have been trying to sell my ranch, but no luck. For God's sake send me fifty dollars." The check came promptly, and Garrett decided to cash it in Las Cruces.

On Friday, February 28, Carl Adamson—Miller's partner and another brother-in-law—arrived at Garrett's ranch. The next day, they hitched Adamson's rented buggy to drive into Las Cruces. Exactly why is unclear. On February 29 Apolinaria waved farewell to her husband for the last time. The men met Brazel somewhere along the trail. Brazel and Garrett argued; Adamson later said that Brazel hinted he might not give up the lease. The trio—some say Rhode accompanied Brazel—went over San Agustin Pass and through the tiny community of Organ. They halted near Alameda Arroyo. While Garrett stood at the rear of the wagon, removed his left glove, and unbuttoned his trousers to relieve himself, one bullet tore through the back of his head and a second entered his stomach.

Brazel confessed to Garrett's murder, calling it self-defense. On March 3 Brazel pleaded "not guilty" in court; Adamson testified he had seen nothing but had heard Garrett threaten, "If I don't get you off one way, I will another." On April 13, 1908, a grand jury indicted Brazel for murder. The trial, held in April 1909, was poorly prosecuted by District Attorney Mark Thompson, who never even asked how a man could urinate and pose a threat at the same time. Brazel was well defended by Attorney Fall and acquitted. Hence, Garrett's death—like Fountain's—remains a mystery and even more controversial.

Was Garrett's death a conspiracy? Many believe so. But who was involved and why? Leon C. Metz, Garrett's biographer, has examined this question. Many observers, he claims, think the conspiracy began in the El

Paso St. Regis Hotel and involved Adamson, Miller, Cox, Rhode, and maybe even Albert Fall. Cox despised Garrett and wanted his land. Thus, he and the others hired Miller to murder Garrett, and Brazel would provide the excuse. He would also confess because he had no family and was generally well liked by everyone.

The conspiracy falls apart, however, because Cox already held Garrett's stock and land. Miller's role, when examined closely, is highly suspect, and attempts to place him at the murder site are difficult to prove. Another theory implicates Rhode or even Cox, arguing that the motive was revenge for a death ten years earlier. Yet Adamson never claimed that Rhode was with Brazel; nor does any eyewitness place Cox there. Other conspiracy stories implicate Lee and Gililland, principal figures in the Fountain case who were already acquitted.

On the other hand, Metz concludes that Brazel indeed killed Garrett; afraid for his life should the goat problem remain unsolved, Brazel "took the safe way out and shot him." Hence, Brazel did not lie when he confessed; he simply did not kill Garrett in self-defense. There were no conspiracies, no money changed hands, there was no ambush, and there were no tremendous inaccuracies in the stories told by Brazel and Adamson.

There is another possible motive, however. Garrett had undoubtedly grown so mean and vindictive that anyone who crossed him—or whom he thought crossed him—genuinely feared for his life. In 1910 Fall said Garrett was a "soured and disappointed man," quarrelsome and insulting. He provoked fights, and everyone feared he would kill somebody. In fact, wrote Fall, a sigh of relief went up after Garrett died. Still, this does not exonerate Brazel as the gunman and may even strengthen his motive.

Regardless, today Sheriff Patrick Floyd Garrett is linked in popular culture with Billy the Kid, not Wayne Brazel or Albert Fountain. The public lacks a clear picture of Garrett beyond his involvement in the single event of July 14, 1881. Because America adores youth, Billy is depicted in film as a misguided, fatherless teenager, a romantic brooder, a simpleton, or a charismatic outlaw, leaving the older Pat Garrett the role of double-crossing friend, father figure, or the heavy hand of law and order. William Peterson, who played Garrett in *Young Guns II* and has been one of the few young actors cast in the role, is an exception. He portrayed the lawman as neither evil nor rigidly upright and, thankfully, not as grumpy. Moreover, Peterson's Garrett strode the dangerously thin line between outlaw and lawman, friend and foe, and is perhaps the most accurate portrayal to date. Still, Garrett's story was only part of Billy's.

In truth, if Garrett has a larger significance in the history of the American West, then perhaps we need look no further than 1880–1881. Indeed, it may lie precisely in his relationship to Billy the Kid. Few men possessed the raw courage to go after Billy and his gang. Sheriff George Kimbrell, sheriff of Lincoln County before Garrett, certainly did not. Nor could the sporadic, local posses, such as the one in White Oaks, effectively track and capture them. Garrett did make New Mexico territory safer for ranchers, businessmen, and ordinary citizens. Sadly, like so many other frontier characters, he was unable to find a niche in the new world he helped create. Garrett envisioned himself a wealthy rancher like Chisum, a land developer like Hagerman, and a politician like Curry, but his temperament, drinking, and gambling stood in the way. He lacked education, social graces, and the financial acumen that, in an era called the Gilded Age, would have rendered all his other flaws less devastating. This rough, in-the-saddle man of action embraced society's fringe, scorned religion, and was either unable or unwilling to make the necessary adjustments to ensure success in polite circles.

On the other hand, Garrett was a tough, diligent lawman long before he failed as a rancher, irrigator, or customs collector. It is difficult not to admire the cat-and-mouse pursuit of the Kid, even if that same tenacity did not convict Albert Fountain's killers twenty years later. Those who view Garrett in a favorable light tend to see a sheriff whose smoking gun killed one of the most notorious men of the nineteenth-century Southwest, not the old, angry man shot while urinating behind a buckboard. In reality, Garrett represents the many individuals who outlived their abilities. In myth, he remains the man who shot Billy the Kid. Considering everything else, Garrett actually might have been proud of such a reputation.

4

Tom Horn

Rogue Frontiersman

Larry D. Ball

In the annals of the American frontier, Tom Horn occupies a prominent, if tragic, place. Although his early years in the West were undistinguished, he emerged from obscurity in Arizona as a scout in the Apache campaigns and earned local applause as a rodeo star, lawman, and detective. Despite possessing many admirable qualities, as well as the skills necessary to survive in the violent conditions surrounding the Indian wars, Tom Horn drifted into an even more callous occupation—that of hired assassin. When finally brought before the bar of justice in Cheyenne, Wyoming, in 1902 for the murder of a fourteen-year-old boy, this once highly praised scout was found guilty and hanged. Despite this unfortunate end, Tom Horn retains a permanent place in frontier legendry.

There was nothing in his early years that pointed to such a regrettable demise. Thomas H. Horn Jr. was born on a farm near Memphis, Missouri, on November 21, 1860. His father, Thomas Sr., was a strong Campbellite (Disciples of Christ) and, according to Tom Jr., resorted to whippings to enforce discipline. An unconfirmed story holds that Tom Sr. was also the leader of a band of swindlers and confidence men and that he eventually fled to Canada to avoid the law.

Young Tom preferred hunting with his favorite dog, Shed, rather than attending church and school. Yet he managed to receive some elementary school education and possessed a quick and alert mind. At age fourteen, in 1874, Tom Jr. left home. Even though he later maintained that he ran away from home, a contrary version holds that Tom Sr. cast the rebellious offspring out, turning him over to Mexican teamsters on the Santa Fe Trail. Working at various jobs as teamster, railroad hand, and cowboy, young Tom made his way to Prescott in Yavapai County, Arizona, where he may have had relatives.

Tom Horn whiled away his time in the Laramie County Jail by braiding ropes and fashioning other cowboy paraphernalia. Courtesy of the American Heritage Center, University of Wyoming.

Tom Horn's activities in the late 1870s are difficult to determine. His autobiography, *The Life of Tom Horn: Government Scout and Interpreter, A Vindication,* written in a Wyoming jail in 1903, provides most of the information about his movements in his early youth. Although Horn wrote in a lively and entertaining manner, he was facing the distraction of the hangman's noose at the time and sought to convince readers that during his Arizona years, especially during his service in the Apache Wars, his conduct had been exemplary—hence the words "A Vindication" in the title. Yet Horn paid little attention to the exact sequence of events and jumbled his facts, almost always according himself a larger role than he actually played and embellishing the truth at times.

Even though Arizona became his home, Horn exhibited a roving disposition and often moved around, in and out of the territory. The young Missourian, who grew into a big, strapping six-footer, spent some time around the army posts of Fort Whipple and Camp Verde. While herding government livestock, cutting wood, and performing other tasks, Horn became acquainted with many soldiers. They often looked out for him and loaned him books with which to further his education. Horn also encountered many Hispanics and Apache Indians around these military installations. Possessing a quick ear and alert mind, he soon spoke Spanish fluently and managed to learn some of the Apache tongue.

Years later, Horn spoke very highly of Al Sieber, a civilian scout for the army, who detected potential in the youth. Recognizing his gift for languages and love of the outdoors, Sieber arranged for Horn to live with the Coyotero Apaches of Chief Pedro, near Fort Apache, in eastern Arizona. Pedro, who grew to like Horn, named him "Talking Boy." Because employment around the army camps was sporadic at best, Sieber took Horn on prospecting trips. Thereafter, Horn could never shake the mining bug and often disappeared into the mountains in search of the mother lode. Horn later claimed that he and Sieber joined the prospecting party of Ed Schieffelin in 1877, the notable mining venture that led to the discovery of Tombstone.

Horn continued to work for various army posts and Indian reservations. In the early 1880s he supervised cattle herds contracted to the San Carlos Apache Reservation. In October 1882 he signed on as a packer for the army and served in this capacity through most of the Apache campaigns. His autobiography provides a vivid description of these often grisly events. Although he would have readers believe that he was a chief scout throughout these years, it was only during his last year with the army, in 1885–1886, that he reached this coveted position. The army often used packers for tasks and may have sent him with Al Sieber or other scouts on unofficial searches after renegade Apaches. These stints as a packer and scout were usually for only short periods of time, and old-timers remembered Horn primarily as a government herder in the early 1880s.

Despite its inaccuracies, Horn's book revealed a brutal, no-holds-barred state of affairs in southern Arizona in the 1880s. Both Indians and whites killed callously and mutilated corpses for effect. In one instance, Al Sieber savagely cut off the head of an Apache wrongdoer in front of Horn. In another, Horn and several Indians killed three Mexican horse thieves and left the corpses at a watering place as a warning to other would-be bandits. Some years later, Horn related one especially gruesome incident to Pinkerton detective Charles Siringo, and although neither Horn nor Siringo was an absolutely reliable source, this story fits into the "wartime" atmosphere of the 1880s. After a battle in which several Apache men and women were killed, according to Horn, he and some soldiers discovered a baby clinging to its dead mother. Rather than carry the baby back to the reservation, Horn dispatched the helpless infant on the spot. "I shot the little brat," he said bluntly to Siringo.

In October 1885 Horn signed on with the army as superintendent of a pack train on what proved to be the final campaign to capture Geronimo. This cagey medicine man and a small group of followers had again taken refuge in northern Mexico. The expedition, however, had a surprise in store for Horn. Soon after the bluecoats departed Fort Bowie on the chase, Chief Scout Al Sieber was suddenly recalled to San Carlos. Before leaving, Sieber recommended that Horn be promoted to chief scout. Although only a "field promotion," in this position Horn performed the duties of scout, as well as Spanish interpreter, for the remainder of the campaign.

In January 1886 Lieutenant Emmet Crawford's column, with Horn as chief scout, encountered a Mexican force also searching for hostiles. The Mexicans—either inadvertently or deliberately—fired on the American force. In the exchange, Crawford was killed and Horn was wounded in the arm. Lieutenant Marion Maus, who assumed command, praised Horn for

General George Crook (seated center) and his staff posed for photographer C. S. Fly of Tombstone, Arizona, at the conference with Geronimo in 1886. Tom Horn, identified as an interpreter on this occasion, is kneeling in the front row, fifth from the left. Courtesy of the Western History Collections, University of Oklahoma.

his bravery in this action. A short time later, the new chief scout accompanied an officer to Geronimo's camp, in an effort to persuade the elusive chieftain to return to the reservation. The Apache leader refused at the time, but submitted of his own volition the following September.

Since the conclusion of the Geronimo campaign, Horn's role in the Apache Wars has aroused much controversy. Some army officers, who resented the presence of civilian scouts, maintained that they were merely nuisances. However, Lieutenant Maus appreciated Horn's services and urged that his name be included in the general order recognizing the bravery of the various participants. The army high command refused Maus's request, asserting that only officers and enlisted men could be so recognized. In this instance, the official memory failed the military, as the army had recognized such persons in earlier such manifestos in Arizona.

With the conclusion of the Apache Wars, Horn left government employ on September 30, 1886, and returned to familiar civilian undertakings—cowpuncher, teamster, miner, and lawman. He excelled in the first occupation, and Arizonans soon considered him a wizard on horseback. At Fourth of July festivities in Globe in 1889, Horn startled spectators with his steer-tying skill. "His dexterity was much admired," said a local journalist. At the subsequent territorial fair in Phoenix, in October, he bested all competitors in this event. In Tucson a few months later, he made "a $500 wager that he could throw and tie a steer in less time than any cowboy in Arizona, New Mexico, or Texas," according to the *Arizona Daily Star.* Apparently, there were no takers at this time.

Tom Horn was known as a man who could take care of himself, but he was not known as a trouble-seeker. Nor was he considered a "quick-draw" artist, although Arizonans regarded him as one of the finest pistol and rifle shots in the territory. His unerring aim, combined with bravery and coolness under fire, made him a formidable adversary. Frank Murphy, a well-known Arizona lawman and friend of Horn, recalled that the former scout shot and killed a Mexican in Cochise County. Although legend holds that the victim was a Mexican army officer and that the cause of the incident was an argument over a woman, Murphy declared that Horn's victim was not a soldier. When the Mexican tried to bully Horn, the latter shot in self-defense. Horn makes no mention of this incident in his memoirs, although he admitted elsewhere that he killed his first man—meaning white man—at the age of twenty-six, which would place this affair in 1886 or 1887. In referring to this shooting, his only remark was that the victim was "a coarse old sonofabitch."

When in need of an experienced fighter, people were still quick to call upon Horn. In 1887 a bloody vendetta erupted in Tonto Basin. This feud, known variously as the Pleasant Valley War or Tewksbury-Graham Feud, involved John D. Tewksbury and his family and partisans on one side and Thomas and John Graham and their supporters on the other. The causes of this bloodletting are still debated, although the Grahams were accused of running a rustling ring, while the Tewksburys were charged with introducing sheep into cattle country.

Tom Horn's part in this regrettable event is difficult to unravel. In his autobiography, he accorded himself the roles of "mediator" and deputy sheriff. Survivors of the vendetta, however, recalled that Horn was an associate of the Tewksbury faction. In fact, he remained a lifelong friend of Ed Tewksbury, one of John Tewksbury's sons. Horn also claimed that the sheriffs of the counties affected by the vendetta—Yavapai, Apache, and Gila—valued his services so much that all three lawmen deputized him at one time to assist in suppressing the fighting. Unfortunately, there is no evidence to support this assertion. Some writers have speculated that Horn, as a Tewksbury partisan, may have participated in the assassination of Martin Blevins, a Graham supporter, in July 1887. This accusation is based upon Horn's admission that he killed his first man at the age of twenty-six; he was in his twenty-sixth year when Blevins was murdered. However, Horn also could have been referring to the shooting of the Mexican that took place around this time.

Although sources for Horn's participation in the Pleasant Valley War are sketchy at best, his course through this bloody affair appears very inconsistent. For a time he hired out his gun to a group of Tonto Basin ranchers who professed a desire to remain neutral. This may account for his claim that he was a "mediator." But when a vigilante movement arose in 1888—

probably organized by these self-same neutral ranchers—to suppress the remnants of both feuding factions, Tom Horn was present in its ranks. In August of that year, he was among the regulators, led by rancher Glenn Reynolds, who lynched three of the suspected rustlers.

When Reynolds was elected Gila County sheriff in the subsequent November elections, the new county lawman called upon Horn's law enforcement and interpreting skills in a controversial trial of several Apache Indians in Globe. These Native Americans—one of whom was Apache Kid—were accused of assault with intent to kill Al Sieber, Horn's old friend. Strangely, interpreter Horn was not present at the trial. The proceedings, which took place in late October 1889, coincided with the territorial fair in Phoenix. Horn's friends, including Sheriff Reynolds, insisted that he enter the steer-tying event. While Horn was away, the sheriff prepared to escort Apache Kid and his comrades to the penitentiary in Yuma. En route, they overpowered and killed the sheriff and his deputy on November 2. In his recollections, Horn asserted that had he been present he might have been able to prevent the assassinations. The prisoners had hatched their plot openly in their native tongue, which the lawmen could not understand. "Had I not gone to the fair I would have been with Reynolds," Horn wrote later, "and could have understood what they [the Apaches] said. . . . I won the prize roping at the Fair, but it was at a very heavy cost." Horn may not have been completely honest with his readers, because two weeks had elapsed between the steer-tying contest, on October 17, and the death of Sheriff Reynolds on November 2. Horn fails to explain what prevented him from returning to Globe in time to join Sheriff Reynold's escort.

A few weeks later, an event occurred that had a profound effect on Horn's life. In December 1889 Cyrus W. "Doc" Shores, sheriff of Gunnison County, Colorado, issued a reward notice across the Southwest for two horse rustlers, Mat Edmiston and Jim Wylie. It happened that Burt Dunlap, a Graham County rancher and Tom Horn's present employer, was also postmaster in Aravaipa Canyon. After reading Shores's reward notice, Dunlap recognized the two fugitives as local cowhands, calling themselves Will and Joe Kirkpatrick. The postmaster informed Shores and arranged to get a deputy sheriff's badge for Horn so he could assist the Colorado lawman.

Writing in old age, Shores recalled his first meeting with Tom Horn in Willcox, Arizona, in January 1890:

> *[Horn was] a tall, dark-complected man with a black mustache. . . . He was around thirty years of age and presented an imposing figure of a man—deep chested, lean loined, and arrow straight. He was*

wearing a plaid shirt, woolen trousers, and high-heeled boots. A wide-brimmed sombrero covered his head.

Only Horn's "dark, shifty eyes" detracted from his impressive image. Even though Shores's description may have been colored by his knowledge of Horn's subsequent career, the rodeo champion clearly had a commanding presence.

Because Deputy Sheriff Horn knew the Kirkpatricks, he was able to lead Doc Shores directly to them and make the arrests without difficulty. Before leaving Horn in Tucson, Shores suggested that he should pursue a career in law enforcement. "With your background as an Indian scout and understanding of the Mexican lingo," remarked the Colorado law officer, "I believe I could get you a job with the Pinkerton National Detective Agency." Horn thought it was a good idea and decided to give it a try. Shores recommended Horn to James McParland, superintendent of Pinkerton's western division in Denver. After seeking letters from persons who knew Horn in Arizona, McParland offered him a job. Horn quickly accepted. In late April 1891 he rode down to Willcox to catch the train for Denver. A writer for the local *Southwestern Stockman* noted his departure. "After a residence of fourteen years in Arizona," said this newsman, Horn professed to have "tired of cowboy life." He was going to Denver to seek his fortunes with Pinkerton.

The fledgling detective's first case turned into an embarrassing muddle. Using the cover name Thomas H. Hale, Horn traced a suspected train robber to Reno, Nevada. But the roles suddenly were reversed when, on May 4, 1891, the sheriff in Reno arrested Horn on charges of robbing a faro game and held him for trial the following June. When the jury could not agree, he was released on bail, pending a new trial in the fall. In a letter to his former employer, Burt Dunlap, Horn protested his innocence and asked for letters from former associates attesting to his good character while he lived in Arizona. Burt Dunlap and his brother, Horace, obliged by gathering numerous testimonials on Horn's behalf. Even General Nelson Miles, who commanded the military force that pursued Geronimo, submitted a letter for Horn.

With a representative of the Pinkerton Agency lending support at his new trial, the jury found Horn not guilty on October 2, 1891. Arizonans were pleased at the news. Globe's *Silver Belt* reported exultantly that Arizona's "boss cattle tyer and knight of the lariat" had been acquitted. It was all "a case of mistaken identity." Privately, William Pinkerton reportedly admitted that Horn was indeed guilty of the robbery, but the agency could not afford such adverse publicity on its record.

Whatever the truth of the matter, Horn continued in the service of the Pinkerton Agency. In between his two trials, Horn joined Doc Shores, his old mentor, in the pursuit of bandits who robbed the Denver & Rio Grande at Cotopaxi, Colorado, on August 31, 1891. The detectives trailed two suspects all the way to Indian Territory before capturing them. After time out for his second trial in early October, Horn traced a third Cotopaxi outlaw, Dick McCoy, through winter snows to a remote village in northeastern Utah. Learning that his quarry was in a local saloon, Horn brazenly walked into the midst of a group of barroom toughs, leveled his gun at McCoy, and placed him under arrest. Even McCoy had to express grudging admiration for the detective's bravado.

Although the length of Horn's tenure with the Pinkerton Agency is not clear, it appears that he remained with the company until 1894. Some years later, Robert Pinkerton recalled that the company employed Horn "principally to follow up rustlers, cattle and horse thieves, [and] stage and holdup men. . . . We found in Horn a most thorough plainsman and trailer, a man of unquestionable courage and good judgment in all that pertained to his class of work." Charlie Siringo, a fellow operative, maintained that the Pinkerton Agency kept Horn on the payroll for baser reasons. Siringo, who later fell out with his employers and wrote several critical books about the agency, alleged that Pinkerton hired Horn because Siringo refused to do the company's "dirty work." Although Siringo's accusations might have been motivated by bitterness, Horn's subsequent career as a hired assassin supported Siringo's contention.

Horn's next assignment took him to Wyoming, where a tense and sometimes violent situation existed between the large cattle companies on one side and small ranchers and homesteaders on the other. The former accused the latter of wholesale livestock theft and of packing juries in order to set any accused men free. The big companies regarded the homesteaders ("nesters") of the Powder River Valley, in Johnson County, Wyoming, as the greatest offenders, although residents of neighboring counties were suspected as well. By late 1891 the barons of the range were resolved to take drastic measures to eradicate rustling.

Horn's arrival in Johnson County coincided with this growing tension. There are indications that he was in the troubled county by late 1891, only a few days after the Nevada courts released him. In late November Horn and another man allegedly ambushed and murdered a suspected cattle thief. The primary assassin was later identified as Frank Canton, the former sheriff of Johnson County. The following April Horn reportedly was party to one of the more bizarre, and potentially lethal, efforts on the part of the large ranchers to suppress rustling. The barons hired an "army" of some fifty mercenaries, armed them with a blacklist, and ordered the gunmen to assassinate or drive the suspected "wielders of the long rope" from the county. However, when the invaders killed two men on their list, an outraged public rose up, corralled the band, and threatened to wipe them out. At this point, the U.S. Army intervened and took the mercenaries into protective custody. Eventually the gunmen were released and left the state. Horn was not among the men arrested. He had the good fortune to leave the invading party just before its downfall.

Within weeks of the abortive "cattleman's invasion," operative Horn, still using the cover name Thomas Hale, was back on the job in Johnson County. When unknown persons ambushed and killed Deputy U.S. Marshal George Wellman in Johnson County on May 10, 1892, U.S. Marshal Joseph Rankin dispatched a posse to the troubled region. Among his deputies was Hale (Horn). After Rankin's men ran into difficulty apprehending the murderers, he attempted to explain his problems to the U.S. attorney general in Washington, D.C. In a letter on this matter in October 1892, Rankin also revealed the reason for Horn's presence in Wyoming:

> *About the time of the killing of Wellman, at the request of the cattlemen, I appointed a man by the name of Hale [Horn] a deputy for Johnson County. He had been obtained by the cattlemen from the Pinkerton Agency at Denver, and was selected by them because of peculiar fitness for the work. He was to remain in Johnson County and watch for the parties against whom warrants were to be sworn out, and also to secure evidence as to who killed Wellman.*

When the marshal attempted to light a fire under Deputy Hale/Horn, the latter reminded Rankin that he was a Pinkerton detective first and a deputy second. Hale said that his supervisor in Denver ordered him "to take no instruction from you [Rankin] whatever. My instructions . . . were to try to drive these men [rustlers] out of the country and not arrest them," he said bluntly. Hale explained that the cattle companies had resorted to this drastic course of action because any effort to prosecute accused thieves would result in a jury of sympathetic small ranchers and farmers releasing them. Hale concluded that "the cattlemen would be in a worse fix" if this should transpire than if no arrests were made at all.

The following year, in 1893, Horn was scouting the Wyoming range for the sprawling Swan Land and Cattle Company. By this time, he was so well known that he had dropped the alias of Thomas Hale, although he may still have been in the Pinkerton Agency's employ. Now Horn used the cover of a working cowhand. He also carried a Laramie County deputy sheriff's badge. In November 1893 Horn deputized several cowhands and arrested five persons suspected of cattle theft. The prisoners included William Taylor, Louis Bath, James Cleve and his wife, Nettie, and Eva Langhoff.

The charges against Nettie Cleve were dropped. The trial of the other four took place in Laramie in January 1894. The jury acquitted Eva Langhoff, but found Bath guilty and sentenced him to eighteen months in the territorial penitentiary. Bath was pardoned after serving twelve months. The charges against James Cleve and William Taylor were also dropped.

Several years later, Horn recalled his chagrin at this courthouse spectacle and concluded that he would no longer rely upon the courts. With the consent of the cattle companies, he vowed to run suspected thieves out of the county or intimidate them into a more law-abiding state. He used various means to frighten suspected rustlers—threatening letters, warning rifle shots, and, finally, outright assassinations. Using techniques that he probably learned in the Apache campaigns, Horn rode the ranges at all times of the night and day, appearing unexpectedly in remote areas. He attempted to create a specter that potential thieves would dread, and he would boast publicly about his feats. Later, Horn's friends asserted that his tendency to boast was merely a tactic to enlarge his reputation as a range detective and that he often took credit for crimes he did not commit. If so, his tendency toward braggadocio would soon get him into much trouble.

Horn left the Pinkerton Agency in 1894 but continued in the employ of Wyoming livestock interests as a range detective. Although enemies of the barons charged that the Wyoming Live Stock Association, the official organ of the big cattlemen, retained Horn's services, this organization denied any such association with such a lethal individual. However, this disavowal did not preclude individual members of the association from privately hiring him. One cattleman whom Horn served was John C. Coble, manager of the Iron Mountain Ranch, northwest of Cheyenne. Coble and Horn became good friends. In the following year, Horn was suspected of murdering two alleged rustlers, William Lewis and F. U. Powell. Both victims were neighbors of the Iron Mountain outfit. Even though the sheriff called in Horn for questioning, the grand jury failed to indict him in either shooting. In regard to the second assassination, Horn reportedly boasted that when he pointed his gun at Powell, the latter was "the scaredest son-of-a-bitch you ever saw."

With Wyoming lawmen harboring such suspicions about him, Horn may have begun to feel that Wyoming was too hot for him. Or, he may have tired of such work. In December 1895 the Solomonville *Arizona Bulletin* informed readers that "Tom Horn, the well known cowboy, who has been in Colorado for five or six years in the employ of the Pinkerton detective agency, has decided to return to Arizona." Back in his old haunts, Horn resumed his former activities as cowhand, miner, and lawman.

In November 1896 William Kidder Meade, U.S. marshal of the territory, asked Horn to join a federal posse in pursuit of William "Black Jack"

Christian's band of train and post office robbers. Although Horn was too busy at the time, he agreed to help the marshal later on. Horn's reply of November 7 revealed that he had, indeed, developed a callous and mercenary attitude toward the taking of human life. He wrote:

> *If the business is not too pressing and you write and explain it to me I will give you any assistance I can. If it [the assignment] concerns the Outlaws on the Border and you are going out with a posse I could not go as I know that with any posse you could get you could not accomplish any thing. . . . No one knows as well as myself the way in which the posse would be handicapped. I can stand a better show to get them by going alone and will go and get some of them at least and drive the rest out of the country if there is any thing in it for me.*

Even though Horn advised Meade to abandon plans to send a posse after the highwaymen, he assured the marshal that he would get results if he took on the task. As he wrote ungrammatically: "*No cure, no pay* is my mottoe. So if I don't get them it costs no one a cent."

Tom Horn continued to invest time and energy in mining ventures. Although he failed to strike it rich, he and one partner, John Harr, made a modest profit from diggings in the Aravaipa Canyon. For some years, miners had longed to explore the southern extremity of the San Carlos Apache Reservation, where coal and other minerals had been discovered. By the 1890s prospectors were illegally prowling this mineral-rich area, while politicians attempted to persuade Congress to set aside the area for mining claims. In 1897 Tom Horn joined this frenzy and informed a Globe newspaper that he had located a promising copper claim. However, his hopes for new wealth were soon dashed. When federal surveyors eventually redrew the reservation boundary, Horn's mine remained a part of the Indian lands, and, disappointed, he had to relinquish his claim.

The outbreak of the war with Spain in April 1898 afforded Horn a new opportunity for a steady income. On April 23 he signed on as a pack master in Tampa, Florida, and landed with the Fifth Army Corps in Santiago, Cuba, a few weeks later. In the absence of sufficient landing craft, Horn and other packers faced a serious dilemma in getting their mules ashore in a timely fashion. According to one source, Horn took the initiative and merely pushed many horses and mules overboard, hoping the animals would instinctively swim to dry land. Apparently, this expediency worked, but Colonel Theodore Roosevelt, whose favorite horses were among those thrown into the water, was very upset.

On August 1 Horn was promoted to chief packer, although the war was over in Cuba, except for the peace treaty. By this time, he had succumbed to yellow fever and was among the thousands of men evacuated to stateside hospitals. When the army discharged Horn on September 6, he made his way to the Iron Mountain Ranch in Bosler, Wyoming, where his former employer, John C. Coble, took him in while he recuperated. Not until January 1899 did Horn feel strong enough to return to work. When he heard that the army was forming new pack trains for the war against Emilio Aguinaldo's rebels in the Philippine Islands, Horn applied for a position as pack master. However, he did not receive the appointment.

The former packer returned to the task he knew best—manhunting. There were still many opportunities in this line of work. On June 2, 1899, six men robbed a Union Pacific train at Willcox Station, a few miles west of Laramie. When several large posses proved unsuccessful in the search for the highwaymen, the railroad authorities employed Tom Horn as a detective, with the assignment to quietly ferret out the bandits. To assist him in this search, Horn summoned Ed Tewksbury, his old friend from the Pleasant Valley War in Arizona. In late July 1899 the two men began an extensive scout that took them through parts of Wyoming, South Dakota, and Nebraska. But the robbers—evidently Butch Cassidy's notorious "Wild Bunch"—were too slippery for even these experienced trackers. Upon his return to Arizona, Tewksbury was forced to admit that they did not even "get sight" of the robbers.

Although this foray into the wilderness after the train robbers afforded Tom Horn some publicity, it had an unexpected consequence. After he and Tewksbury abandoned their manhunt, rumors persisted that they had actually killed two of the Wild Bunch, one of whom was allegedly the notorious Harvey Logan, alias Kid Curry. At first, Horn made no effort to dispel this report, but Kid Curry, who considered Horn a mere tinhorn and braggart, angrily threatened to kill him on sight. Not until January 1900 did Horn admit that he and Tewksbury had inadvertently fallen upon the trail of two small-time rustlers in a remote section of northwestern Wyoming. When the two suspects, Tex Blair and a man named Monte, opened fire on the detectives, the manhunters killed both men. Tewksbury was wounded in the exchange, and Horn hastily buried both outlaws and rushed his comrade to the nearest town for medical attention. In commenting on this incident, the *Cheyenne Sun-Leader* was naturally concerned about these unnecessary deaths and the absence of a coroner's inquest, not to mention the absence of any sign of remorse on the part of detective Horn.

By midsummer 1900 Horn had returned to his old line of work as a stock detective. Ora Haley, whose vast spread stretched over southwestern Wyoming and northwestern Colorado, retained Horn's services. The detective's task was to drive rustlers out of the Brown's Hole region of Haley's

Colorado holdings. Many years later, Hi Bernard, Haley's foreman at that time, recalled that his boss and other cattle raisers decided on this action in a conference in Denver. In carrying out his assignment, Horn used the alias of Hicks, the name of some of his relatives. Horn was suspected of assassinating two alleged livestock thieves, Madison (Matt) Rash and Isom Dart, the latter a black man. Before shooting Rash, Hicks/Horn took the unusual step of filing a formal complaint against him in a local court. The complainant signed his real name, Thomas Horn. The reason for this action is unclear. Upon returning to Cheyenne, Horn had the temerity to boast to a newspaperman that he had suppressed rustling in the Brown's Hole region, although he did not admit to the killings.

Instead of shuttling off to Arizona as he had done after his difficulties five years earlier, Horn returned to Cheyenne. By this time he had earned a sinister reputation in the state, especially among homesteaders and small ranchers. Whether Horn was as effective at range riding as his reputation led people to believe is questionable. Some observers regarded him as a blowhard who often claimed credit for many deeds that he did not perform. However, there is no doubt that Horn was experienced in the ways of the wild and that the Apache campaigns had taught him how to endure the discomforts of the "cold camp." At the same time, people who knew Horn well believed that he had killed men. He employed any means at hand to create an atmosphere of fear and intimidation as a means to suppress rustling. Such blustery behavior may have been another means to reinforce his occupation as a hired assassin. "Killing men is my specialty," Horn reportedly quipped, "and I have a corner on the market."

Horn's decision to remain in Wyoming eventually proved fatal. On July 18, 1901, an assassin took the life of Willie Nickell, the fourteen-year-old son of Kels Nickell, a rancher near Iron Mountain. A few days later, someone—presumably the same gunman—shot and wounded the father, who eventually recovered. Deputy U.S. Marshal Joe LeFors, a former livestock detective who was familiar with Horn's activities on the range, took up the Willie Nickell case. In order to get close to Horn, LeFors used the ploy of arranging for his employment as a stock detective in Montana. This enabled the deputy marshal to cultivate a social relationship, which included frequenting bars and the red-light district. One evening in January 1902 LeFors cleverly maneuvered Horn—by now deep in his cups—into admitting to the assassination of Willie Nickell. This "confession," taken down in shorthand by a hidden stenographer, led to his arrest and ultimate undoing.

In October 1902 Horn stood trial in Cheyenne for the murder of Willie Nickell. It was a media event, with many journalists hovering around the courtroom. These eager reporters not only reported every aspect of the proceedings, but some critics accused them of "making" the news as well. Furthermore, the public was clearly divided between the big cattle companies and the smaller fry. Many Horn partisans, who were convinced that the experienced range rider would not be so careless as to assassinate a young boy, alleged that he was being railroaded, and the public demanded that someone should pay.

Even though Horn's friend, John C. Coble, mobilized the powerful cattlemen and provided him with the best attorneys, the manhunter's case did not go well. His lawyers presented a lackluster defense. Nor did the defendant do himself any favors when on the witness stand. Even though Horn maintained that his "confession" was not that at all—he was merely "joshing" with Deputy Marshal LeFors—the defendant's cavalier manner convinced many observers otherwise. He laughed at the wrong places and acted very casual at times. When the subject of his relationship with Glendolene Kimmell, an attractive schoolteacher, came up, he made offhand and slighting remarks about women that outraged the female public. The association of Kimmell with Horn's case has given rise to much speculation that the two were lovers, but there is no evidence to support this contention.

Horn steadfastly maintained his innocence of the murder charge, yet he admitted on the stand that his duties as a livestock detective demanded the use of techniques against rustlers—short of assassination—that circumvented the courts. In fact, Horn left the impression that he, and his employers, placed themselves above the law. On Friday, October 24, 1902, the jury rendered a verdict of guilty, and the judge sentenced Horn to hang.

Coble and the cattle interests continued to fight on Horn's behalf. An appeal of Horn's conviction to the state supreme court was to no avail, and Governor Fenimore Chatterton also refused to commute the sentence. With time running out, the condemned man made a clumsy effort to break out of jail in August 1903, but he was quickly recaptured. Three months later, on November 21, 1903, the forty-three-year-old frontiersman was hanged. Even if the Wyoming jury had not convicted Horn, escape from his fate may have been unlikely because the Colorado authorities had already announced their intention to bring him back to stand trial for the Rash and Dart murders in Brown's Hole.

Since his death in 1903, Tom Horn has become a part of frontier legend. This legend is not always pretty, nor is it always consistent. Yet Horn could exhibit an engaging side. Veterans of the war in Cuba recalled how Horn encountered two Arizona soldiers who were suffering from yellow fever and getting no medical attention. He took them into his tent and saw to their proper care. In Wyoming he cared for a cowhand who had been

Even when confined to a jail cell, the tall and athletic Horn was an imposing person. He is shown here awaiting execution in the Laramie County Jail in Cheyenne, Wyoming. Courtesy of the American Heritage Center, University of Wyoming.

wounded in a shooting incident when no one else would do so. When the unfortunate man died, Horn saw that he had a proper burial. This complex man could also be counted on to keep promises. For example, when Horn told a lady in Wyoming that he would bring her a gift from Arizona, she soon forgot about the promise. But he returned with the gift of an Indian basket. As Horn got older, he may have regretted having no children of his own. In his later years he enjoyed sitting on the street in Cheyenne and talking with young people.

Since his Arizona days, Horn had possessed a sense of humor and enjoyed playing pranks. His antics could be rough around the edges. William Chapin Deming, a Wyoming newspaperman and public servant, observed Horn at the Inter-Ocean Hotel in Cheyenne during the 1901 Thanksgiving season. Although somewhat tipsy, Horn was playfully throwing his lariat over bellboys and customers.

Horn could also be mean and surly. He exhibited such behavior especially when he had been drinking heavily. Such binges became more frequent as he got older. Cyrus Shores, the Colorado sheriff and an associate of Horn, had the opportunity to observe both sides of Horn's personality. When they first met in Arizona, Shores was taken with Horn's sense of humor and bravery. However, Shores had an opportunity to observe Horn's darker personality when they took up the long chase after two train robbers in 1891. As trail fatigue began to set in, Horn became selfish, demanding, and moody. When the fugitives sent back threats against the detectives' lives, Horn became furious. When they captured the outlaws in Indian Territory, Horn tried to kill one of them on the spot. Only the timely interference of a woman prevented the angry Pinkerton agent from carrying out his threat.

Exactly what led Horn to this regrettable stage in his life is impossible to determine at this late date. Perhaps he simply lacked a conscience. Possibly, his departure from home at an early age and exposure to the harsher side of frontier life helped shape his jaundiced outlook on life. One writer,

John Rolfe Burroughs, concludes that all a person has to do to understand how Horn went wrong is to read Horn's description of the Apache Wars in Arizona. These grim and free-for-all campaigns hardened him and provided the training for his subsequent life as a hired assassin. Dean Krakel, perhaps the keenest student of Horn's personality, suggested that Horn might have had a psychiatric condition such as a split personality. After all, there were two Tom Horns.

In one area, Horn did reveal a singular consistent attitude throughout his life—a reverence for men of wealth and power. Jay Monaghan, whose *Tom Horn: Last of the Badmen* (1946) remains the most complete biography of this contradictory personality, noted that Horn spent much of his life "serving the rich and the powerful," and that he became "an instinctive vassal of the vested interests." Such a subservient attitude may have arisen from his humble origins or from the fact that he failed to accumulate property in his own right. Yet he seemed to perceive no difference between the U.S. government paying him for killing Apaches and wealthy cattlemen remunerating him for assassinating alleged livestock thieves.

Tom Horn's place in western legend falls primarily on the shadowed side. His years as a livestock detective and killer-for-hire shadow any other accomplishments. In some respects, Horn resembles another legendary frontier character, Thomas E. "Black Jack" Ketchum. A notorious southwestern highwayman, Ketchum was hanged in New Mexico for train robbery in 1901, only two years prior to Horn's execution. Unlike other frontier personalities who won fame as mankillers, such as Wild Bill Hickok and Wyatt Earp, Horn and Ketchum were cold-blooded murderers. They did not give their victims a chance. There was something particularly appalling about Horn, who killed from ambush and at a distance. Furthermore, Horn and Ketchum climbed the gallows, leaving some doubt as to the well-being of their souls, an outcome that not only saddened but discomfited many westerners.

Charles Horn encountered the problem of his brother's uncertain religious status when he claimed the body after the hanging. He transported Tom's corpse to Boulder, Colorado, with a view to interring his brother with relatives. However, local ministers hesitated to preside over services for a person reputed to be an unrepentant murderer, and they thought it improper even to permit the body inside an established church. Finally, Edward G. Lane, pastor of the First Baptist Church, agreed to officiate at the last rites of Tom Horn, even though many members of his congregation objected. Although he conducted the funeral service, he insisted on doing so in the mortuary chapel, rather than in the church sanctuary.

Even after his death, Horn continued to create controversy. When Laramie County sheriff George Smalley proposed placing other inmates in

Charles Horn, standing hatless, watches as the body of his brother, Tom, is loaded into a hearse for shipment to Boulder, Colorado. Courtesy of the American Heritage Center, University of Wyoming.

Horn's former cell, the prisoners quickly raised objections. They feared bad luck if they were forced to sleep in the room of a man who had come to such a deplorable end. On the other hand, sideshow promoters were just as quick to exploit the ghost of the hanged man for profit. Numerous promoters pestered Charles Horn with offers for his brother's body, but the grieving sibling angrily rejected all comers. On one occasion, he threatened to bloody the nose of one aggressive entrepreneur who awakened him late one night with an offer. The saddened brother placed Tom Horn's body in a Boulder cemetery, where it remains to this day.

The matter of Tom Horn's guilt or innocence in the death of Willie Nickell still arouses passions and much controversy. An indication of the intensity of this debate occurred in September 1993, when Horn's case was retried in Cheyenne. The prime mover of this judicial event was Chip Carlson, a Wyoming resident and biographer of the convicted assassin. With the support of Horn's descendants, who stoutly maintain that he was railroaded, Carlson obtained an order from the Wyoming Supreme Court for these new proceedings. In the widely publicized proceedings, which even captured considerable space in *The Times* of London, Tom Horn was acquitted. Even though the acquittal had no legal standing, Horn's descendants took the court's action as a vindication of their frontier ancestor.

Whatever the facts of his case, there is much in Tom Horn's life to provoke interest and debate. Writers and readers undoubtedly will continue to find Horn an intriguing subject well into the twenty-first century. The appearance of two Hollywood movies based loosely on his life in the 1980s is also testimony to this phenomenon. Whether we attempt to explain Horn's tragic demise, as many have, by arguing that he was a frontier character who had outlived his times or by concluding that he alone must bear the responsibility for his fate, his name remains forever a part of frontier legend in the American West.

5

DOC HOLLIDAY

Vigilantism with Honor

GARY TOPPING

It is easy to give Doc Holliday no more place in history than that of the Earp brothers' evil genius. As the Earps struggled to rise out of their past in the demimonde of card parlors, saloons, and gunfights, and into the respectable world of politics and law enforcement, Holliday's shadow cast a constant gloom over them, reminding both of their dark worlds of earlier times. It is true that both Holliday's and the Earp brothers' careers seemed to move on contrary tangents, for Holliday left the respectable profession of dentistry for the faro table just as the brothers were abandoning the saloon for law-abiding society. Nevertheless, although Holliday blasted his way into history as he plied Virgil Earp's shotgun with deadly effect at the OK Corral, his life and career are meaningful in their own right.

John Henry "Doc" Holliday in the early 1880s. Courtesy of the Western History Collections, University of Oklahoma.

In an interview late in life, Holliday acknowledged having earned some notches on his gunbelt, but pointed out that he took the law into his own hands only in cases where the law was otherwise absent and while awaiting the emergence of a more stable and peaceful social order. This is, of course, a standard defense of vigilantism, and though Doc Holliday was known occasionally to cross the line into vengeful retribution, the argument has its points.

It is of much more than passing significance that John Henry "Doc" Holliday (1851–1887) was a southern aristocrat. His father, Major Henry B. Holliday, was a lawyer, a planter credited with introducing what became the lucrative pecan industry in southern Georgia, and a soldier, who led a famous unit called "Fannin's Avengers" in the Mexican War and the 27th Georgia Infantry in the Civil War. His mother, Alice Jane McKey, was a Georgia transplant from South Carolina. A famous beauty with musical talent, she was the archetypal southern belle. Official records of the precise birth date of their son near Griffin, Georgia, were among the casualties of General William Tecumseh Sherman's scorched-earth campaign of 1864, but a notation in a recently discovered family Bible places the event on August 14, 1851.

The birthing itself was fraught with peril and closely attended, for Alice Holliday had recently lost a frail daughter who lived only six months in 1850. The couple desperately sought success this time. Fortunately, the major's brother, Dr. John S. Holliday, was a renowned physician and surgeon, and his effective supervision of the delivery was rewarded by the addition of his name to that of the father at the baby's baptism, which took place in the town's Presbyterian church on March 21, 1852.

Tragedy marred the birth nevertheless. Karen Holliday Tanner, a family member, reports a tradition that the baby was born with a cleft palate and harelip that robbed the infant boy of his ability to nurse and, unless corrective surgery could be performed, would render normal speech impossible. Ironically, for one who would become a legendary consumer of whiskey in his adulthood, the baby's early feedings were laboriously administered from a shot glass. When the child was eight weeks old, Holliday family solidarity paid off once again. Another relative, Dr. Crawford W. Long, one of the early pioneers in the use of ether anesthetic, agreed to perform the surgery, assisted by the boy's uncle, and successfully mended both the palate and the lip.

The operation had no guarantees and only gave the boy a chance at a normal adulthood. The young John underwent countless hours of speech therapy administered by his mother, who devised special word charts to exercise the boy's pronunciation of problematic letters. The sessions were arduous and robbed the boy of many of youth's carefree hours. They also built an enduring bond between mother and son and corrected his speech well enough that any residual defects were masked by his natural southern accent, and none of his eventual western acquaintances commented on it. No doubt those hours also developed his withdrawn personality, his self-sufficiency, and his stoicism that emerged in adulthood and continued to sustain him through a life of physical suffering and threats of external danger.

The Hollidays personified, fought for, and suffered as a result of their southern culture. Like the realities of the frontier West, which Doc later came to personify, the realities of southern culture have become obscured by myth. It is worth trying to brush aside some of that myth to understand the real world of Holliday's youth in order to understand what he brought with him to the West.

The Mind of the South (1941), which earned for its author, W. J. Cash, the eternal enmity of southern romanticizers, presents an unflattering profile of a southern ethos with individualism and violence at its core, rather than cultured leisure and gentility. At the heart of that ethos was "the bald, immediate, unsupported assertion of the ego, which placed too great stress on the inviolability of personal whim, and which was full of the chip-on-shoulder swagger and brag of a boy—one, in brief, of which the essence was the boast, voiced or not, on the part of every Southerner, that he would knock hell out of whoever dared to cross him." Such a person, Cash goes on, was not one to await delayed resolution of conflict through negotiation or litigation. "What the direct willfulness of his individualism demanded, when confronted by a crime that aroused his anger, was immediate satisfaction for itself—catharsis for personal passion in the spectacle of a body dancing at the end of a rope or writhing in the fire—now, within the hour—and not some ponderous abstract justice in a problematic tomorrow." In those southerners who went west, the dueling pistol in the hand of an Andrew Jackson, the bloodied cane wielded by a Preston Brooks, and the shoulder-holstered Colt and waistpocket sheath knife carried by Doc Holliday form a seamless continuity as the Code of the South became the Code of the West—a new frontier continuing an old one.

The immediate circumstances of Holliday's boyhood could only have heaped coals upon the smoldering propensity for violence in that southern ethos. The spectacle of Sherman's swath of total destruction would have imprinted an indelible resentment on the psyche of an impressionable twelve-year-old son of a Confederate officer. An even greater humiliation, though, came with the military occupation of the South during Reconstruction, when a federal garrison of African American troops was established in Valdosta, the nearest town to the Holliday estate. The inevitable sting of that lends a morsel of credence to an unverifiable legend that the teenage Holliday drove a group of black youngsters out of a favorite swimming hole, probably by shooting over their heads. The story was perhaps invented, kept alive, and maybe even augmented into a wounding and even a killing of one of the boys by Holliday himself, who was far out on the western frontier, where verification was impossible and where having a reputation as a dangerous man with a gun would have served his needs well.

In 1866, barely after his father's return from the war, Holliday's mother died, and his father almost immediately remarried. Rachel Martin, the bride, was only eight and a half years older than young John Henry Holliday. The act enraged the son. Not only was this an assault on his Oedipal attachment to his mother, nurtured through their lengthy and private speech therapy sessions, but it also violated his sense of loyalty. The latter would be a controlling motivation during his adulthood. During her last days, Holliday's mother reverted to the Methodist faith of her youth, and the young man, no doubt partly as an act of rebellion, also abandoned his father's Presbyterianism and embraced the religion of his mother. The result was a permanent rift between father and son, a rift that shaped a new future for him apart from the plantation and even apart from the South.

For an aristocratic southern male of Holliday's time, there were few career possibilities. The most likely was to succeed his father as patriarch of the plantation. That now was impossible. Another was the military, but that also was unthinkable in view of the humiliation the federal military had recently inflicted upon the South. That left the professions. At first, Holliday was inclined to follow his uncle into medicine, but he found that his uncle had become disillusioned with the medical profession because of its backward resistance to ether anesthetic. On the other hand, dentistry embraced anesthesia, and the uncle encouraged the young man into what he regarded as a more progressive field. In some ways dentistry was only beginning to work its way to respectability among the professions, and most practitioners resembled Frank Norris's fictional McTeague—untrained, unsophisticated molar extractors with few qualifications beyond possession of a pair of forceps and a strong arm. However, the young Holliday took his professional aspiration seriously and had the money to get the best training available. Thus, he found himself in Baltimore, which boasted the two finest dental schools in the country. Holliday graduated, not from the prestigious Baltimore College of Dental Surgery, but rather from its upcoming rival, the Baltimore Dental College. As a practicing dentist, Holliday was good and enjoyed the work's challenges to his quick intellect and the dexterity of his delicate hands.

At this time, harbingers of his future notoriety were beginning to manifest themselves. For one thing, Holliday seems to have learned to drink during his dental training. Even more ominously, upon his return to Griffin, Georgia, to open his first dental practice, he was diagnosed with advanced consumption (tuberculosis), a widespread malady evidently promoted by malnutrition in areas where southern agriculture had been most devastated by the war. It may, in fact, have been the disease that took his mother's life. A perverse irony exists in the possibility that she may have passed it on to her son at the very time she was trying to give him a normal life through the speech therapy. The only way to prolong his life, Holliday was told, was to seek a drier climate. He left for Dallas, probably in 1872.

Over the next couple of years, Holliday wavered between the respectability of the dental profession and the shady life of the gambler and gunfighter. It is known that he practiced dentistry and that he enjoyed working inside the tight confines of a patient's mouth with his dexterous fingers. His practice evidently languished, though, perhaps either from patients' shyness about subjecting themselves to close proximity with his constant cough or because of his growing fondness for the gaming table. Holliday would have found that handling a deck of cards proficiently was an intriguing challenge equal to that of dental surgery and, if adequately mastered, far more lucrative. During Holliday's boyhood, a slave woman named Sophie Walton had taught him and his cousin a card game called "Skinning," in which deft card handling and the mental discipline of card counting were critical to success. Through long sessions at the table, Holliday developed and improved his skill. Gradually, he drifted away from dentistry. Although this was not the last time he would practice his old profession, it was quickly becoming less of an important factor in his future plans and the new world he was beginning to inhabit.

A plethora of games were available on the frontier, offering lucky miners or hot-blooded cowboys fresh off the trail a generous selection of ways to part with their earnings. Professional gamblers also enjoyed a wide range of choices to suit their skills and could ply their trade in a wide variety of locales. In addition to the cattle towns of Texas and Kansas, the mining frontier created communities in Colorado, Nevada, Arizona, and other western states and territories where new wealth and games of chance came together. A circuit eventually developed on which gamblers traveled from town to town, seeking new sources of wealth or escaping unpleasant episodes of the past. Doc Holliday soon became one of its familiar fixtures.

Although Doc Holliday occasionally played poker, his primary game was faro. Among the various frontier gambling practices, faro was the king, and "faro artists," such as Doc Holliday, were the aristocrats of frontier gamblers. "Faro" is a corruption of "Pharaoh," which derives from the images of Egyptian kings often depicted on the backs of the imported decks of cards used in the game. Further symbolism included the solitary tiger, which designated an ace. Faro games were advertised by tiger signs on the street, and playing faro was called "bucking the tiger." Many an unskilled pasteboard pusher learned the expensive lesson that the faro tiger, under the whip and spur of a faro master like Doc Holliday, was a mean mount indeed.

The unique excitement of faro derives, in the first place, from the fact that all cards are played face up. So the strategies of the players are openly observable by all, and competition is intense. Also, card counting (i.e., keeping track of the cards previously played, which gives a progressively precise indication of which cards are left) is a part of the game. In fact, the dealer has an assistant called the "casekeeper," whose role is to keep a running list of cards played. This aspect encourages betting, for the odds in favor of the player increase as the game proceeds.

Only the dealer handles the cards, which are dealt one at a time out of a springloaded box. He deals them onto two piles in front of him—a "lose" pile and a "win" pile. In the center of the table is an imprinted diagram showing each of the thirteen cards in the suit of spades. Bettors place chips on the denomination they think is going to come up next in the win pile or, by covering their chips with a penny or copper token, the lose pile. Each "turn" consists of the dealer exposing two cards, the first of which goes on the lose pile, thus exposing another card in the box, which goes on the win pile. The first card in the box, which of course is exposed when the box is first loaded, is called "soda," and does not count. Similarly, the last card, which is called "in hock," does not count, thus leaving fifty cards that are played in twenty-five turns. If the same denomination appears in both the win and lose piles in a given turn, it is called a "split," and any bets on that denomination are divided between the house and the player. The greatest intensity of play occurs when only three cards (including the one "in hock") are left. At that point the dealer introduces a new betting opportunity by inviting the players to "call the turn," which means to guess the order of appearance of the three cards and to place an additional bet accordingly. In an honest faro game, it is estimated that the house will take 2.5 percent of all money bet, a profit that was divided between the dealer, the assistants, and the gambling establishment. But how honest were the games?

A presumption of a generally honest game was necessary among potential players if a gambling house expected to stay in business for long, for everyone who gambles hopes to win. Because the game's odds favored the house over the long run, a dealer like Doc Holliday would find little need to cheat. However, on the occasions when a bad run of cards occurred, which can happen in any card game, the house and players alike expected that a skillful dealer would employ techniques designed to "readjust" the odds. Such readjustments were a risky business, placing a mortal premium on the dealer's skill. If he were caught, there would be immediate trouble, even though all parties assumed that such an attempt would be made.

One of the virtues of faro, from the dealer's standpoint, was the variety of opportunities it offered for nefarious manipulation of the deal. Because the dealer alone handled the cards, there were always ways in which he could slightly nick cards of a certain denomination, deal "seconds" (i.e., not the top card), palm a card, or use a rigged deck or dealing box. Doc

Holliday's nimble but strong fingers, trained first in Sophie Walton's Skinning games, then in performing intricate dental procedures in tight quarters, naturally lent themselves to the netherworld of crooked cards. On various occasions, Holliday made immense amounts of money at faro, and we have to assume that some of his fortune, at least, was a tribute to his sleight of hand.

Practitioners of such black art had to be able to protect themselves with weapons. Almost anyone can laugh off losses in a few hands of low-stakes faro early in the evening and move on, but in the marathon late-night sessions where Doc Holliday made his best money, after free-flowing alcohol had loosened the purse strings but tightened the tempers, a string of losses could provoke suspicions of dishonesty and sudden eruptions of violence. With their lives depending on their ability to defend themselves quickly and decisively when such an encounter became inevitable, many frontier gamblers turned themselves into walking armories with a dozen or more weapons of various types stashed from boot top to coat collar.

Holliday's choice of arms was much simpler and more conservative. Because he carried a shotgun on two famous occasions, Doc Holliday has gone down in history as having a preference for the scattergun. It is true that he used Virgil Earp's sawed-off shotgun at the OK Corral, opening a fatal hole in Tom McLaury with his double salvo of buckshot. It is also true that a banker suddenly thrust a shotgun into his hands during the Earp posse's tense exit from Tombstone under the ready guns of John Behan's rival posse after Wyatt Earp's murder of Frank Stilwell.

In fact, though, Holliday eschewed the shotgun and used one only reluctantly under the duress of the moment. Unprepared for the suddenness with which the OK Corral shootout precipitated, he was carrying only one of his two sixguns. He accepted Virgil's shotgun only as an emergency equalizer against the firepower he expected to face. In the Tombstone departure, he was the only member of the Earp faction without a shotgun. Evidently, he thought it less trouble to accept the weapon proffered from a bank's protective arsenal than to waste time protesting. Anyone who has fired a large-gauge shotgun knows the ferocious recoil it produces. Although a sawed-off barrel offers the attractive feature of a shot pattern that will devastate anything in the general direction of the muzzle, it was simply too much gun for the emaciated Holliday. Also, the black powder used in those big guns produced so much smoke that it obscured the target in case a second shot became necessary. At the OK Corral, in fact, Holliday thought his double-barreled blast had missed McLaury, leading him to follow up with his sixgun and waste a shot he might have wished for later.

Instead, on the street and at the gambling table, Doc Holliday carried only three well-concealed but instantly accessible weapons. Two were nickel-plated Colt revolvers, one carried high on his right hip and the other in a shoulder holster. To those he added a waistpocket sheath knife. The latter might seem a dubious choice for a fight across a card table, but it is nevertheless possible that Holliday sometimes found a quick slash with a sharp knife faster than drawing and cocking a pistol.

How dangerous was Doc Holliday? One can be certain that he participated in nothing close to the thirty gun or knife fights with which he was credited after his death. For one thing, it was in his own interest to promote an image of himself as a rough customer in order to discourage casual challenges. Also, western myth has a habit of exaggerating stories after the fact so that virtually all frontier heroes have received credit for more dramatic feats than their historical due.

Doc's Dallas years, however, ended both in violence and legal trouble, beginning with a bloodless exchange of shots with a man named Charles W. "Champagne Charlie" Austin on New Year's Day 1875, and ending with an arrest for gambling a few months later. Thus began Holliday's life as a fugitive, wandering around "the circuit" of gambling centers from one legal jurisdiction to another to avoid prosecution or simply waiting until the short memories of understaffed law enforcement agencies allowed him to return to a previous scene of violence.

On this particular occasion, Doc went briefly to Denison, Texas, on the border of the Indian Territory, but found it offered few pickings for a professional gambler. He then moved on to Fort Griffin, Texas, a camp-follower community for Fort Richardson, whose federal troops were finally pacifying the Comanches and Kiowas. His stay there was brief, though he would return later. On June 12, 1875, he was arrested for gambling but skipped town before the case came to trial.

His hasty departure this time was a ride of legendary proportions from Fort Griffin, Texas, to Denver, Colorado, via Pueblo, a solo journey over eight hundred miles of largely waterless and trackless terrain, crawling with the very Indians whom the Fort Richardson soldiers were trying to subdue. It was an amazing feat that creates yet another image of Doc Holliday far from the frail, consumptive ex-dentist with delicate hands and a pallid complexion. Holliday was, in fact, a master horseman and outdoorsman who competently negotiated immense distances on horseback, either in flight from the law or in pursuit of an income.

The years 1876–1877 found Doc Holliday wandering among Denver, Cheyenne, and Deadwood, South Dakota. It may have been in the latter community that he first met Wyatt Earp, who spent the fall of 1876 there, though such a meeting is undocumented. By the summer of 1877 he had returned to Texas, where, during a brief stay in Breckenridge, he got into a violent controversy with a local gambler named Henry Kahn. An argument over a card game provoked Doc to beat Kahn savagely with his cane, and when the two encountered each other later in the day, Kahn fired at Holliday, wounding him severely. Recuperating in Fort Worth, Doc was visited by a cousin, George Henry Holliday, who nursed him back to health and tried to convince him to return to Georgia. Instead, Doc returned to Fort Griffin.

Fort Griffin was the archetype of a western boomtown. Its population of cowboys, buffalo hunters, Indians, and soldiers was supplied and preyed upon by the usual seedy army of traders, gamblers, and prostitutes, against which the town's meager law enforcers made little headway. Doc hung out his shingle in the saloon of John Shanssey, an ex-boxer and teamster who had been mayor of Yuma, Arizona, before following the "circuit" to Texas. It may have been Shanssey who introduced Holliday to two people who would play major roles in his life as he emerged from obscurity to claim center stage as a western outlaw.

The first was a prostitute known as Big Nose Kate, more formally known as Kate Elder. She was born Mary Katherine Harony to a medical doctor who emigrated from Hungary in 1860. When her parents died in 1865, Kate went to live in a foster home, from which she soon escaped and embarked upon a life of wandering. In St. Louis she assumed the name of Kate Fisher and became a prostitute. She probably met Wyatt Earp in Wichita in 1874 while working in a whorehouse run by James Earp's wife. She then followed the Earps to Dodge City, where she changed her professional name to Kate Elder. From there she moved to Fort Griffin.

What began as a relationship of convenience between Kate and Doc became one of concubinage, and the two remained together off and on until Doc's death. Theirs was a tempestuous and perhaps abusive relationship. Kate was an independent professional who plied her trade without benefit of madam or pimp. She enjoyed her work and practiced it, to Doc's frustration, even when he was able to support them both in grand style. Kate saved Doc's life during their flight from Fort Griffin, but almost lost it for him later in Arizona through her drunken and coerced testimony against him in connection with the Benson stagecoach robbery. She died alone and destitute in a pioneers' rest home in Prescott, Arizona. Nonetheless, she was proud of her relationship with Doc Holliday and shared his most lucrative and notorious years.

Shanssey also may have introduced Doc to Wyatt Earp, if the two had not already met in Deadwood. Earp was just breaking into law enforcement at the time, and passed through Fort Griffin in search of some unspecified rustlers (not incidentally, a train robber named Dave Rudabaugh, who had not yet committed the crime that, as legend has it, put Wyatt on his trail). A saloon was obviously a good place to make inquiries, and when Shanssey himself had nothing to report, he referred Earp to Doc Holliday. By this time, Holliday was well acquainted on the gambling circuit and had access to news that Earp occasionally found useful.

Thus began one of the most famous friendships in western history, and one of the oddest. As previously mentioned, the two men's careers were moving on exactly contrary curves at the time they met—Earp toward the respectable professions of law enforcement and politics and Holliday away from professional respectability and toward the shady world of the saloon and the card table. Although Earp spent a fair amount of effort in subsequent years trying to escape the sinister suspicions of his association with Holliday, he never betrayed the gambler. His loyalty may have rested on the fact that Doc saved his life in a confrontation with some rowdy Dodge City cowboys, though the episode may be fictitious. There is no question, however, that Doc amply earned Earp's loyalty at the OK Corral and later stood with him against John Behan's posse when the Earps shipped Morgan Earp's body out of Tucson. In addition, the two had other things in common beyond their principles of loyalty. Both were descendants from good southern families, and their refined manners would have certainly drawn them together (the Earps had roots in North Carolina and Kentucky, and although Wyatt was born in Illinois and some of the brothers fought for the North in the Civil War, the genteel manners remained). Both men also possessed greater than ordinary intelligences—a rare attribute that set them apart from the riffraff of the frontier.

Fort Griffin was a rough enough place that trouble was virtually inevitable for a man of principle like Doc Holliday. The principle in Holliday's case was his insistence that all participants in a card game should keep their eyes only on their own cards. Once again there are no primary sources for the incident, but what seems to have happened is that a popular local gambler named Ed Bailey kept trying to get an advantage over Holliday in a poker game by sneaking looks at the discard pile, a transgression for which one would customarily lose the pot. Holliday warned him to stop, but as Holliday raked in his winnings from one hand, Bailey went for his gun. Holliday lunged with his knife, and Bailey, who was no more lucky against that weapon than he had been at cards, wound up dead on the floor.

Clearly, Bailey had been cheating and had attacked Holliday, so Doc chose arrest over flight, assuming he would be vindicated and released to gamble in Fort Griffin again. But he had miscalculated Bailey's popularity in the town. A substantial group of Bailey's friends decided to take justice into their own hands, and a lynch mob threatened to break into the jail and hang Holliday. At this point, the resourceful Big Nose Kate came to Holliday's rescue by starting a diversionary fire in a building across town, then getting the drop on the single officer left in charge of Holliday and forcing his release. The couple hid in some willows near town all night, until friends brought them some clothes and a couple of horses. They set out at a gallop for Dodge City, Kansas, four hundred miles away, where they would find at least one friend, Wyatt Earp.

Although Doc's relationship with Big Nose Kate did not involve matrimony, it was close enough to it that when they arrived in Dodge City in December 1877, he decided to make an attempt at domesticity and professional respectability by unpacking his dental tools and going into business. It did not last long. Whatever Doc's chances may have been for success as a dentist, Kate was the problem this time. The bright lights, the music, and the big money available in the saloons were a much bigger lure to her than dull domesticity, and soon both Kate and Doc were back at their previous trades.

Domesticity was not all it promised for Doc, either. For a lengthy period in 1878, while he and Kate were having a spat, he pulled up stakes and tried his luck in Colorado, where the Leadville mining boom was just beginning. By September, though, he was back in Dodge City. It was then that he saved Wyatt Earp from a couple dozen cowboys who had the drop on him, by sneaking around behind the cowboys and ordering them to surrender. It was even then an awkward arrest, for Earp had to "buffalo" one of them (subdue him by hitting him in the head) with his pistol, and Doc shot another in the arm. It was, as one of his biographers observes, Holliday's only shot fired on behalf of law and order, but it seems to have aroused some civilized instinct in him. He was known for the rest of his time in Dodge City as Wyatt Earp's backup man.

Although he and Kate got back together briefly in Dodge City, Holliday learned that she had plans to make a fortune entertaining the trail drivers of 1879 when they hit town. Holliday decided to avoid the humiliation and to seek his own fortune following the new Atchison, Topeka & Santa Fe Railroad into New Mexico. It was a brief episode, lasting perhaps from June to August, and is significant mostly because it was the last time he attempted to practice dentistry in Las Vegas, New Mexico. Rejoined by Kate, he divided his time between the dentist's chair and the card table in a saloon he built for himself, and the couple began enjoying some genuine happiness. Although they intended to make Las Vegas their permanent home, they were tempted to try their luck in the new mining towns of Arizona, where Wyatt Earp and four of his brothers were going.

Doc caught up with the now ex-lawman somewhere on the trail and rode with him as far as Prescott. Although their ultimate goal was Tombstone, Prescott was a wealthy mining camp in its own right and the recently designated territorial capital. Enough cash was changing hands on that town's infamous Whiskey Row that Doc left the Earp party for a while to claim his share of Prescott prosperity. During the three months he spent there, he added a reported $40,000 to his holdings. Armed with that bankroll, Holliday left Prescott and arrived in Tombstone in February 1880, while Kate elected to try her fortunes in the hotel business in Globe, Arizona, and to pay Holliday periodic visits in Tombstone.

Tombstone, Arizona, was a classic western boomtown, and the stories of its incredible wealth, colorful inhabitants, and explosive violence have become staples in the western myth. In February 1878 Edward L. Schieffelin, an ex-soldier of Fort Huachuca, discovered the silver veins that gave the town its wealth and fame, in defiance of both the Apaches and the warnings of his former messmates who told him that "instead of a mine, you'll find a tombstone." The first settlers took up residence in 1879, and the town grew faster than a colony of rabbits. By the time Tombstone became the seat of Cochise County in 1881, conservative estimates placed its population at seven thousand. Some scholars estimate its peak at more than twice that figure. The town burned down in June 1881 and again in May 1882, but its inhabitants rebuilt almost instantly and Tombstone kept growing. Although the town rapidly acquired accoutrements of civilization in the form of a telegraph line, gas lights, a school with 250 students, and two newspapers, its mythic image as an archetype of Wild West life is substantiated by the fact that two out of three buildings in 1881 were saloons or gambling halls, and the town reputedly had no less than 150 liquor outlets.

Tombstone's complicated social and legal circumstances can be sketched briefly here, not only because they have been delineated in detail many times elsewhere, but also because Doc Holliday was almost totally uninterested in those circumstances and was involved in them only through his loyalty to the Earps. His goal was simply to play cards, make money, and live out the brief remainder of his truncated, consumptive life as comfortably as possible. If the respectable Tombstone residents scorned and shunned him, he repaid their contempt with nonchalant indifference to their opinions and their social and political affairs, sticking single-mindedly to his faro table.

In short, Tombstone was a battleground between two basic factions. On the one side were the "cowboys" or rustlers, led by Newman H. "Old Man" Clanton and his sons Billy and Ike and involving their colleagues Tom and Frank McLaury. After "Old Man" Clanton's death, leadership of that faction passed into the hands of Curly Bill Brocius and the politically ambitious John Behan. Their legal base after 1880 rested on Behan, who won election as sheriff when Tombstone became the county seat, and their main publicity came through John Rule's newspaper, *The Nugget.* On the other side were the Earp brothers—Jim, Morgan, Virgil, and Wyatt—and Doc Holliday, whenever they called upon or needed him. Their legal base came at first from Wyatt's having been appointed in Tucson as both deputy sheriff and deputy marshal until the 1880 elections, then from Virgil's election as chief of police. Wyatt was also secretly an agent for Wells Fargo to guard the silver shipments for which the company was responsible. The Earp faction was supported by Mayor John P. Clum's newspaper, *The Epitaph.*

What had the potential of being seen clearly as a county faction versus a city faction became hopelessly muddied by the involvement of personal rivalries between Wyatt Earp and John Behan, who were both after the same woman and shared the same political ambitions (Wyatt as a Republican, Behan as a Democrat) as well as numerous other forces. Whatever legal legitimacies either side claimed were little more than tools of ambition and personal animosity. In the wake of emotions fueled by irresponsible journalism and the consumption of vast quantities of liquor, money, and sex, any impartial and binding institutions of civilization were too far distant to matter.

The intricacies of Tombstone's factionalism, ambitions, and overlapping and ambiguous legal jurisdictions did not interest Doc Holliday, who settled in behind a faro table to do what he did best. Ultimately, though, he became involved in various altercations as he had been everywhere else he had lived. He had a run-in with Behan over gambling and came to Nellie Cashman's defense when Frank McLaury complained about the food in her boardinghouse. Both quarrels placed him, as he would have wanted, in the Earp camp. For the most part, he followed the nocturnal routine of a typical professional gambler, rising late in the morning, taking his main meal in the early afternoon while he perused the available news, and preparing to begin his workday in the late afternoon as customers began drifting into the saloons and gambling halls. Although he pandered to (and preyed upon) the worst inclinations of Tombstone citizens, Holliday nevertheless brought a touch of class to the community by his quiet demeanor, his southern gentility, his wry humor and intelligence, and his love for the fine clothes he wore (he eschewed the conventional black garb of the gambler, though he wore a dark suit and light gray overcoat at the OK Corral).

The chain of events that led to the ultimate clash between the two factions began March 15, 1881, when four masked men robbed the stagecoach making its way from Tombstone to Benson, Arizona. Wyatt Earp, a federal marshal, had jurisdiction in the case because the stage was carrying mail, but Sheriff Behan tagged along anyway. At the scene of the crime they discovered that the robbers had murdered a man named Bud Philpot, whereupon Behan asserted his jurisdiction, murder being the greater of the two crimes. As things progressed, there were allegations that both factions were implicated in the incident. Four of the Clantons' riders were the leading suspects, but one was a friend of Doc Holliday from his Las Vegas days. There were even suspicions that Holliday himself was an accessory, if not directly involved. It was true that Holliday had been out of town at the time of the murder, but he had an alibi that he had ridden to Charleston, Arizona, for a card game. Wyatt, who was hoping to establish a reputation by securing clean arrests and convictions, now found things complicated by Holliday's involvement. He needed to get Holliday exonerated not only for Doc's sake, but also to clear himself of possible association with a criminal.

Wyatt turned to the Clantons for help. He offered Ike Clanton a bribe if he would turn on the robbers, bringing them to a trial that would clear Holliday. Before that could happen, however, one of the suspects, who had been arrested by Behan, was allowed to escape and leave the territory, while the other three were killed during yet another crime. Before he died, Bob Leonard, Holliday's Las Vegas friend, confessed to the stagecoach robbery and murder on behalf of himself and the other three suspects, without clearly vindicating Doc.

Ike Clanton's betrayal therefore was no longer needed. The offer came back to haunt him, however, when one of Wyatt's friends learned of the deal and began broadcasting the story. Ike's own life then fell into jeopardy when the story got back to Curly Bill Brocius and John Ringo, who by this time were the real leaders of the Clanton-McLaury-Behan faction. These two leaders were not pleased to learn of a potential traitor in their entourage. It was at this point that the Clantons and McLaurys decided to get rid of the Earps in self-defense. When he learned of the deal, Doc Holliday was as angry with Ike as Ike feared Curly Bill and Ringo would be with him, for Ike had violated his loyalty to his friends—the greatest possible transgression to the Georgia gentleman.

By this time, Doc had his own problems. Big Nose Kate, during one of her fights with Holliday, went out looking for sympathy and encountered John Behan, who was only too happy to listen to her story. He and saloon keeper Milt Joyce plied the woman with drink until she was willing to sign an affidavit implicating Holliday in the Benson stagecoach incident. Holliday was arrested, bound over for trial before Judge Wells Spicer, and released on a $5,000 bond. Doc won his case, both because the Earps got Kate to sober up and recant her coerced testimony, and because his alibi of the Charleston card game had enough corroborative witnesses to persuade the judge. Kate had saved Holliday's life at Fort Griffin, but her testimony against him in Tombstone, by his reckoning, must have balanced the ledger.

By mid-October 1881 it was apparent that it would take a miracle to avoid violence between the two factions, and miracles were in short supply. Several members of the Clanton-McLaury faction caught Morgan Earp unarmed on the street and warned him that he and his brothers and Holliday would be killed if they did not leave Tombstone. Holliday himself wreaked vengeance on Milt Joyce for his part in Kate's deposition by shooting him in the hand. Fortunately for Joyce, Holliday was seriously drunk from celebrating his court victory, and his aim was impaired. Irate at Ike Clanton's violation of his loyalty to his family, Holliday castigated him publicly. Then, on October 25, upon learning of Ike's oath to kill him, Holliday caught him at the Occidental Saloon and invited him to turn his words into action: "Ike, I hear you're going to kill me. Get out your gun and commence." Ike protested that he was unarmed, and Morgan and Wyatt Earp separated the two. Later in the evening, though, Wyatt ran into Ike again after the latter had a fair amount to drink and warned him, "Doc will kill you." Ike's response was ominous and set the stage the next day for the greatest gunfight in the history of the American West: "You had the best of it tonight, but I'll have my friends tomorrow. You be ready for a showdown."

October 26 dawned clear and cold, but it was afternoon, as per his usual schedule, before Doc Holliday saw the light of day. He was awakened early by Kate, who had just learned from Mary Fly, wife of Camillus Fly, who ran the boardinghouse where they were staying, that Ike Clanton had been up all night and had just called, gun in hand, for Holliday. Doc dressed hastily and met the Earps at Hafford's Saloon at the corner of Fourth and Allen Streets. There he learned that the Clantons and McLaurys were waiting for the Earps on Fremont Street, in a vacant lot a few doors west of the OK Corral and that they intended to resolve the conflict then and there. Holliday insisted on joining them.

Doc was having a bad day with his tuberculosis and was walking with a cane. When he insisted on joining the party, though, Virgil Earp talked him into exchanging the cane for a shotgun, which, with the sixshooter he regularly carried, gave him formidable armaments. All were ordered to keep their guns out of sight so as not to provoke violence in case it could be avoided, so Holliday pulled one arm out of a sleeve of his gray overcoat and carried the shotgun underneath. He and the three Earps walked up Fourth Street and turned west onto Fremont.

On their way, the party encountered Sheriff John Behan, who demanded time to talk to the Clantons and McLaurys to try to disarm them, and preceded the Earp-Holliday group to the vacant lot. There he spoke with the other group, which consisted of Tom and Frank McLaury, Ike and Billy Clanton, and Billy Claiborne, a friend of the Clantons. He returned to intercept the Earps and Holliday at about the point on Fremont Street where they first came into view of the vacant lot. Later, Behan and the Earp-Holliday group had different recollections of the words that passed between them, but the Earps and Holliday understood Behan to have said that he had disarmed the others, and they continued down the street.

When the Clanton–McLaury party came into view, it was apparent that no one had been disarmed. Claiborne and other spectators headed for cover, and the Earps and Holliday found themselves facing only the Clanton and McLaury brothers. Virgil called to them to hand over their guns, but it was too late, and only the sound of cocking pistols answered him.

Each side claimed the other opened fire first. Frank McLaury was the most dangerous shot, and Wyatt Earp went for him, hitting him in the stomach but not killing him. Holliday's target was Tom McLaury, who was partially obscured from view as he struggled behind his horse to get a Winchester rifle out of his saddle scabbard. But Holliday got him into the clear in time and gave him both barrels from the shotgun. The shots were fatal, but Holliday thought he had missed and went for his revolver. By this time Ike had taken flight, and Morgan and Virgil Earp had both been hit. Billy Clanton and Frank McLaury took a lot of killing before the job was over. Billy took three bullets, one in the chest, one in the wrist of his gun hand, and another in the stomach. As he went down, he shifted his gun to the other hand and continued shooting until it was empty. Frank McLaury tried to hide behind a horse, but Holliday shot him in the chest as Morgan Earp's bullet got him in the head. One of Frank's bullets grazed Holliday in the hip. In the end, both McLaurys and Billy Clanton lay dying. Only Ike Clanton, who had fled, and Wyatt Earp were unscathed. The most famous shootout in western history was over.

The majority of Tombstone residents were outraged by the violence, and the propaganda surrounding the funeral of the McLaury brothers and Billy Clanton tended to turn that outrage against the Earps and Doc Holliday. Thus, a hearing into the matter held by Judge Wells Spicer focused not on Virgil Earp's possible overstepping of his authority as police chief, but on the alleged personal vendettas of Virgil and his deputies. In fact, Virgil and Morgan Earp were excused from the hearings because of their wounds. Although Wyatt and Holliday were suddenly jailed in the midst of the hearings as the weight of testimony seemed to be going against them, they were able to present witnesses who ultimately demolished the prosecution's case—that the Clantons and McLaurys were unarmed, that the attack was unprovoked, and that Behan himself had the matter under control.

They were not to have peace, however, even then. Shortly after Christmas 1881 Virgil Earp was ambushed by shotgunners on the street, who maimed

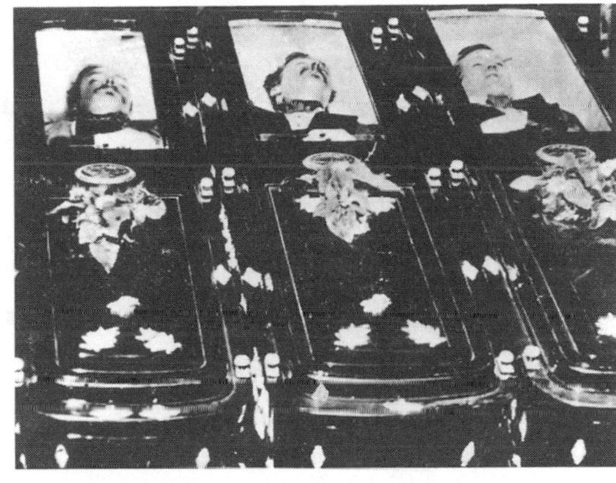

Casualties of the OK Corral gunfight: (left to right) Tom and Frank McLaury and Billy Clanton. Doc Holliday killed Tom McLaury and probably helped kill the other two. Photograph no. 17483, courtesy of the Arizona Historical Society.

his left arm. At about eleven o'clock on the night of March 19, 1882, Morgan Earp was killed in ambush through a window in a bar where he and Wyatt were playing pool. It was apparent that every member of the Earp faction was going to be murdered similarly if they stayed in Tombstone, so they decided to abandon their ambitions in that community and leave town altogether. Packing up what was left of their families, the Earps and Doc Holliday set out for Tucson, where they could put Morgan's body and the wounded Virgil aboard a train for California, where the Earp parents were residing.

Unfortunately, the Earps found the situation in Tucson no less dangerous than that in Tombstone. Although they had taken a posse of their friends along as an escort, they found that they had been preceded in Tucson by Ike Clanton and a group of his supporters, who had every potential of ambushing them, if not engaging in open combat. Even after Virgil and his wife and Morgan's remains were boarded safely on the train, Wyatt and friends were not out of the path of violence. While Wyatt and Holliday ate supper, Wyatt saw Frank Stilwell, who he was sure had been the one to ambush Morgan. Grabbing a shotgun, he ran after Stilwell and shot him dead with both barrels. After having exonerated themselves in one incident of violence, they now had another to worry about.

At that point, Wyatt and Doc decided to wage a vendetta against the remaining members of the Clanton faction, simply killing as many as they could before leaving the territory. In the several deaths that followed, Holliday was never clearly implicated as more than an accessory. But the law clearly wanted to talk to him about that aspect, so he, Wyatt, and their posse decided to cross the line into Colorado. While Wyatt and the others sought obscurity in the small community of Gunnison, Holliday headed straight for Denver, where he figured he would have better chances to make a living.

Holliday was in the state capital only a day or so before a mysterious character named Perry M. Mallen, who claimed to be an Arizona law officer, arrested him and held him for extradition. If extradited, it was obvious that Holliday would be either tried and executed or simply executed as an act of vigilante justice. Wyatt Earp learned of Holliday's peril and contacted his old colleague, Bat Masterson, who was a law enforcement officer in Pueblo, Colorado, asking him to issue a warrant for Holliday's arrest for a con scheme he had allegedly perpetrated in that community. Thus, outside Denver, Bat could arrange for Holliday's acquittal and escape. Although not immediately successful, Bat enlisted some powerful friends in Denver to support Holliday's case and eventually did secure his release into Bat's custody. It had been perhaps Holliday's closest brush with the law. His clever escape led to the coining of a term among Colorado news reporters—"Hollidaying," which meant inventing a phony charge to avoid prosecution on a real one.

The last five years of Doc Holliday's life were relatively uneventful. He spent a brief period gambling in Deadwood, South Dakota, but found himself lured back to Colorado by the wealth being produced in its famous mining camps. He was almost too late, though, for that wealth was rapidly running out by the time he arrived in Leadville in 1883, and it was all a faro dealer—even an expert like Doc Holliday—could do to piece together a living. Personal problems added to Holliday's financial problems as well. He had to fight off recurring pneumonia in addition to the tuberculosis, and the ample dosages of whiskey medication could not have enhanced his performance in the intricate game of juggling faro cards. Symbolic of these hard times is a shooting scrape he engaged in with Leadville's police chief, Bob Allen, whom Holliday shot in the hand after Allen nagged him to pay up a $5 loan. It was a small-stakes game for sure.

By the mid-1880s Leadville and the other mining camps on the old "circuit" were moving out of the frontier phase. The quick riches of the mines were giving way to the more steady returns of commerce, and the old gambling halls and houses of ill repute were yielding to middle-class respectability. Leadville and Denver were even linked by a railroad, which Holliday used to move between one card game and another. Ironically, the new means of transportation may have caused his physical demise just as the new urban refinements were killing the frontier world in which he had made his living. No longer was there a need for those long horseback rides in the sunshine and fresh air that had kept his consumptive lungs functioning between the long stints in smoky card rooms, and his health began to give out.

In May 1887 Doc Holliday took up residence in the Hotel Glenwood in Glenwood Springs, Colorado, a resort community on the Colorado River where sulphur springs were reputed to work wonderful cures on consumptives. Unfortunately, they had the opposite effect on him, irritating his affliction rather than curing it. There is an undocumented and almost certainly false legend that Holliday asked to be baptized into the Roman Catholic Church when he realized his death was near, as a favor to his cousin, Mattie Holliday, a nun in the Sisters of Charity in Atlanta, with whom he reputedly had corresponded steadily over the years. Whether as a Methodist or a Catholic, Doc Holliday died on November 8, 1887, at approximately ten o'clock in the morning. A devil-may-care way of life, and the man who had symbolized its desperation as perhaps no other had ever done, vanished almost simultaneously.

The sparse documentary record of Doc Holliday's life has allowed bountiful opportunities for historians to debate almost any biographical point they wish. The magnitude of disagreement over such matters, though, is nothing compared to the polar opposites of opinion over the larger significance of his life. On the one extreme are the outlaw-lawman buffs who can happily spend a lifetime pursuing physical memorabilia and factual minutiae regarding the colorful personalities and violent episodes of the frontier. On the other side, academic historians haughtily disdain such material, preferring to see it quarantined within the pages of *True West* or *Frontier Times,* lest it contaminate the scholarly historical journals. To the former group, Doc Holliday's hypnotic allure is endless; to the latter, his life was filled with trivial and insignificant events.

The work of scholars like W. Eugene Hollon, Richard Maxwell Brown, and Robert M. Utley suggests a middle ground where the research zeal of the buff and the interpretive skill of the academic might come together productively. These and other historians are posing provocative questions about the nature of a social environment that would call forth a Doc Holliday or a Billy the Kid. What forces can produce a circumstance where basic social order simply breaks down? Or, what are the possible consequences when the institutions of social control are not exactly absent, but reside in partisan factions who mete out partial justice?

Because of such partisanship, Doc Holliday could not afford the luxury of depending on official agencies of law enforcement. Out of necessity he carried his law in his shoulder holster, but it was a form of law nonetheless. One should consider seriously his protestation that everyone he killed deserved killing. Here was no practitioner of random, capricious violence, but rather a skilled craftsman who sought nothing more than an opportunity to practice his trade peacefully.

Doc Holliday was a practitioner of the vigilante justice that one sees historically everywhere there has been a frontier. Of course, no truly civilized society can rest upon the capriciousness of such justice, which depends utterly upon the wisdom of its executor. There are, however, historical instances in which it has been preferable to simple armed chaos in which every man's hand is against his neighbor. Perhaps the race riots and urban gang warfare of our own day have given us enough of a taste of that kind of world that we can begin to appreciate Doc Holliday as a representative figure in a transition to something better.

6

Joaquín Murrieta

The Many Lives of a Legend

Richard Griswold del Castillo

The story of Joaquín Murrieta has been told many times, in historical narratives, poetry, novels, films, and songs. Perhaps his continuing appeal to the imagination arises from the many mysteries surrounding his life and death, as well as his being an underdog who suffered injustices and fought against impossible odds. This Mexican, who lived during the gold rush in California, has inspired a generation of Chicano activists who see him as a victim of Anglo racism and as an avenger of the rights of the Spanish-speaking peoples in the United States. In this way, Murrieta is a hero to the Chicano movement in the United States as well as to Latin Americans and Europeans critical of North American aggression and colonialism.

Although the historical details of Murrieta's life remain unclear, his reputation endures, raising the question about the problematic relationship between history and myth. Altogether, Joaquín has enjoyed many lives in the imaginations of novelists, folklorists, and historians. The problem is to decide for ourselves which incarnation of Murrieta's life helps us make the most sense of our contemporary life.

Joaquín Murrieta was a Mexican immigrant who came to California in search of gold in the 1850s. After witnessing the murder of his brother and the rape and murder of his wife, he set out to avenge these wrongs. For several years, he and a group of other Mexicanos and Californios (former Mexican citizens) stole horses, robbed miners, and killed more than twenty-four people, mostly Chinese immigrants and Anglo Americans. As a result of this violence, the state of California created the California Rangers, a special mounted police force, whose sole purpose was to apprehend Murrieta dead or alive. The state government placed a price of $1,000 on his head.

After several months of searching the foothills for Murrieta, the rangers, led by Captain Harry Love, surprised a group of Mexican vaqueros in Cantua Canyon. The rangers killed several Mexicans, and Captain Love claimed that one of them was Murrieta. To prove his claim, he chopped off Murrieta's head and brought it back for identification. Even though Love gathered a number of testimonials certifying that the head was indeed Murrieta's, some doubted that the Mexican had been killed. To this day many believe that he escaped and returned to his home in Sonora, Mexico.

An early sketch of Joaquín printed in the Pictorial Union *in April 1853, during the height of the manhunt for Murrieta. Undoubtedly, this image was an imaginary reconstruction. Courtesy of the California History Section, California State Library.*

Nearly every part of Murrieta's story has been grist for skepticism, historical debate, political activism, and controversy. In fact, more ink has been spilled exploring the "true" history of Joaquín Murrieta than that of any other Mexican or Chicano historical figure in the United States, with the notable exception of César Chávez. At least one hundred places in California have the name "Murrieta" attached to them. Today, a group called La Asociación Internacional Descendencia de Joaquín Murrieta, an international organization of individuals who claim to be descendants of Murrieta, is dedicated to preserving, protecting, and honoring the memory of their famous forefather and to telling the truth about his legacy.

For many Chicanos, Joaquín Murrieta is seen as a resistance fighter. In revolutionary Cuba and pre-perestroika Russia, he appeared in textbooks and life-size statues as an example of third-world people's revolt against imperialism. World-famous Chilean poet Pablo Neruda saw in Murrieta the struggle of Latin American people to be free of North American hegemony. At the same time, Anglo-American novelists, history buffs, and some academics consider Joaquín Murrieta as an overly romanticized, bloodthirsty bandit-murderer or as a fictitious character, who, because he never existed, is more properly a topic of folklore and literary study. This contradictory and ambiguous legacy springs from a verifiable series of events in gold rush California.

A purported photograph of Joaquín Murrieta Orozco taken near Murphy's Diggings and originally in the possession of Marshall Hill. The photo is currently in the archives of the Old Times Museum in Murphy's Camp. Courtesy of Calaveras County Historical Society.

Beginning in 1853, newspapers in northern California reported that a Mexican "desperado" named "Joaquín," accompanied by several confederates, was robbing and killing miners in Calaveras and Mariposa Counties. The subsequent documentation of the Joaquín story presents many twists and turns. One must ask: Why have these events captured the imaginations of people around the world? What is true about the story of Joaquín Murrieta? Was he a people's hero or a bandit-killer? Because there are many versions of Murrieta's history, what is presented here is hardly beyond dispute. In fact, even today the full story of Joaquín Murrieta's life remains to be written.

The people of Sonora, Mexico, have long known the intimate details of the Murrieta family genealogy and of Joaquín's life, after his alleged death at the hands of Captain Harry Love. The small town of San Rafael de Alamito de Murrieta in the municipio of Trincheras, Sonora, Mexico, claims to be Murrieta's birthplace. The local town council erected a monument that marks his date of birth sometime between 1824 and 1830, born the son of don Juan Murrieta and señorita Juana Orozco. The plaque states simply that Joaquín Murrieta Orozco "fought in California against the north American forces" and that they "called him a bandit and killer," but the Californios knew him simply as "El Patrio," which in English means "the native."

Manuel Rojas, a Mexican scholar, has researched the early life of Joaquín Murrieta by interviewing the surviving members of the Murrieta family in Trincheras and by searching the regional parish archives. Rojas gives Joaquín's birth date as August 16, 1828. Joaquín is also listed as one of ten children. By tradition, the Murrieta men learned farming and bronco busting, as well as gold mining in the surrounding countryside. Rojas believes that Joaquín went to school, where he learned to read and write. He is remembered as a "huero," a light-skinned, fair-haired, tall Mexicano—unusual but not unknown characteristics for people of northern Mexico, where Spanish, American, and French adventurers roamed.

Rojas documents births and marriages of the Murrieta family and lists Joaquín and his companion, Carmen Feliz, as godparents to a child baptized on December 10, 1849. That winter many friends and relatives left for the California gold fields. Joaquín Valenzuela was one of those who departed. Later, he and others from Sonora were reunited in California as members of Joaquín's "gang." After Christmas 1849 Joaquín and his brother Jésus, both married, left their hometown for California. Jésus left his wife and children at home, but Joaquín, married recently to Carmen Feliz, took his wife with him. He had just turned twenty-one.

As they crossed the Mexican desert in the winter of 1850, a Papago Indian guide led them to the necessary watering holes. After reaching the junction of the Colorado and Gila Rivers, the brothers crossed at Yuma and made their way to Salvación, a military post, later known as Calexico. From there they entered the Los Angeles basin, where they came to rest at the San Gabriel Mission. Finally, by the spring of 1850 the two brothers arrived at Murphy's Camp, on the Stanislaus River in the southern Sierra. There the Murrieta brothers staked out a claim and visited the nearby Mexican mining communities of Sonora and Hornitos.

In California during the early years of the gold rush, native Californians and Indians were among the first victims of the American immigrants who coveted their lands. In 1848 the United States, upon concluding its war with Mexico, negotiated the Treaty of Guadalupe Hidalgo, which promised to protect the property and human rights of Mexican citizens who were "acquired" by the United States. But the Mexicans, now citizens of the United States, were not spared violent reminders of their second-class status. During the first decades following the war, lynchings, murders, kangaroo trials, riots, and robberies involving Mexican Americans emphasized the point. Competition for mining claims and gold only intensified the levels of violence. As Mexican, Latin American, and Asian immigrants entered California in larger numbers, their presence added fuel to the fire.

The discovery of gold on January 24, 1848, in Coloma stimulated a worldwide migration to California. Among the first arrivals, almost a year before the Americans arrived, were miners from northern Mexican states like Sonora, Chihuahua, and Sinaloa. Many of these men brought their families with them, unlike the American 49ers, who tended to leave their families behind. These Mexican miners, the "48ers," brought gold- and silver-mining experience with them, having worked in Mexican mining camps. Rodman Paul's history of gold mining in California explains how miners from Sonora, in particular, returned to their home state every winter and then came back to California in the spring, beginning an annual family migration to the gold country.

Most Mexican and Latin American miners established themselves in the southern mines, including the California counties south of Sacramento. It was here that most of the anti-Mexican violence occurred. Mexican and Latin American miners helped teach the newly arrived Americans, who had no experience with mining gold, how to extract the metal from stream beds and ore deposits. But within a short time, resentment about the presence of these "foreigners" erupted into violence, especially in 1849, when Americans started arriving in larger numbers. Americans were angry that many of the best claims already had been staked out by the "Sonorans," as they called all the Mexican miners. The fact that many of the mining towns, like Hornitos and Stockton, became multilingual in business dealings grated on the Anglo-Americans, who regarded this development as unpatriotic. On July 4, 1849, acts of violence broke out against the foreigners, beginning with attacks on Chilean merchants and neighborhoods in San Francisco, then spreading to the mining camps. Historian Malcolm Rohrbough describes how, in the camps near Stockton, Yankee miners ousted the Chileans by passing a code of laws forbidding foreigners from mining. Intimidation and violence ensued, and the Anglos confiscated the Chileans' property and sold it at public auction. In November 1849 Mexican miners along the Calaveras River were attacked by a vigilante group that, after ousting them from their claims, "fined" each miner an ounce of gold. A few days later sixteen Chileans were rounded up and accused of murder. They were given a summary trial, and then three were lynched. Other acts of violence occurred throughout the diggings in the winter of 1849.

Many native-born Mexican Americans, who were citizens of the United States, fell victim to these antiforeigner prejudices and laws. One estimate places about thirteen hundred Californios in the gold regions in 1848, with a similar number returning in 1849. That year the military governor of California, General Percifor Smith, responding to nativist fears that foreigners were taking all the gold out of the mining regions, announced his "trespass" orders, which prohibited noncitizens from mining gold on public property. He appealed to American citizens to help him enforce his policy, and under the protection of the military, Anglo-American miners robbed and harassed foreigners. After a riot, French immigrant miners were also driven from the gold camps. Irish and Australian miners became targets of vigilante violence in San Francisco and elsewhere in the diggings, and Chinese miners provoked paroxysms of hate and paranoia in late 1851 and were also driven out of the gold camps.

In April 1850 the California legislature, in response to the pressure from the 49ers, passed the Foreign Miners tax law, which required that all non–

U.S. citizens pay a tax of $20 a month for the privilege of mining gold. Soon, hundreds of unofficial "tax collectors" emerged to extract money from the foreigners. If they did not have the money, their property was confiscated and sold at auction. Later, because of pressure from foreign governments, the legislature repealed the act and replaced it with a tax of $3 a month. By the mid-1850s most of the foreigners had been driven from independent gold mines and claims. Those who remained were working for American miners as laborers, or they labored for the large corporations that began to develop deep shaft mines in California and Nevada.

During the height of this antiforeign hysteria, Murrieta and his wife and brother entered California. Within a few months, an incident took place that triggered Murrieta's career as an outlaw. In May 1850 at Murphy's Camp in northern California, Murrieta's brother, Jésus, purchased a mule from a couple of Anglo-Americans, who, in turn, accused him of stealing the mule. A meeting of the local "court" speedily convicted and hanged Jésus. A few days later, according to the accounts of Mexican historians, a group of Americans attacked Joaquín at his gold claim. Believing him dead, the invaders raped and killed his wife, Carmen Feliz.

Although no documents verify these specific injustices, all historical accounts since the publication of John Rollin Ridge's novel *The Life and Adventures of Joaquin Murieta: The Celebrated California Bandit* (1854) have cited these possible events as motives for Murrieta's rampage of violence. In some accounts Murrieta is credited with systematically hunting down and killing every member of the group who participated in the crimes. The date of Murrieta's rampage is in question, however. Some historians date the murders in 1853, just prior to the newspaper reports in San Andreas County about a new wave of robberies and killings attributed to a man named Joaquín. Whatever the specifics, Joaquín Murrieta was certainly a victim of violence along with hundreds of other foreign miners in California. These dramatic events set the stage for Murrieta's war of revenge against the American.

Scholars and novelists who have written about Murrieta agree that more than one Mexican outlaw was called Joaquín. Much confusion and certainty surrounds this conviction. Remi Nadeau, who wrote a judicious study titled *The Real Joaquin Murieta* (1976), notes that in 1851 a man named Joaquín Murrieta stole twenty-nine horses from a ranch near Los Angeles. (Nadeau uses the California spelling of the last name; Mexican authors universally spell it Murrieta.) In 1852 Murrieta was specifically named in a court document regarding the murder of General Joshua Bean, a well-connected American, former mayor of San Diego, and owner of a local saloon and store in San Gabriel. Although witnesses said that they saw Joaquín kill

General Bean, Ana Benitez, a New Mexican woman, testified that Joaquín Murrieta had been with her the night of the murder. She named Cipriano Sandoval as the murderer. Within a few days, a lynch mob hanged Cipriano and several other Mexicans who claimed to know Joaquín. Two days before the hangings, the Tejon Indians reported that they had taken stolen horses from a man named Joaquín Murrieta and a band of Sonorans.

According to the Mexican historian Rojas, some time in 1852, after the death of Joaquín's wife and brother, Murrieta organized an "Acordada" (a secret pact) among Mexicans and Latin Americans for self-protection. Their slogan was "All or nothing." They numbered about twenty-two members and their names have been gathered by Mexican and U.S. scholars. Rojas listed two "Joaquíns," Joaquín Valenzuela and Joaquín Ochoa Moreno. Frank F. Latta, an Anglo historian who did a great deal of fieldwork interviewing surviving eyewitnesses, compiled detailed biographies of sixty-two members of Murrieta's "gang," including five individuals whose anonymity he protected. His enlarged list included four Joaquíns, including the Joaquín Valenzuela just mentioned, but Latta added Joaquín Juan Murrieta, Joaquín "el Famoso," and Joaquín Botellas. Author John Rollin Ridge, a half-Cherokee Indian named Yellow Bird, listed five Joaquíns, including Murrieta and adding Joaquín Carillo. Altogether, in addition to Joaquín Murrieta, there may have been five Joaquíns who were part of Murrieta's band.

This discussion of names is important because most newspaper reports attributed the murders and robberies to a "Joaquín," but not specifically to Joaquín Murrieta. Nadeau suggests that, at the time, American miners tended to blame every robbery and murder on the Mexican "Joaquín." In 1853, when California governor John Bigler posted a $1,000 reward for the capture of "Joaquín," he named "Carillo," a man described as "a Mexican by birth, 5 feet 10 inches in height, black hair, black eyes, and of good address." Later, the state assembly bill authorizing the California Rangers to capture "Joaquín" recognized that there were five wanted men. The bill spoke of a "party or gang of robbers commanded by the five Joaquíns, whose names are Joaquín Muriati, Joaquín Ocomorenia, Joaquín Valenzuela, Joaquín Boteller, and Joaquín Carrillo." Allowing for misspellings, all the Joaquíns that later historians mentioned are accounted for, but the bill also omitted a few.

Contemporary evidence suggests that a band of "outlaws" existed with more than one member named Joaquín. All of the deeds attributed to one man may in fact have been committed by more than one Joaquín. In addition, the original reward was for a Joaquín Carillo, not Joaquín Murrieta. Murrieta was mentioned by name for the first time in 1853, but only as one of a list of five men, all of whom were equally wanted by the government.

Manuel Rojas's informants told him that Murrieta organized his guerrilla group into four squadrons with lieutenants reporting directly to him. One of these lieutenants was Joaquín Valenzuela. During the spring and summer of 1852 they stole horses and drove them back to Sonora, where, according to eyewitnesses, they intended to raise a larger force to reinvade and reconquer California. Frank Latta, who relied on his interviews with eyewitnesses to retrace Murrieta's horse trail from the San Joaquín Valley to Sonora, Mexico, mapped the band's watering holes and probable resting spots.

In 1852, before Joaquín's appearance in the gold country, the most notable member of "la Acordada" was Valenzuela, a veteran of the U.S.–Mexican War who had fought with a guerrilla group headed by Francés Celedonio Domeco de Jaruta. Endorsing the "Plan de Jaruta" and refusing to accept the Treaty of Guadalupe Hidalgo, this band continued to fight against Americans in Mexico after the peace treaty was signed. After the betrayal and execution of their leader, Valenzuela and several other members of the guerrilla army fled to California. Eventually they joined Joaquín Murrieta, bringing with them their slogan of defiance, "All or nothing," as well as the notion that the U.S.–Mexican War had never ended.

On January 29, 1853, the *San Joaquín Republican* reported murders, horse thefts, and robberies, which were attributed to a band led by "Joaquín, a very desperate man." This was the first notice of Joaquín's activities in the gold camps. The rapid movement of the gang and escalation of violence was truly amazing. Nadeau has painstakingly reconstructed the movement of Joaquín and his men in *The Real Joaquin Murieta*. The newspaper reported that, nine days earlier, three Mexicans had robbed a group of Chinese miners of their gold dust while, simultaneously, three other Mexicans had robbed other Chinese miners, stabbing one of them. On January 21 Joaquín's band killed an Anglo-American at Yackee Camp and murdered another nearby along with a Chinese. Giving chase the next day to a Mexican suspected of horse theft near San Andreas, a posse of American miners soon were fighting it out with a gang of eleven Mexicanos. Later that day a Mexican band entered Yackee Camp, shooting at everyone and killing one American. That night they attacked two more Americans inside a quartz mill. Within a week, one Chinese and four Americans had been killed. In retaliation, the entire Mexican population of the San Andreas region was forced to leave their homes. In the resulting chaos, two Mexicans were lynched and one was shot. The entire region was in an uproar, with all Mexicans suspected of being part of Joaquín's gang.

After a few days of peace, the violence erupted again on February 7 near Angel Camp, when a Mexican suspected of being one of Joaquín's men was lynched after "confessing" to spying for Murrieta's gang. The next

Years later an artist sketched the head of Joaquín Murrieta, supposedly as it appeared when it was on display in San Francisco. This sketch appeared in the Overland Monthly, *November 1895. Courtesy of the California History Section, California State Library.*

day, Joaquín's men attacked and killed two Chinese miners. Then, again outrunning a posse, they robbed a group of Chinese and shot two of them. For the next week, Joaquín's men avoided capture, killing Chinese and Anglo miners as they eluded local posses. By the end of February Joaquín and his band had killed thirteen people and stolen more than one hundred horses. Murrieta and his band seemed to escape no matter how many people pursued them. On one occasion, a posse surrounded a tent where Joaquín and his men were supposedly hiding. Miraculously, they escaped by shooting their way out, wounding several of the attackers in the process. The next day, Joaquín's men moved on to Mariposa County to hide out. When discovered once again, they managed to shoot their way to freedom, killing more Americans and Chinese. By now, angry and terrified miners were urging Governor John Bigler to offer a reward of $1,000 for Joaquín Carillo, dead or alive. Those living in the towns where the attacks had taken place complained that this reward was still not sufficient.

The legendary escapes of Murrieta and his men contributed to the growth of his reputation, especially among the Mexicanos and Latinos who lived in nearly all the Mexican mining camps, like Hornitos. During the weeks following the spate of violence in Mariposa County, Murrieta and his men sought refuge there. Undoubtedly, many lionized him as a hero who had made the Americanos afraid of Latinos.

Ultimately, someone recognized Murrieta while he was playing monte in a local saloon. He was drunk and boisterous. A couple members of his band entered and carted him off, preventing him from being easily captured. A few days later, a group of Americans tried to take him prisoner, but Murrieta shot it out with them and escaped. Finally, on March 10 a person identified Murrieta at a fandango in Quartzberg, located near Hornitos. Even though a general shootout followed, with several Americans being killed or wounded, Murrieta again escaped unharmed.

The mounting casualties proved that Murrieta and his men were truly terrorizing the gold camps. Some observers estimate that as of March 1852 the gang was responsible for forty-one killings: twenty-eight Chinese and thirteen Americans. Because most of the victims were Chinese and most of the murders took place during Murrieta's escape, it is unlikely that revenge was Murrieta's main motive. Initially, retribution may have been the motive. But soon it became a matter of self-defense or greed, as in the case of the shootings of the Chinese. Obviously, then, the image of Joaquín Murrieta as a bloody avenger is exaggerated. He was a fugitive who had to shoot it out to escape capture.

By May 1852 the California legislature had decided to form a special police force to capture or kill Joaquín Murrieta and his men. These were the California Rangers, headed by Captain Harry Love, a Texan and veteran of the U.S.–Mexican War, whom historian Hubert Howe Bancroft described as "a law-abiding desperado." According to another historian, Remi Nadeau, Captain Love liked killing people. He had a good deal of experience in killing as a veteran of the Indian wars in Texas. Like many other Anglo Texans, Love thought that the only good Mexican bandit was a dead Mexican bandit. In fact, his prisoners had a habit of being shot while trying to escape. The authorizing bill that established the rangers allowed Love to employ twenty men who were to be paid $150 each for three months of service. There was no additional bounty for killing Joaquín; the original reward of $1,000 remained. Among those who signed up for the California Rangers, only one, William Wallace Byrnes, claimed to have seen Joaquín Murrieta in person. During his service in the U.S.–Mexican War, Byrnes had been taken prisoner and jailed in a mission in Sonora. There he came to know Murrieta, who was then a student at the mission. Others, however, have said that Byrnes knew Murrieta because he had frequently played cards with him in the mining camps.

Captain Love and the California Rangers began their operations in May 1853. Unable to find any trace of Murrieta, they instead set about capturing horse thieves, including one whom they claimed was Murrieta's brother. Seemingly, every suspicious Mexican was somehow related to Murrieta. Predictably, while on the way to jail in Stockton, Love's prisoners tried to escape and were killed. Nadeau quotes Ranger Bill Howard about this incident: "It took too much trouble to carry prisoners about with us and when we were sure of a man being a bandit we shot or hung him."

Murrieta and his men were nowhere to be found because they were making their way south through the San Joaquín Valley. Yet several people claimed to have sighted Murrieta. A Mexican rancher reported that Murrieta and several of his men had asked for food and that during the dinner conversation Murrieta told him that he was indeed the wanted man and that no one would ever take him alive. Murrieta told the rancher the story about the rape and murder of his beloved wife and about his early career of vengeance.

The Mexican rancher described the man as having four revolvers and a bowie knife and wearing a long beard as a disguise. In the story presented in the local press, the reporter named the bandit "Joaquín Muliati."

Also in May 1853 the *San Joaquín Republican* reported that Joaquín and his men were in San Luis Obispo. A month later, news came that he had taken advantage of the hospitality of one Andre Ibarra, wounding a family member and tying up the rest. Finally, on July 4 readers learned that Murrieta and his men were south of San Diego across the border at a rancho named Buena Vista. A few persons suggested that the posse should invade Baja California to wipe out this nest of robbers and put an end to Murrieta.

Meanwhile, Captain Love and his men slowly proceeded south, capturing Mexican horse thieves and their horses as they went. They stopped briefly in San Juan Bautista to capture a man who was supposedly Murrieta's brother-in-law, to help in locating and identifying the bandit chief. Finally, after riding five or six days, Love reached a place called Arroyo Cantua, located some twenty-seven miles west of present-day Fresno, in the California coastal range. Supposedly, this site was near Murrieta's hideout, a rancho called Molino Vallejo. According to Frank Latta's research, Murrieta and his men had rustled more than three hundred horses for shipment south to Mexico. A large group of men were branding horses when Love and the rangers entered the canyon. Prudently, as Love was outnumbered two to one, he decided to register the names of the Mexican horsemen on the pretext of collecting a tax from them later. Love collected eighty-three names that day (Latta believes all of them were probably false). He then left with the rangers riding south, with the intention of returning to surprise the Mexican horsemen.

The next day, Murrieta's men hurriedly drove their horses south, leaving about fifty behind because they had stampeded earlier in the rush to leave. Near Bakersfield, at Tejon Pass, according to Latta, Joaquín Valenzuela (not Joaquín Murrieta) decided to double back and get the horses they had left behind, because each was worth several hundred dollars in Mexico. According to Latta's research, Joaquín Murrieta also left his gang and returned to his rancho, where he planned to pick up his lover, Rosa, and then take a boat to Mexico.

Captain Love and the rangers had followed the horse trail of the Murrieta gang to Tejon Pass. There, the signs became confusing, indicating that one group of Murrieta's gang had headed south to Mexico, while two groups had doubled back north. Love's men decided to follow the northern trail. Eventually, they encountered a group of Mexican horsemen camped at Arroyo Cantua near the Diablo Range on the Tulare Plains. On July 25, 1853, a battle ensued between Love's rangers and Murrieta's men. Among the combatants was the famous "Three-Fingered" Jack Garcia or "Tres Dedos." According to historians Theodore Hittell and Hubert Howe Bancroft, and as reported in various newspapers, Tres Dedos was really Manuel Garcia, who had lost one of his fingers in a shooting incident during the U.S.–Mexican War. "Three-Fingered" Jack, as he was known to the Americans, actually had four fingers. He had a violent career as a guerrilla fighter during the U.S.–Mexican War in California, as a member of Solomon Pico's gang of outlaws, and as an escaped convict.

Joining Tres Dedos was Joaquín Valenzuela and perhaps thirty other Mexicanos. Love's rangers apparently surprised the Mexicanos, who were guarding the horses, and then surrounded the main body of Murrieta's men. As they began asking questions, Bill Byrnes, who supposedly knew Murrieta by sight, cried out, "This is Joaquín boys! We've got him at last." Within a few seconds the man identified as Joaquín and "Three-Fingered" Jack began shooting and running. In the flurry of shots from the rangers, Manuel Garcia was killed. Two other Mexicanos were wounded and died soon after. As for the man identified as Joaquín Murrieta, he jumped on a horse and sped down the arroyo with rangers pursuing and shooting wildly. Finally, the rangers managed to disable Murrieta's horse. As he fled on foot, he was shot in the back three times. According to Ranger Howard, who later wrote an account of this fight, Murrieta was not dead and pleaded in Spanish for his life, "Don't shoot any more. I'm dead." Nevertheless, in their excitement, the rangers kept shooting and riddled the man with bullets.

As the smoke cleared, four men lay dead or dying. The rangers had taken two prisoners, but the rest of Murrieta's men had fled. None of the rangers had been wounded. To prove that they had killed the wanted man, Captain Love chopped off Murrieta's head. For good measure, the rangers decided to do the same to "Three-Fingered" Jack and to remove his mutilated hand as well. According to contemporary descriptions, the Joaquín they killed had blue eyes and light brown, slightly curly hair. This description differed from the official one of Joaquín Murrieta in the wanted poster, who had black hair and brown eyes. These differences did not seem to bother the posse, and they began their journey to Sacramento to collect their reward. Along the way they discarded "Three-Fingered" Jack's head, because it was too mutilated by bullets and was decomposing rapidly. Unfortunately, one of the prisoners reportedly "fell" from his horse while crossing a creek and drowned. At Fort Miller the rangers stopped to put the remaining head and hand in jars filled with brandy to preserve them until a reward could be collected. The remaining prisoner, and the only one who could positively identify Murrieta, was lynched a few weeks later, supposedly by pro-Murrieta partisans to prevent his betraying his companions.

From the outset, many people doubted that Love and the rangers had killed Joaquín Murrieta. These doubts were especially evident in the northern California Mexican barrios where Murrieta had already become a gigantic folk hero. Others also questioned the killings. In August 1853 a Mexicano in Los Angeles told an *Alta California* reporter that Americans had attacked him and his companions. In the conflict, four of the Mexicans had been killed, including Joaquín Valenzuela. The San Francisco *Herald* also reported that Joaquín Valenzuela, not Murrieta, had been killed. The *Alta* wrote in early August, three weeks after the Arroyo Cantua shootout, that Joaquín Murrieta and his men were resting at Mission San Fernando as guests of Andrés Pico.

To silence doubters and to secure his reward, Captain Love gathered a number of affidavits from those who reportedly knew the bandit. Love went around with the grisly brandied head, showing it to witnesses and getting them to sign pieces of paper. Nadeau examined each of these testimonies and concluded that all were questionable in proving that Joaquín Murrieta had been killed. Most were based on hearsay evidence, some contradicted known facts about Joaquín, and others were signed merely with an "X." As Nadeau points out, none of the affidavits positively identified the head as that of Joaquín Murrieta. Meanwhile, the head and hand remained in Love's possession, and he went on tour charging $1 per person to view the trophies. In San Francisco, while the head was on display, a man claiming to be Joaquín Murrieta wrote to the local newspaper, saying, "I still retain my head." The *San Francisco Chronicle* concluded that the whole debacle was a hoax and that Joaquín was "enjoying the cool breeze of Sonora, Mexico, without his head, since that is here."

Nevertheless, Governor Bigler came through with the $1,000 reward for the death of Joaquín Murrieta. Later, the assembly voted an additional reward of $5,000 out of gratitude. Yet reports that Love had killed the wrong man persisted in the American newspapers. As late as 1856 eyewitnesses were reporting that Murrieta was indeed living in Sonora, Mexico. Supposedly, Joaquín's sister saw the head, confirming that it was not her brother's.

None of the twentieth-century historians who have delved into the evidence are convinced that Captain Love killed Joaquín Murrieta in July 1853. Frank Latta's oral interviews with survivors convinced him that an Indian named Chappo from Monterey was the man whom Love beheaded. Meanwhile, Nadeau suggests that the man Love killed was probably an anonymous Mexicano who had the misfortune of getting caught up in the fight. Mexican historian Manuel Rojas believes that Joaquín Valenzuela was the man who was beheaded. But other authors, including John Rollin Ridge, Ireneo Paz, and Pablo Neruda, maintain that Murrieta was indeed killed and beheaded on that fateful July day in 1853, a tragic end to a heroic figure.

In contrast, Manuel Rojas maintains that Murrieta was in hiding at his brother's house in Los Angeles when he learned of the killings at Arroyo Cantua. Immediately he decreed that his guerrilla group be disbanded, and that José María Ochoa, the man whom the rangers had taken prisoner, should be killed because he had revealed the plans of the "Acordada" to the gringos. Murrieta reportedly divided up the horses among his men and left for Mexico with his new wife, Ana Benitez. According to Rojas, Joaquín first went to Tecate in Baja California, where he became a rancher until 1883. Then he moved to Cucurpe, Sonora, near his birthplace, where he died "near the end of the 19th century." This undramatic ending is the story that La Asociación Internacional Descendencia de Joaquín Murrieta promotes. Although Mexican and U.S. scholars conclude that Joaquín Murrieta probably was not killed at Arroyo Cantua, most people continue to believe that his life tragically ended there. With the gory image of his head, pickled in brandy, the events surrounding his death would stir imaginations for the next 150 years. The legend of Joaquín Murrieta grew out of fictionalizations of his life, which, in turn, changed his history.

The first fictional interpretation, based on some historical fact, was *The Life and Adventures of Joaquin Murieta: The Celebrated California Bandit* by John Rollins Ridge, published in 1854. Ridge's family had been removed from Georgia along with thousands of other Indians to follow the Trail of Tears to present-day Oklahoma. When the author was a young man, his father and grandfather were killed by rival tribal factions, and later Ridge himself killed a man in self-defense. He fled to California during the gold rush and worked as a deputy clerk in Yuba County. In his spare time, Ridge wrote for San Francisco newspapers and wrote his small book on Joaquín Murrieta, based on newspaper reports and stories. It was a literary reconstruction, including conversations between Murrieta and his men. Ridge embellished what was known about Murrieta by having the bandit leader rescue fair maidens and by including nonexistent gunfights and escapes. In Ridge's interpretation, Murrieta became a Robin Hood of the Sierra. Ridge's version of Murrieta's adventures reappeared repeatedly in other novels and histories. In fact, his book became the standard "history" of the celebrated outlaw and the primary text cited by California historians.

After the Murrieta story appeared in popular magazines, such as the *Police Gazette* in 1859, replete with illustrations, it soon became the subject of a play by Charles Howe. This drama of five acts was titled *Joaquín Murrieta de Castillo* and was performed in San Francisco. The legend was beginning to take on a life of its own. Soon the West Coast poet Cincinnatus Hiner Miller adopted

Joaquín's first name to become Joaquín Miller, probably to add to his fame. Miller wrote a long poem about Murrieta, which was published in England.

Eventually, dime novelists of the late nineteenth century utilized Murrieta's life story. For example, Joseph Badger wrote *The Pirate of the Placers, or Joaquín's Death Hunt* and a sequel, *Joaquín the Saddle King: A Romance of Murrieta's First Fight.* This tradition of popular novels continued into the twentieth century, with more than a score of lurid tales offering telling details that were added and subtracted. For example, the name of Murrieta's lover changed from Rosita to Carmela and then to Mariana.

At the beginning of the twentieth century, the Murrieta story attracted attention in Chile, where author Robert Heyenne published *El bandido chileno Joaquín Murieta en California* (Santiago, 1900), a novel-history about Murrieta that later became the template for an epic tale that Pablo Neruda told. This same story was republished in a plagiarized version by "Professor Acigar" in Barcelona, Spain, and then republished in Mexico, changing Murrieta into a Mexican by birth. In 1904 Ireneo Paz, the mother of the famous Mexican poet–philosopher Octavio Paz, wrote a literary history of Murrieta titled *Vida y adventuras del mas célebre bandido sonorense, Joaquín Murrieta: Sus grandes proezas en California* (1904). This volume was later translated into English and published in Chicago in 1937. As these works appeared, the story became more and more complex: Paz had Murrieta capturing a schooner near Sacramento and briefly becoming a pirate; Murrieta moved freely about in various disguises, even once as a spectator at the trial of one of his compadres; new names emerged as members of Joaquín's gang—Pedro Sánchez, Juan Borilda, Joaquín Blanco.

The greatest writer to tell the Murrieta saga was Pablo Neruda in his play *Fulgor y muerte de Joaquín Murieta,* published in 1974. In the preface, Neruda claimed that he discovered incontrovertible evidence that Joaquín was a Chileno. In telling his story, Neruda added new literary elements: Murrieta's right-hand man was an Indian chief; the gringos were anti-Catholic; there were omens of impending death; and when Murrieta was decapitated, his head continued to talk and taught listeners a song urging honor and respect for Latin Americans.

Other treatments of the life and death of Joaquín Murrieta have surfaced in Mexican communities on both sides of the border, in popular ballads known as *corridos.* These popular histories related Murrieta directly to common people. Although many versions of corridos about Joaquín Murrieta existed, scholars did not begin collecting and studying these surviving fragments until 1948. The first recorded versions were sung by the Hermanos Sanchez y Linares in 1934, then again by Lalo Guerrero in 1948. Most of the folk songs characterize Murrieta as the traditional macho hero, a man suffering injustice and confronting his difficulties with pistol in hand. One version says that Murrieta was an orphan and that he came to California in 1850 with his wife, Carmelita. All versions portray Murrieta as entirely justified in his career of revenge and violence, with most emphasizing that his was a war against the Anglos. Similar to other romantic heroes of the people, Murrieta is shown as representing the feelings of the Mexicanos in California.

The Joaquín Murrieta story has appeared in several movies. *Joaquín Murrieta* (1964), produced in English by the Spanish studio Pro Artis Iberica, was directed by George Sherman and starred Jeffery Hunter as Murrieta. In Mexico the Churabusco studios produced a Spanish-language version titled *La verdadera leyenda de Joaquín Murrieta* (1985), which won a Mexican film award for its script.

Finally, Murrieta made another transition to the contemporary era in Rodolfo "Corky" Gonzalez's epic poem *I Am Joaquín.* A former middleweight boxing champion who became a Chicano political organizer in Denver during the 1960s, Gonzalez wrote the poem to inspire a generation of Chicano youth looking for their identity. The "Joaquín" in Gonzalez's poem represents not only Murrieta but all Chicanos in the United States who have experienced racism and oppression. The recurring phrase "I am" in the poem precedes the many incarnations of Joaquín, as revolutionist, as Indian warrior, as Spaniard, as mestizo, and as despot, dictator, and betrayer. Here Joaquín Murrieta becomes a symbol of the difficult struggles of the Mexican people in the United States as well as a symbol of the complexities of their cultural heritage. The poem became the narrative for the first film of the Chicano movement, *I Am Joaquín* (1969), produced and directed by Luis Valdez. In this film, the powerful visuals accompanying the dramatic reading by Valdez imbedded the image of Joaquín Murrieta in the heart of the Chicano movement.

In conclusion, one must ask: What is there about the life of Joaquín Murrieta that inspires his countless reincarnations in the imaginations of succeeding generations? From the unsympathetic view, Joaquín Murrieta, if he existed at all, was a murderer who preyed on defenseless Chinese miners and Anglos. His acts of violence cannot be justified according to a Judeo-Christian ethic. Yet because he is long dead, it is safe to romanticize him.

For non-Latinos, Murrieta is a protean western outlaw whose escapades can be appreciated for their daring and boldness, much in the same way as those of Billy the Kid or Jesse James. Indeed, there is a fascination with "bad" men in American history: the outlaws of the Wild West, the bootleg gangsters, the Mafia. Murrieta's story follows this tendency. If we instinctively identify with an underdog who challenges the system, then Murrieta becomes a nineteenth-century Californian version of Robin Hood, although there is no account of his giving to the poor. Instead, he gave to himself and to his men, who started out poor.

Latino parents who do not want their children to look upon Murrieta as a role model can still admire his courageous challenge to ethnocentric Anglos, who were engaging in their own acts of robbery and murder. In this view, Joaquín Murrieta was the Mexican's avenging angel in California. He defied the odds, outsmarting the Americanos at every turn, until the end. Meanwhile, the members of La Asociación Internacional Descendencia de Joaquín Murrieta can proudly trace their bloodlines back to this famous man and claim that they too are part of a quixotic history, one that contains many twists and turns in fact and fancy.

In the end, though, the facts of Joaquín Murrieta's life remain a mystery, and perhaps this is the secret to his enduring appeal.

7

BILLY THE KID

Thunder in the West

RICHARD W. ETULAIN

The wiry youth dashed out of the burning adobe home on a hot New Mexico evening in July 1878. Miraculously dodging the murderous fire of partisans bent on gunning him down, the daring teenager raced out of the firelight and into the safety of nearby darkness. Running through the hail of bullets and avoiding the deadly fire that mowed down several of his compatriots, the Kid sprinted out of the town of Lincoln, only to reappear a few weeks later as the rumored leader of a gang of rustlers bent on revenge and control. In one way, Billy the Kid escaped into the safety of darkness; in another, he emerged from the shadows of others to become a noted outlaw of the Southwest.

The story of the adolescent gunman Billy the Kid and his notorious career has mesmerized readers and listeners around the world for more than a century. Sometimes regarded as a Robin Hood stealing from the rich to help the poor, as a lone individual holding out against the corrupt Santa Fe Ring, Billy was inducted early on into the pantheon of Wild West heroes. In the 120 years since the dramatic apex of the Lincoln County War, Billy the Kid has exploded into a gigantic mythic figure. He challenges General George Custer, Buffalo Bill Cody, and Wyatt Earp as the most well-known character to gallop out of the Old West. In the last several decades, scholars and popularizers alike have continued to expand the Kid's reputation as one of the most intriguing superheroes and archvillains of the Wild West.

Nothing in Billy's mysterious beginnings suggests he would become a notorious national or even international character. In fact, the Kid's origins are as uncertain and sketchy as an orphan's. Despite years of diligent research, scholars and others interested in Billy the Kid have failed to turn up

Billy the Kid, the only known authentic photograph; here reversed as a tintype. Courtesy of Lincoln Heritage Trust, Lincoln, New Mexico.

a universally accepted birth date, birthplace, or birth name. Many agree, however, that he was likely born in the New York City area in November 1859, that his mother was Catherine McCarty, and that he was first named Henry McCarty. (A few biographers accept Billy's birth date as 1858, because he told a census taker that he was born in Missouri during that year.) In 1867 Catherine McCarty resided in Marion County, Indiana. Three years later, Catherine and her two sons, Joseph and Henry, were in Wichita, Kansas, where Catherine bought a town lot and filed on a plot of ground just outside town. Upon selling the land, Catherine, Joseph, and Henry, and their friend, William Antrim, left Kansas. According to some sources, they stayed briefly in Denver and then moved to New Mexico. On March 1, 1873, in Santa Fe, Catherine and Antrim were married, with her two sons among the witnesses. As Catherine's tuberculosis worsened, the new family moved south to Silver City, where Catherine took in boarders and Antrim did odd jobs between his prospecting forays, which often took him out of town for several weeks at a time.

A partial portrait of young Henry emerges from contemporary accounts, reminiscences taken from his boyhood friends as much as a half century later, and bits and pieces from other scattered sources. Remembrances of Henry in Silver City picture him not as an unusual youth but as a lively chum who attended school, loved and respected his mother, and got along with his stepfather. Everyone spoke of him as small in size, boyish, and energetic. Some recalled his mischievous ways, his smiling face, and his prominent two front teeth. His teacher, Mary P. Richards, reportedly a superb instructor with an English education, recalled Henry as "a scrawny little fellow with delicate hands and an artistic nature." For Richards, Henry was "no more of a problem in school than any other boy growing up in a mining camp." Henry's boyhood friends remembered his love of dancing and singing and his interest in books, especially dime novels and other sensational adventure stories.

Then tragedy struck. Gradually succumbing to her illness after spending four months bedridden, Catherine McCarty Antrim died on September 16, 1874. The new family quickly disintegrated. Although clearly not an abusive stepfather, William Antrim seemed little interested in nurturing his stepsons and instead farmed them out to the homes of their friends. First, joining a group of rambunctious young boys known as "the Village Arabs," Henry started gravitating toward petty crime. A year after his mother's death, he was arrested for stealing clothes from a Chinese man. The local paper reported that "it's believed that Henry was simply the tool of 'Sombrero Jack,' who done the actual stealing whilst Henry done the hiding." While in jail, Henry escaped up the jail cell chimney and headed for Arizona.

For nearly a century, Henry Antrim eluded biographers between his disappearance from Silver City and his reappearance two years later in southeastern New Mexico. Now, thanks to the tireless research of lay historians Robert N. Mullin and Jerry Weddle, we can trace Antrim during his two years in Arizona. Without money, a job, or connections of any sort, Henry, or Kid Antrim, as he soon became known, roamed from ranch to fort to camp in southeastern Arizona. When he seemed unable to keep a job on a ranch—"he was a light-weight," one foreman said—Henry wandered toward the Camp Grant area, loitering around the hotel, store, and hog ranch that sprang up nearby. Honing his skills as a dealer and gambler, Henry also fell in with John McKay (or McAckey), an ex-soldier, and together they became adept at horse stealing, which would become a career long occupation for Henry. Working in tandem in late 1876 and early 1877, Henry and McKay stole horses for their own use or to sell. On two or three occasions, Henry was arrested, but he proved a master of tricky escapes.

It was in Arizona that Henry killed his first man. In mid-August 1877 he came to a cantina near the boundary of the Camp Grant military reservation. Soon after he arrived, a burly blacksmith named Frank P. "Windy" Cahill, known for his loose tongue, began bullying Antrim. Cahill called Henry a "pimp," and Henry retaliated, calling the blacksmith a "son of a bitch." A wrestling match ensued, and the heavier Cahill, hurling his youthful opponent to the floor, began to pummel him. Henry grabbed the .45 stuck in his belt, shoved it into the belly of his antagonist, and pulled the trigger. As Cahill rolled aside in agony (he died the next day), Henry jumped up and raced outside, vaulted onto a nearby horse, and galloped toward New Mexico. An inquest was quickly called and concluded that "the shooting was criminal and unjustifiable, and Henry

Antrim alias Kid, is guilty thereof." Although his act might eventually have been considered justifiable self-defense, Henry Antrim fled eastward, fearing for his life.

In the early fall of 1877 the seventeen-year-old Antrim returned to New Mexico a changed man. Now calling himself William H. Bonney (the origin of the new last name remains unclear), he learned how to survive on his own. Adept with horses and guns, he struck new acquaintances as self-assured, adventuresome, and courageous, despite his boyish appearance. He especially impressed observers with a tenuous mixture of bravado, fearlessness, and joviality. A recent graduate of the go-it-alone and the rest-be-damned school in Arizona, Bonney headed into a tumultuous arena that continually tested his endurance during the four years remaining to him. In all aspects, his was a short, violent life.

When Bonney entered Lincoln County, he rode into one of the most lawless areas of the American frontier. Within a few months, Lincoln County erupted in war, which rushed to a fiery climax in the summer of 1878. But the county remained riven with violence. Until his death in July 1881, the Kid played an increasingly central role in the imbroglio.

Except for the Native Americans who had resided there for centuries, southeastern New Mexico was largely new territory for everyone. As early as the 1850s and 1860s Mexican/Hispanic families began to settle fertile areas near streams. By the mid-1860s Texas cattlemen moved onto the rangelands west of the Llano Estacado, finding they could sell their beef to the military, who, in turn, fed Indians on the Bosque Redondo or Mescalero Reservations. In 1869 Lincoln County was created. Nine years later, in 1878, when the Lincoln County War broke out, the county contained twenty-seven thousand square miles and was said to be the largest county in the United States.

By late fall of 1877, when Billy arrived, Lincoln County was experiencing several of the major problems that plagued the pioneer West. As Marc Simmons, the leading historian on New Mexico, has written: "political corruption, range wars, feuds, land frauds, and cattle rustling . . . brought their full measure of grief to New Mexico's citizenry." Distance, isolation, and inadequate legal systems exacerbated the already tense situation.

Among the major actors in Lincoln County between 1878 and 1881, Billy Bonney was the latest to arrive. In the late 1860s John Chisum, one of the early Texas cattle barons, had moved herds into New Mexico and Arizona. At the outbreak of war, Chisum, now the "Cow King of New Mexico," had hired nearly one hundred cowboys to look after his eighty thousand cattle ranging over much of the southeastern quadrant of New Mexico. In fact, by 1878 Chisum may have been the largest cattle raiser in the United

States. For nearly a decade he had been a major supplier of beef to the military for reservation Indians and for adjacent mining boomtowns.

The next enterprising soul to arrive was Lawrence G. Murphy. At the end of the Civil War, Murphy mustered out of the service and opened a trading store at Fort Stanton. Ambitious, hardworking, and willing to bend governmental and legal guidelines to his own benefit, Murphy had become the entrepreneurial czar of the area. He controlled trade at Fort Stanton and the beef supply for the Mescalero, even though he was not officially in charge of the latter. By 1873 the army had had enough of Murphy and his questionable activities and threw him out of the fort. Relocating nine miles away in Lincoln, now the county seat, he quickly controlled business dealings from his new site. With close financial and political ties to the so-called Santa Fe Ring of lawyers, politicians, and businessmen in the territorial capital, Murphy and his lieutenants, Jimmy Dolan and John Riley, became known as "The House" in Lincoln and its surroundings.

Before Billy appeared on the scene, two other major protagonists arrived and soon loosely aligned themselves with Chisum and even more directly opposed Murphy and The House. Alex McSween, a lawyer from the Midwest, came in March 1875 with his redoubtable wife, Susan. After initial contacts and negotiations with Murphy, McSween swung away from that group. Meanwhile, Englishman John H. Tunstall, then in his early twenties, arrived in early November 1876, hoping to set up his own competing ring to supply beef and financing for the Lincoln area. Before long, Tunstall was forced to go *mano-a-mano* with Murphy and company.

A war for political power and economic control of Lincoln County threatened to explode when Murphy and his political and legal friends arrested Chisum and McSween in late December 1877 as they traveled east on business. When territorial and county officials accused McSween of misusing funds from an insurance policy of one of Murphy's deceased partners, they revealed their close ties to Murphy as well as their growing opposition to the Chisum, McSween, and Tunstall faction. Concurrently, McSween and Tunstall organized a bank, and the Englishman bought a ranch from which to supply cattle to the military. Billy Bonney directly entered the scene in late 1877 or early 1878 when he signed on as a rider for Tunstall.

A series of tragic events in the first months of 1878 brought on the Lincoln County War and triggered Billy's central involvement in the conflict. These violent occurrences were among the most sensational of the decade-long battles, earning Lincoln the dubious reputation of having the most dangerous main street in the country. The series of conflicts between the two warring camps became increasingly violent, with each side bent on destroying its opposition, at any cost and by almost any means.

The shooting stage of the Lincoln County War began with the killing of John Tunstall in February 1878. For his opponents, the Englishman, through his new bank and his courageous (if not foolhardy) newspaper attacks on what he considered illegal actions in the county, was becoming a troublesome stumbling block. James J. Dolan (Murphy's heir) and his supporters vowed to curb Tunstall's influence. That avenue became possible when Dolan used his influence through the courts and Lincoln County sheriff William Brady to attach the holdings of Tunstall and McSween. Riding to Lincoln to defend his position, Tunstall was shot down in cold blood on the evening of February 18. Later that night, Billy Bonney, who had been accompanying Tunstall to Lincoln, rode with other Tunstall supporters to report the violent death. It is said, too, that Billy vowed revenge on Tunstall's murderers.

Billy was not long in retaliating. When he and Richard Brewer, Tunstall's ranch foreman, were deputized to find those who killed the Englishman, they stumbled on Billy Morton and Frank Baker in a Dolan cowcamp. The Regulators, as some of Tunstall's and McSween's allies now styled themselves, quickly captured Morton and Baker, the former known to be among those who gunned down Tunstall. The captives knew they were unlikely to survive the trip to jail. As Morton and Baker feared, several Regulators shot them down "when they tried to escape." Most likely Billy took an active part in the killings. In fact, he was becoming increasingly a part of the faction opposed to Dolan and The House. For the first time, Billy learned the meaning of camaraderie, with a group he admired and enjoyed. As his friend, George Coe, said of Billy, he "wasn't known then as a warrior. . . . But he grew bigger and bigger."

John H. Tunstall, English newcomer to Lincoln County, New Mexico. Courtesy of Lincoln Heritage Trust, Lincoln, New Mexico.

Billy's growing thirst for revenge took an unfortunate twist six weeks after the death of Tunstall. On the morning of April 1 Sheriff Brady and a deputy fell before the murderous gunfire of the Regulators, including Billy Bonney, who hid behind the gate of a corral facing Lincoln's main street when they fired their shots. In their assassination of Sheriff Brady, Billy and his cronies broke with a strong frontier code that might allow a killing in a hand-to-hand battle, but not the treacherous murder of a respected lawman. Brady's killing was clearly an assassination, and it was for this murder that Billy eventually would be sentenced to die.

Alexander A. McSween, Lincoln County lawyer. Courtesy of Lincoln Heritage Trust, Lincoln, New Mexico.

For the next three and a half months, Billy continued to ride with the Regulators and other McSween partisans. Although changes eventually brought about new local law officials and a new commander at nearby Fort Stanton, as well as a federal investigation of the Tunstall murder, the two groups of bitter opponents in Lincoln County waged their interrupted war. As Robert Utley, the leading biographer of Billy the Kid, notes, "Lincoln County escalated toward a climax."

That climax came in the Five-Day Battle in mid-July on the main street of Lincoln. Those fiery days are among the most dramatic events in the history of the frontier West, competing with Custer's Last Stand, the assassination of Wild Bill Hickok, and the gunfight at the OK Corral as archetypal episodes of a Wild West. Those sensational days in Lincoln also vaulted Billy Bonney to the forefront of the Lincoln County battles. Afterward, until his death three years later, he remained a central player in the complex civil war.

The notorious confrontation in Lincoln in the summer of 1878 drastically redirected power relationships in southeastern New Mexico. The deadly conflict up and down the town's main street also reoriented partisan leadership in the county. If the shootout became the apex of the Lincoln County War, it likewise ushered in a new kind of social turmoil that raged for several years. In all these happenings, Billy Bonney played a conspicuous role.

When increasing numbers of heavily armed Dolan and McSween supporters swarmed into Lincoln on July 14 and 15, residents realized that a showdown was imminent. In the first days thereafter, shooting was scattered and rather ineffective. But the tide noticeably turned when Colonel Nathan Dudley, commander at Fort Stanton, accepted Dolan's charge that the McSween contingent had fired on a soldier from the fort. On July 19

James J. Dolan, Emil Fritz, William Martin, and Lawrence G. Murphy. Courtesy of Lincoln Heritage Trust, Lincoln, New Mexico.

Dudley marched a force of his officers and more than thirty enlisted men into town, accompanied by a howitzer and a Gatling gun. Pointing the cannon in the direction of one group of McSween supporters, Dudley ordered them out of town. After that retreat, Dolan's forces clearly gained the upper hand, aided by the presence of the soldiers and abetted by Lincoln sheriff George "Dad" Peppin.

The eye of the conflict now focused on the McSween house, where less than fifteen supporters remained, including McSween himself and Billy Bonney. Twice, Susan McSween walked through the dangerous gunfire to entreat Dudley to spare her husband and her home. The colonel refused and looked the other way when Peppin's men succeeded in setting fire to the wooden sections of the McSween residence. After the women and children fled, the fire burned its way room by room until finally cornering the men in the kitchen. Taking charge, Billy Bonney planned an initial pell-mell dash by half of the group, whom he would lead out the back way. He was convinced that the first breakout would attract the attention and guns of Dolan's and Peppin's men and thus allow the second group, including McSween, to rush to safety.

Death crouched, waiting outside the burning home. Most of Billy's group eluded the spray of bullets as they ran the gauntlet, through the firelight and out of sight down a sharp bank to the Rio Bonito. Rather than take advantage of this distraction, the second group seemed to freeze. McSween, hiding in the shadows of the backyard, pled to surrender but refused to do so when an opponent moved toward him. One shot rang out, followed by a storm of bullets that mowed down McSween and other members of his group. McSween was immediately killed. As his riddled body lay just outside his burning home, Dolan and Peppin supporters celebrated into the night.

In the months following the shootout of midsummer 1878, the roles of the leading protagonists changed, as did the patterns of subsequent conflicts. Two of the major opponents of The House, Tunstall and McSween, had fallen before the guns of Dolan and others, and a third, John Chisum, seemed to withdraw, keeping his riders from participating in the turmoil. Meanwhile, L. G. Murphy, who divested control of The House, moved to Santa Fe, where he died of cancer in October 1878. The war in Lincoln financially ruined Jimmy Dolan, and Santa Fe resident Thomas Catron assumed control of the bankrupt House, an act that symbolized the declining power of the anti-McSween contingent. Although Dolan maintained his alliances with Peppin and Colonel Dudley and continued to harass his opponents, his hammerlock on Lincoln began to loosen.

The changes were no less dramatic for Billy Bonney. After hiring on as a rider for Tunstall and then serving as something of a bodyguard for McSween, Billy now had to find a new occupation. During the next three years he became the leader of the old Regulators and obviously a participant in the cattle- and horse-stealing raids that plagued ranchers like John Chisum. After a few false starts, Billy slowly gravitated away from Lincoln and toward Fort Sumner.

Over the next few months, Billy seemed unable to decide how to support himself. He wandered indecisively. To secure an immediate livelihood, he and remnants of the Regulators stole livestock, usually cattle and horses, and sold them to buyers in the Texas Panhandle. But when Billy's comrades, Doc Scurlock and Charlie Bowdre, abandoned Lincoln and resettled in Fort Sumner to work for Pete Maxwell, and when other former Regulators moved to Texas, Billy's group of cronies were reduced to a handful. For a brief period, Billy threatened to give up his nomadic life, to move back to the Lincoln area, and perhaps to take up land that he talked of working before Tunstall's death.

If these were Billy's true inclinations, the bubbling controversies and conflicts that erupted in the Lincoln area in late 1878 and early 1879 dashed his hopes. The impact of the changes became clearer when Frank Warner Angel, a federal investigator sent to report on the Lincoln County vendetta, blamed Governor Samuel Axtell for much of the war. Angel's criticisms, added to previous charges against the governor, led to his dismissal and to the appointment of Lew Wallace, a former general in the Civil War, as his replacement. When Wallace arrived in New Mexico in late September 1878, he hoped to cool off belligerents with a general pardon for all insurgents who were not under grand jury indictment. But Wallace had not counted on the legacies of conflict that stirred fresh disputes. For example, when Susan McSween returned to Lincoln at Thanksgiving time, she was accompanied by a brash, outspoken lawyer named Huston Chapman, who was even more combative and wrongheaded than McSween herself. Together, they sought revenge against Colonel Dudley for his part in the Five-Day Battle.

Despite these swirling controversies, Billy and the other partisans seemed interested in making peace. Billy even contacted the Dolan partisans and asked for a peace parley. Everything seemed to be proceeding toward a truce until the evening of February 18, 1879, when a boozed-up Dolan henchman met the recalcitrant Chapman on Lincoln's main street. An unidentified shot rang out, and Dolan's gunman shot Chapman, leaving the dying lawyer, his clothes still burning, lying in the street. The hours-old treaty collapsed, with Billy and several others who had witnessed the killing surreptitiously leaving town.

Chapman's murder finally jolted the lethargic and hesitant Governor Wallace into action. In the first week of March he made his promised but long-delayed trip to Lincoln to see if he could bring peace to the troubled area. Wallace now seemed another person, moving quickly and decisively. He pressured Edward Hatch, the military commander of New Mexico, to replace the stubborn, controversial Dudley, which Hatch did, despite an outcry from Dolan supporters. Then Wallace urged Hatch to round up all those partisans, including Billy and his closest friends and their opponents, not covered under the governor's amnesty provisions. Learning of the governor's presence in Lincoln, Billy wrote the executive a letter on March 14, offering to testify against Chapman's murderers. As he told Wallace, he would "appear at Court" and "give the desired information"—if the governor would "Annully those indictments" hanging over his head. Billy continued: "I have no Wish to fight any more[;] I have not raised an arm since Your proclamation."

The governor quickly responded, opening perhaps one of the most intriguing correspondences in the entire history of the Old West. Telling Billy he had "the authority to exempt [Billy] from prosecution," Wallace urged the Kid to meet for a private conversation. Billy took the governor at his word and came alone late in the evening of March 17 to the home of Squire Wilson, the justice of the peace. More than twenty years afterward, his memory undoubtedly colored by time and literary license, Wallace described to a reporter Billy's appearance with a Winchester rifle in one hand and a pistol in the other. Billy left the secret meeting convinced that Wallace had promised him a pardon if he would testify against Chapman's killers in the upcoming grand jury and court trials. The pardon never came, despite Billy's fulfilling the initial parts of the bargain.

For the next three months, Billy put his life in the hands of the political and legal leaders of Lincoln County and of the territory of New Mexico. On March 21 Sheriff George Kimbrell, in a planned maneuver, arrested Billy and cohort, Tom O'Folliard, and jailed them first in Lincoln and then at Fort Stanton. When the grand jury convened in April, Billy kept his word and testified against Chapman's murderers. He also testified against Colonel Dudley the next month before a court of inquiry called to examine charges against the commander for his controversial actions during the previous year. In providing this evidence against Dudley, Dolan, and their friends in high places, especially against District Attorney William Rynerson and the biased Judge Warren Bristol of the U.S. District Court, Billy considerably heightened the danger of his situation. Meanwhile, Wallace seemed to abandon Billy (whom he superciliously referred to as that "precious specimen") when he returned to Santa Fe. Billy received no pardon, the grand jury granted a change of venue to Doña Ana County on Billy's case, and he came under vicious attack during the Dudley hearings in May and June. Convinced that Wallace had reneged on his promise and that Dolan supporters Rynerson and Bristol planned to hang him on charges for killing Sheriff Brady, Billy and his friend, Doc Scurlock, "escaped" from Lincoln on June 17, 1879. When Billy's murder trial was changed to Doña Ana, he later told a journalist, he knew that he "had no show and so . . . skinned out."

After Billy left Lincoln, he surfaced in northern and eastern sections of the territory. In late July a friend (who recalled the incident years later) met Billy in a hotel near Las Vegas. There he was introduced to a "Mr. Howard," whom Billy later identified as the famous Jesse James. A few weeks afterward, Billy stopped in Lincoln to attend a *baile* (dance) at Susan McSween's. At that time, Billy told his close acquaintance Frank Coe that "he was tired of dodging and had run from them [his opponents] about long enough." Obviously, Billy had no way of realizing he would be on the dodge the rest of his days, despite his evidently genuine wish to avoid that nomadic lifestyle.

During the next year, from the fall of 1879 to late 1880, Billy's life fell into an undesigned pattern. Fort Sumner, and on occasion the mining boomtown of White Oaks, increasingly became his hangouts. The former fort, which had become a conglomeration of Mexican/Hispanic ranchers and farmers as well as a haven for dislocated cowboys and other frontier flotsam, functioned as an ideal place for Billy for other reasons. Located strategically between cattle ranches in the Texas Panhandle and the military beef markets of Fort Stanton and the Mescalero Reservation, Fort Sumner became a retreat and rest station for Billy. Stealing beef in west Texas, he and his cronies then often sold the stock to go-between Pat Coghlan, who bought the questionable animals and immediately sold them for a higher price to the military. Between raids, Billy could count on his friends—Hispanics and Anglos alike—in the Fort Sumner area to provide a bed and food until the next beef check.

Fort Sumner became a place of recreation, where Billy seemed to have won over several willing señoritas with his smile, good humor, lively dancing, and gentlemanly manners. Billy loved the bailes, enjoyed dancing with the vivacious Mexican/Hispanic women, and may even have fathered several children with two or three of the young Hispanas. It was also in Fort Sumner, in January 1880, that Billy killed his second man. Joe Grant, a drunken Texan, challenged Billy in a deadly shooting contest, but when Grant's pistol misfired, Billy spun around and shot Grant three times.

In the fall of 1880 one occurrence foreshadowed important changes in Billy the Kid's peripatetic life. Tired of the rustling raids by Billy and other cattle thieves, large ranchers like John Chisum and Captain Joseph C. Lea urged Pat Garrett, a former Texas buffalo hunter, to move to Lincoln and to run for county sheriff. As they hoped, Garrett won the election in early November. A few weeks later, Garrett set out to round up Billy and his rustling sidekicks. For the next eight months, Garrett tailed the Kid like a determined, persistent bulldog.

Several events in December 1880 warned Billy that his free, independent ways were coming to an end. For one, even though Billy wrote again to Governor Wallace to proclaim his innocence, the governor announced a $500 reward for Billy's capture. A few days later, Garrett's posse, lying in wait for the rustlers in Fort Sumner, gunned down Tom O'Folliard, a demise that Billy narrowly avoided. Tracking Billy's retreating men through the snow, Garrett's posse surrounded them near Stinking Springs, a few miles east of Fort Sumner. After one of Billy's closest friends, Charlie Bowdre, fell before Garrett's guns and the cornered rustlers suffered through several hours of freezing cold and hunger, they surrendered. Realizing Fort Sumner could not house the dangerous captives, Garrett took the prisoners to Las Vegas and then on to imprisonment in Santa Fe.

Now the precariousness of Billy's situation seemed to take hold of him. On New Year's Day 1881 he wrote again to Governor Wallace. Two weeks earlier, before his capture, Billy had written to Governor Wallace that he, now called Billy the Kid, was not "the captian [*sic*] of a Band of Outlaws"; there was, he told Wallace, "no such Organization in Existence." Billy wished that "some impartial Party" would "investigate this matter." If so, "they would find it far different from the impression put out by Chisum and his Tools." Now, on the first day of 1881 he wrote another letter to Wallace, saying, "I would like to see you a few moments if You can Spare time." Knowing the days were slipping away, Billy wrote three more letters, with the last one, sent on March 27, betraying Billy's sense of urgency and frustration: "for the *last time* I ask. Will you keep Your promise. I start below tomorrow." Wallace answered none of Billy's letters.

The next day Billy's captors took him to Mesilla, straight into the jaws of frontier justice. On April 6, 1881, Billy faced murder charges in the federal court, presided over by his nemesis, Judge Bristol. Billy's defense attorney, Ira E. Leonard, quickly and convincingly pointed out the inadequacies of these charges. They were immediately dismissed. Two days later, with new lawyers, Billy again appeared before the court, this time on territorial charges for the murder of Sheriff Brady. Bristol not only stacked the jury with members unsympathetic to the Kid, but he limited their decision to first-degree murder or acquittal. He also instructed the jury that it need not be proved that Billy fired the shot that killed the sheriff, only that he was present when Brady was shot. Not surprisingly, the jury quickly returned a guilty verdict. On April 13 Billy was sentenced to hang one month later in Lincoln. Despite legend to the contrary, Billy did not respond to the death sentence while in the courtroom. He did tell a reporter for the local newspaper, however, that he thought it "hard" that he "should be the only one to suffer the extreme penalties of the law." Billy was the sole person convicted of Brady's murder.

Less than a week later, on April 21, Billy arrived in Lincoln under heavy guard. He was jailed in what had been the former Murphy-Dolan store. Watched over closely by deputies James W. Bell and Robert Olinger, Billy had less than one month to live. Although manacled hand and foot and chained to the floor of a second-story jail cell, Billy never seemed to despair despite his bleak prospects. Those who visited him between his capture the previous December through his time in the Lincoln jail remarked on his cheerfulness, his smiles, his joking about his circumstances. Perhaps, rather than focusing on his incarceration, Billy fixed his mind on escaping. If so, that opportunity came quickly. On April 28, roughly two weeks before he faced his date with the gallows, Billy the Kid surprised his captors by killing the two deputies and riding untouched out of Lincoln. He would enjoy another ten weeks of freedom before he met his death, delivered by Pat Garrett in a darkened room in Fort Sumner.

Although Billy's dramatic escape from the Lincoln jail ranks with the most storied events of the American Wild West, the details of the startling incident remain vague and mysterious. Did Billy, as biographer Walter Noble Burns argued in his account in the 1920s, outsmart Bell during a card game, grab the deputy's gun, and then kill Bell and Olinger? Or, did he, as Robert Utley asserts in the best biography on Billy the Kid, slip out of his handcuffs, use them as a vicious weapon against Bell, and kill the two guards? Or, as strong local memory has it, did Billy receive a secret message that a gun awaited him in the privy, a weapon he used to kill Bell before snatching up Olinger's shotgun to end that deputy's life? Whatever the exact manner of escape, Billy dispatched Bell and Olinger, his third and fourth killings, and rode unscathed and uncontested out of Lincoln.

When Pat Garrett, who was in White Oaks on business, heard of Billy's escape, he is rumored to have said, "Now I'll have to do it all over again." Governor Wallace added to the motivations of Garrett and other pursuers by offering a $500 reward for the Kid's capture. The governor also signed the Kid's death warrant. Organizing several different posses, Garrett rode throughout the county, but without success. Although rumors located the Kid in several places in the area, Garrett failed to locate him. Some observers thought Garrett was doing little to capture the Kid. Then, stronger evidence surfaced, suggesting that Billy had returned to Fort Sumner, his favorite hideout after the Lincoln County War. Even though Garrett doubted the accuracy of that report, he and two of his deputies rode into Fort Sumner.

Meanwhile, Billy had been lying low. Riding west out of Lincoln after his dramatic escape, he then turned east and north. During Billy's journey, several friends urged him to escape into Mexico, but he rode instead toward Fort Sumner. What drew him in that direction? Did he feel safe there? Could he depend on his friends to shelter him from pursuers? Or, as many have maintained, was there a sweetheart, perhaps Paulita Maxwell or Celsa Gutiérrez, who drew him? Possibly all these needs prompted him to go back to Fort Sumner. Without money, acquaintances, and a support group, Billy decided to stay in Fort Sumner, an unwise if not understandable decision.

On July 14, 1881, Garrett and his two deputies, John Poe and Thomas C. "Kip" McKinney, rode into Fort Sumner to see if Billy was in the area. After failing to gain information from other sources, Garrett decided to visit Pete Maxwell before leaving town, even though it was nearly midnight. The son of deceased land baron Lucien Maxwell, Pete lived in the fort's former officers' quarters. Well acquainted with the layout of the house, Garrett told the two Texas deputies to remain outside while he walked through the open door into Pete's bedroom. He awakened Pete and asked him if he had seen Billy.

Less than a minute after Garrett entered the bedroom, a man in stocking feet approached the Maxwell home. When Billy spotted the two Texans, men unknown to him, he spoke to them in Spanish, the language of most residents of Fort Sumner. *"¿Quien es? ¿Quien es?"* (Who is it?) Not wanting to identify themselves, Poe and McKinney said nothing.

What happened next has become a part of western legend. Billy moved swiftly into the bedroom and advanced toward Pete Maxwell's bed. As he questioned Maxwell about the men outside, he may also have seen another indistinct figure near Maxwell's bed. The Kid hesitated—a fatal moment. Garrett, recognizing the voice of the intruder, pulled his pistol and fired twice. The first shot, hitting the Kid just above the heart, killed him almost instantly. Fearing that Billy might still be alive, Garrett and Maxwell dashed out of the room. A few moments later, Pete Maxwell and others reentered the bedroom to find the Kid dead on the floor.

The next morning a coroner's jury concluded that Garrett had killed the Kid in line with his official duties. On the afternoon of July 15, 1881, Billy was buried next to his comrades, Tom O'Folliard and Charlie Bowdre, in the old military cemetery at Fort Sumner. All had fallen before the lethal guns of Pat Garrett or his lieutenants.

Even before his death in mid-July 1881, Billy the Kid appeared in several essays and books. Most of these early accounts, including those in dime novels and articles in sensational magazines, depicted Billy as a dangerous outlaw, if not a vicious killer. Not until the 1920s and 1930s did a more positive image of Billy emerge. Some biographers, historians, and filmmakers have portrayed him as part of a long line of Robin Hood–type heroes, robbing the rich and arrogant upper class and aiding the poor and powerless. During the latter half of the twentieth century, detractors and aficionados of Billy the Kid have continued to see him through these conflicting interpretive lens.

Other writers present a more complex picture of Billy the Kid. Biographers Robert Utley and Frederick Nolan, for example, find the satanic murderer or innocent Robin Hood images too simplistic. They opt instead for more oxymoronic truths: Billy as the bad-good man, the gunman-friend, the desperado-companion. Rather than having a black or white hat, Billy wears a gray one.

This complex and ambivalent frontier hero has a long history. As far back as eighteenth-century Daniel Boone, historians and biographers have presented conflicting pictures of frontiersmen: Boone as the courageous, intrepid explorer and vanguard of civilization; Boone as the illiterate, ne'er-do-well wanderer; Boone as an ambivalent mix of positive and negative characteristics. Later, George Custer, Wyatt Earp, and Wild Bill Hickok elicited similar conflicting images.

If clashing representations of Billy the Kid echo ambiguous reactions to other heroes of the Wild West, his experiences in the Lincoln County War and afterward also illuminate what historian Richard Maxwell Brown calls the "Western Civil War of Incorporation" in his book *No Duty to Retreat* (1991). In Professor Brown's provocative schema, the post–Civil War West often hosted murderous shootouts between "incorporation gunfighters" (Wild Bill Hickok, Wyatt Earp, and Tom Horn) and "resister gunfighters" (Jesse James, the Younger gang, and the Dalton brothers). The Lincoln County War and later events in that area exemplify Brown's depiction of violent conflict on the Gilded Age frontier. As the agent of the incorporating law-and-order desires of John Chisum, Joseph C. Lea, and, in some respects, Thomas Catron and Lew Wallace, Pat Garrett set out to vanquish Billy the Kid, a major resister to the incorporation cattlemen, lawyers, and politicians. In this illuminating picture, Billy's death and the victory of Garrett, like the defeat of the Clanton and McLaury factions three months later in Tombstone, Arizona, represent the triumph of settlement, civilization, and incorporation over the older ways of individualism, anarchic freedom, and disorder.

Even more important, interpretative frameworks, such as Brown's, enlarge the significance of Billy the Kid and the Lincoln County War. True, the outlaw's story as a stirring narrative continues to draw thousands of readers. But accounts of Billy's role as resister will certainly raise other notable questions of social and political importance. Such questions may lead, for instance, to a layered examination of what Billy the Kid and the Lincoln County War reveal about frontier, regional, and even national conflicts during the 1870s and 1880s. One might even fruitfully compare Billy the Kid with Ned Kelly (1855–1880), the famed bushranger who also violently resisted the forces of incorporation on the other side of the world in Australia. Such biographical and historical projects will help clarify the meaning of Billy's life even as they illuminate his times.

But Billy the Kid's life has come to signify much more than the story of a slim, young outlaw living out his brief life on an isolated southwestern frontier. As in the stories of Custer, Wild Bill, Buffalo Bill, and Calamity Jane, legend becomes larger than life. Wanting to know and experience a magical Old West, Americans have kept Billy symbolically alive. No one has better encapsulated this emotional urge than historian Paul Andrew Hutton when he writes: "Billy the Kid just keeps riding across the dreamscape of our minds—silhouetted against a starlit Western sky, handsome, laughing, deadly. Shrewd as the coyote. Free as the hawk. The outlaw of dreams—forever free, forever young, forever riding." Perhaps we may still find out when Billy was born, the identity of his biological father, and what really happened on that midsummer evening in 1881. But the Billy who still lives, who still captures our imagination, who continues to be reinvented by every generation, is the metaphorical outrider still lighting out for the territory ahead.

8

BELLE STARR

"Queen of the Bandits"

GLENDA RILEY

Her mother called her Myra Maybelle or, more affectionately, May. Her second husband addressed her simply as Belle. A balladeer, however, dubbed her a "two-gun woman." And journalists and self-styled historians labeled her the "bandit queen."

It was the latter group—what contemporary Americans call "the media"—that convinced generations of Americans that Belle Starr was a rough-riding, hard-shooting, mean-mouthed outlaw. During her lifetime and especially after her death, dime novelists and yellow journalists proclaimed Belle Starr the most daring and wily female gunslinger the American West had ever known. They copied Belle Starr anecdotes from each other, reprinting them so often that folklore soon became fact, passed on by word of mouth from one generation to another. Some writers even replicated themselves, reissuing their work every decade or two to reach a new group of readers. The illustrations they used and reused also took on a dreary repetitiveness.

It was not until the 1940s that a few Starr chroniclers examined the oft-repeated myths and questioned their validity. Others, however, continued the sensationalistic tradition. In 1982 Oklahoma writer Glenn Shirley clarified many of the dates, issues, and controversies. After comparing details of the Belle Starr saga with newspaper reports, court documents, and other written evidence of her day, Shirley argued that Belle Starr could not have committed even a small proportion of the crimes and other exploits attributed to her. Although the Belle Starr who emerged from Shirley's pages was far less dashing than the romanticized Belle of fictionalized history, her life became more complex, interesting, and even poignant.

Belle Starr was a woman caught between a number of cultures: those of women and men, of the lawful and lawless, and, finally, of Anglos and

Indians. She vacillated from one to the other, acting feminine on some occasions and masculine on others. She often supported the law and occasionally broke it. She upheld Anglo beliefs at times, while defending Indian customs at other times. As a result, Belle Starr's contradictory personality and life provided considerable room for journalistic embroidery. Unfortunately, she left behind virtually no letters, diaries, or memoirs to contradict tall tales or offer insight into her actions.

At the same time, Starr participated in her own romanticization, not so much by her deeds but by the image she projected. Especially in her later years, she liked to play the "bad girl," to shock the good folks of the neighborhood, including the ladies. She toted two guns, even though she also favored long, flowing skirts. She always rode sidesaddle, and the folds of her skirt draped to the best advantage over the side of her horse. Starr's partial rejection of women's culture, however, proved a costly miscalculation, as such isolation not only cut her off from female society but from a network of female support. No evidence suggests that she ever had one truly intimate woman friend. Nor did she ever join any of the myriad women's clubs that proved so important to the lives of numerous nineteenth-century women, especially of her background.

Belle Starr had developed a contentious approach to life. Rather than seeking communication and compromise, she was likely to ignore people, erupt into a rage and curse anyone who opposed her, or follow an offensive course of action. True, she lived in trying times and places—frontier and Civil War Missouri, Reconstruction-era Texas, and Indian Territory (later Oklahoma)—but she never learned an effective way to deal with upheaval and conflict.

Moreover, Starr ran with bad men. Perhaps she had reformer instincts. After choosing undesirable male companions, she often spent considerable energy attempting to change them. When her efforts failed, she frequently supported her husbands and lovers in questionable activities, or at least stayed out of their way. As a result, she buried several men who met brutal ends—until her last husband buried her after an assassin's bullets brought her down in the middle of a muddy road in 1889.

Belle Starr was born Myra Maybelle Shirley near Modoc, Missouri, on February 5, 1848. As a young child, she absorbed a skewed view of life. Her father, John Shirley, was a stubborn and single-minded man. The son of Samuel Shirley and his first wife, John moved to Tennessee with his father after his mother's death. But when his father remarried, John left home and migrated to Indiana. In 1818 John married Nancy Fowler. The union, which lasted less than a decade, produced two children and ended in divorce. In 1829 John remarried but soon divorced again. Sometime during the 1830s John Shirley married a third woman, Elizabeth Hatfield, then in her teens and kin to the feuding Hatfields and McCoys. After the Sarcoxie War of 1837 drove the Osage Indians out of Missouri, John Shirley and Elizabeth homesteaded eight hundred acres of land on which he grew corn and raised hogs and horses.

Studio photograph of Belle Starr, taken at Fort Smith, Arkansas, 1887. Courtesy of the Western History Collections, University of Oklahoma.

Census and family records indicate that John's son, Preston, and daughter, Charlotte Amanda, by his first wife, were part of the household. To this family group, Elizabeth, or Eliza, as she was known, added John Addison M. in 1841, Myra Maybelle in 1848, and Edwin Benton in 1849. Thus, in her most formative stage of life, Myra experienced a concept of family based on multiple marriages and that included half brothers and sisters, as well as parents of disparate ages. At the same time, it is unlikely that she knew her grandparents or other far-flung relatives.

John Shirley's ambition to be more than a farmer created additional variations in his family's situation. He gained title to his land in 1848 and began selling portions of it in 1850. In turn, he used the income to purchase lots in nearby Carthage, Missouri, on which he built a tavern and livery stable called the Carthage Hotel. The Shirley family left their rural home to become town dwellers, and, by virtue of his relative wealth, John Shirley assumed the honorific title "Judge." In addition, the 1860 census indicated that Eliza bore two more sons, Mansfield and Cravens.

Carthage, a town of less than five hundred people during the 1850s, had a definite personality. It was a raw frontier hamlet that attracted many proslavery southerners. When the first newspaper, which adopted the grand-sounding name *Star of the West and Southwest News,* began publication in 1859, it advocated slavery. The Shirleys themselves were slave owners, holding between two and four slaves. In addition, because Carthage was on a new route to Santa Fe, it hosted a stream of traders, miners, and other travelers. John Shirley's tavern especially provided a stopping point for southern planters, merchants, itinerant preachers, lawyers, and litigants. During her formative years, young Myra found a ready audience in this checkered company. Many visitors seemed willing to coddle and applaud the sprightly, dark-haired child and her antics.

At the same time, John and Eliza Shirley attempted to raise their daughter properly. John's fine library beckoned, while Eliza's piano waited. When the Carthage Female Seminary was established in 1855, the Shirleys enrolled Myra as one of its first pupils. Because numerous parents feared that the frontier would "barbarize" their daughters, such private seminaries and academies for "ladies" were common. They offered a "good English education," instruction in such "female accomplishments" as ornamental needlework and playing the piano, and exposure to feminine graces. Myra also spent some time at a private school held in the Masonic Hall in Carthage's central square. As a student, she demonstrated a quick wit and ready intelligence. She could, however, be combative. A schoolmate recalled that even at age ten, Myra "would fight anyone, boy or girl, that she quarreled with."

Moreover, Myra did not carry her instruction in women's culture into her leisure time. Such female occupations as making cross-stitch samplers and keeping daybooks seemed to hold little allure for her. Myra's only sister, Charlotte Amanda, who was twenty years her elder, offered little in the way of female companionship and guidance. Although Myra's mother was apparently educated to some degree and assumed the airs of a southern lady, it is unknown whether she pressed young Myra to follow her example. Perhaps she was too busy helping her husband run the Carthage Hotel.

Even though Myra developed some proficiency playing the piano, she clearly preferred the outdoors and the company of her brother, John Addison, whom the family called Bud and who was the most important single influence in Myra's youth. He taught Myra her exceptional skill with firearms and goaded her to ride every horse in her father's stable of fine mounts. It was Bud who accompanied Myra on her rambles through the countryside surrounding Carthage. It was Bud who seldom walked away from a dare, who passed his sense of adventure on to his younger sister.

Meanwhile, during the 1850s the catastrophic events of imminent civil war swirled around the Shirley family. Abolitionist evangelist John Brown swept through the area, while Missouri and Kansas fought their own private war over slavery. After the Civil War began in 1861, Missouri tottered on the brink of joining the Confederacy. The state decided to avoid declaring secession unless President Abraham Lincoln's government attempted to coerce the South back into the Union, a middle-ground position that lasted until Fort Sumter fell in April. When Lincoln called for

Missouri volunteers to fight for the Union cause, Missouri's governor refused to act.

As John Shirley watched Missouri disintegrate into internal warfare between Union and Confederate sympathizers, he ranted at his family. His eldest son, Preston, a staunch Secessionist, migrated to Texas. Bud took a different tack. As a horde of Jayhawkers, Border Ruffians, and Quantrill's Raiders crisscrossed Jasper County, Bud Shirley, with his father's approval, joined the fray. Bud became a bushwhacker, dedicated to making life intolerable for Union supporters.

Myra followed her brother's lead. Even though Belle Starr biographers routinely state that women were barred from such activities, Myra operated unofficially. Like thousands of women in the South and North, who served as spies, scouts, and saboteurs, Myra aided Bud by relaying intelligence information across the lines. It took months, and sometimes years, of hard experience for troops to recognize that petticoated, hoopskirted women were not as harmless as they appeared. Hoopskirts could, and did, conceal everything from maps to medicine. In addition, Myra brought to her undertakings unusual talents as a rider and shooter.

Despite accounts in numerous biographies, however, the daring Myra did not save Bud from arrest and possible murder by a wild ride across fields and hills. Near the end of the war, in late June 1864, Bud fell at the hands of the militia while, according to Carthage citizen Sarah Musgrave, leaping "over the fence" to escape arrest. Bud Shirley, she stated, "fell dead on the other side." Musgrave added that the following day Myra "appeared at Sarcoxie . . . with a belt around her waist, from which swung two big revolvers, one on each side." According to Musgrave, Myra Shirley planned to avenge her brother's death.

Before Myra could take action, however, she saw her home life disrupted once again. An embittered and frightened John Shirley sold his Carthage holdings and moved his family to Sycene, south of Dallas, Texas. Although little is known of the Shirleys' Texas journey, Myra probably drove one of the family wagons. Behind the departing Shirleys, Carthage was burned and sacked; along the way, chaos and poverty prevailed. Indian refugees, would-be settlers, and scoundrels of every sort lined the roads. As the family passed through Dallas–Fort Worth, they saw bustling business establishments lining the rutted streets and vying with one another for trade and people's entertainment dollars. Myra was about to learn what the term "wide open" meant.

Once in Texas, John Shirley settled near his son, Preston, where he established a small, diversified farm and resumed raising horses. Although the Shirleys kept to themselves, they quickly alienated their neighbors by filling their water barrels until the well was nearly empty, thus leaving little for the next person until the well refilled.

Meanwhile, Myra faced a difficult adjustment. At the one-room school, she behaved badly and garnered a reputation for irritability and recklessness. At home, Myra helped with domestic chores and childcare while she listened to her father rail against carpetbagger rule and the arrests of former Confederate guerrillas, even though Union guerrillas had received amnesty. John also spoke of such notorious fugitives as Jesse and Frank James, who had once ridden with Quantrill but had since turned to a life of crime to support themselves.

Sometime in 1864 Myra met a few of what her father considered heroic yet mistreated men. More specifically, the James brothers and four of their band traded on Cole Younger's acquaintance with the Shirleys back in Missouri, as well as on standards of southern hospitality, by stopping in Sycene to seek brief refuge with the family. It was at this time that Myra supposedly fell in love with Cole Younger and was pregnant with his child by the time the group departed. Younger himself, however, denied any romantic liaison with Myra. In a prison interview after Belle's death, Younger stated, "I knew the lady slightly some years ago, but it has been many years since I have seen her." When Belle's daughter, Pearl, later used the name Younger to disguise her identity, the action convinced many observers that Younger's statement was pure chivalry and that he had indeed fathered Belle's first child.

On the contrary, writer Glenn Shirley's probing research indicates that, although young Myra did fall in love with what she termed a "dashing guerilla," the man in question was James C. Reed, who had known Myra briefly in Carthage. After Jim Reed's widowed mother moved her brood to Texas, Jim and Myra began their courtship. Although a variety of writers have devised colorful stories about John Shirley's supposed opposition to the match and the couple's elopement, no one has remarked on the resemblance Jim bore to Myra's slain brother, Bud. Like Bud, Jim was handsome and dashing, handy with weapons, an expert rider, and a risk taker. At age seventeen, Jim had joined Quantrill, but he escaped Bud's fate and emerged with his life intact. Eighteen-year-old Myra was intrigued and infatuated. On November 1, 1866, she married twenty-year-old Jim in Collins Country, Texas. Jim Reed, not Cole Younger, fathered Myra's first child, Rosie Lee, born in September 1868 and nicknamed Pearl when Myra took to calling Rosie her "pearl."

During those early years of marriage, Myra tried to be a devoted wife and mother. She followed Jim to a farmstead in Missouri, traveling to Sycene for a brief visit after the slaying of her roguish brother, Edwin, by Texas

Rangers. She soon returned to Missouri, where she lavished attention on Pearl. A neighbor, Gertrude Higgins, remembered that Myra attended Bethel Baptist Church with her finely dressed daughter, doting on the child rather than watching the minister.

Unfortunately, Jim Reed was less satisfied with life. He found farming monotonous and preferred horse racing and gambling in Fort Smith, Arkansas. Jim also spent time in Indian Territory just west of Fort Smith, where he fell in with the extended family of the notorious Cherokee Tom Starr; stolen horses and cattle surely passed through Jim's hands. Also, because white fugitives abounded in Indian Territory, where Anglo law had difficulty reaching them, Jim met the James brothers and others of their ilk. One contemporary observer claimed that the James gang even invited Jim to join their 1868 raid on a bank in Northfield, Minnesota, but that "he was married to Belle then . . . and she wouldn't let him go."

Even in 1869, after Jim participated in the assassination of his brother's killer and the couple fled to California, Myra still had hopes of a stable family life. Although Jim did not, as rumored, associate with the James brothers and their band in California, his source of income remains unclear. On February 22, 1871, Myra gave birth to a son, James Edwin, who was nicknamed Eddie. The following month, federal officers charged Jim with passing counterfeit money and discovered that he was a fugitive from a murder charge in Arkansas. Once again, Myra packed up her belongings and her family. While Jim fled the authorities, she moved her brood back to Texas.

Ever hopeful, Myra encouraged Jim to resume farming. Cole Younger recalled that Myra declared that "she was tired of roaming the country over and wanted to settle down." The Shirleys gave Myra and Jim a portion of farmland, while Younger drove some of his cattle northward to Texas. He never saw Myra Maybelle Shirley Reed again.

Despite Myra's efforts to gain respectability, Jim's activities foiled her. In the August 10, 1874, issue of the *Dallas Commercial,* a reporter described Myra as "a highly educated and accomplished lady," but "no influence seemed sufficient to check" Jim Reed's "viciousness." The *Commercial* went on to accuse Jim of stock thievery, holding up people, and "cold-blooded murder."

Now under indictment for murder in Texas as well as Arkansas, Jim Reed departed for Indian Territory. Leaving her children at her parents' Sycene home, Myra went with her husband, either out of duty or a sense of daring. Despite her presence, Jim continued his criminal endeavors, including participating in the infamous Grayson robbery. On November 19, 1873, a group of bandits relieved the aged Indian judge Watt Grayson of $30,000 in gold coins. Although some believed that Myra, dressed in men's clothing, accompanied her husband, witnesses offered no evidence of Myra's presence. They remembered no female robber dressed as a man. When Jim eluded the charges against him by escaping back to Texas, Myra again trailed behind.

After the couple reached Texas, Myra finally drew a line. Berating Jim for leading such a corrupt life, she left him and joined her children at her parents' home in Sycene. The *Dallas Commercial,* however, reported that the real cause of Myra's desertion was Jim's seduction of "a young girl named Rosa McComus." Subsequent articles revealed Jim Reed's continuing involvement in robberies, often under a variety of aliases. The newspaper also made additional references to "the poor girl" whom Reed had promised to marry and to his unfortunate wife and children. Thus, Myra Reed not only had to endure emotional turmoil and the collapse of her marriage, but she had to do so publicly with the eyes of Dallas upon her.

On August 9, 1874, Myra learned that Deputy Sheriff John T. Morris had shot and killed her husband. Although legend says that Myra refused to identify Jim's body so that Morris could not claim a reward, she did no such thing. In fact, witnesses verified Reed's identity and Morris collected $1,700. Myra probably never saw her husband's body, and her feelings regarding Jim's demise remain unknown. Whether she lamented or celebrated Reed's departure from life is an unsolved puzzle.

When Judge Watt Grayson tried to recover some of his stolen money from Myra, however, she made no attempt to protect her dead husband's reputation or to revise the past for the sake of her children. Myra testified that her husband had indeed stolen Grayson's money. According to Myra, Jim and two other men told her "they had accomplished their object and had the money to show for it, and they sat down upon the ground and began counting it." She added that Watt Grayson was out of luck, for Jim "spent or disposed of all he had" and left her "in a destitute condition."

A lesser woman might have given way to despondency at this point, but not Myra Shirley Reed. Nor did she take up a life of crime and brutality to avenge her many disappointments and losses. Although the *Daily Commercial* admitted that Dallas lacked "a sufficiency of men to effectually preserve the peace and the salary now paid the officers [is] not sufficient to maintain men decently," Myra apparently did not consider exploiting the situation. Rather, she reacted in a way expected of a nineteenth-century wife and mother who had been wronged in ways beyond her control. She returned to Sycene and retreated into the circle of her family, undoubtedly hoping for a happier future.

Little is known of Myra and her children until 1876, when Myra sent a letter to her in-laws in Vernon County, Missouri. Addressing the Reeds as "Dear Mother and Brothers and Sisters," Myra revealed that death and turbulence continued to cloud her existence. "My poor old father has left this world of care and trouble," she wrote. In addition, because her youngest brother, Cravens, who was known as Shug or Doc, "got in trouble" he had to flee, leaving her mother with only grandson Eddie as protector. "Mother," Myra added, "is going to move away from here in a few days and then I'll be left alone. Eddie will go with her, and I don't know that I shall ever see him again." She described Eddie as "manly" and "quick-motioned," who "very much" resembled his father.

When Myra turned to the subject of her daughter, she disclosed her own frustration. The child attended school in Dallas and, despite family opposition, pursued a brief stage career. Myra explained that "I wanted her to be able to make a living of her own without depending on any one." Clearly, Myra resented women's economic dependence on men. Although her father had led her to expect ongoing support from a husband, Jim had let her down. Now, although Myra rented out her portion of Shirley land, she said she would realize "nothing from my farm" that year and was thinking of selling the parcel. Unsurprisingly, Myra concluded the missive on a somber note: "I am far from well. I am so nervous this evening from the headache that I can scarcely write."

Myra's letter to the Reeds indicated that rather than traipsing around Dallas, dropping in on saloons, and playing the role of a wild woman, Myra Shirley Reed suffered in relative silence. Her situation soon worsened. Myra's mother moved to Dallas but did not take Eddie. Instead, he lived with the Reeds until he reached twelve years of age. Alone and untethered, Myra sold her farm and appeared to spend her time visiting family members. She next turned up in the mining camp of Galena, Kansas, where she lived with Bruce Younger, half brother to Cole Younger's father. As early as 1876 the *Joplin News* had speculated that Younger participated in the recent James gang's attack on a Missouri Pacific train. Myra had to be aware of Younger's reputation, yet she could not seem to escape her fascination or affinity for men who walked outside the law.

One resident remembered that when Myra appeared in Galena "around 1879" she "dressed like other women . . . nothing loud or flashy." The town's ladies found Myra unacceptable because of her connection with "tinhorn gambler" Bruce Younger. According to this particular Galena resident, Myra and Bruce usually stayed in Galena's Evans Hotel and were regulars on Redhot Street, the hub of dance halls and saloons. He did not think the couple had married: "people like them didn't get married much in those days." He was probably right; no marriage license appears to exist.

Evidently, Myra, now bereft of a husband, the daily presence of her children, and the ongoing support of her mother, had drifted into a half life. Although the son of a Galena hotel owner remembered that Myra's mother, daughter, and youngest brother occasionally stayed with her, Myra lacked a firm anchor. In addition, societal dictates of the era encouraged women to marry. Apparently, Myra was not one of those women who could live alone. Or perhaps eroded self-esteem convinced her that she had no place in the world, except as the companion of an unsuitable man. Maybe she believed she had fallen so low that Bruce Younger *was* suitable for a woman such as she. Still, the hotel keeper's son described Myra as "a mighty good-lookin'" woman, well educated, quietly dressed—not tough like the newspapers made out—while another Galena observer remembered Belle as "always well behaved." Obviously, she was not suffering from depression, nor had she yet assumed the colorful, public stance that would characterize her during the last years of her life.

The turning point in Myra's life came when she reestablished her earlier acquaintance with the Starr family of Indian Territory. Perhaps Myra and Bruce Younger resided briefly, as one chronicler claimed, in Indian Territory, where she would have come in contact with members of the Starr clan. At any rate, Myra found herself drawn to Tom Starr's son, Sam, a charismatic, handsome, nearly full-blooded Cherokee who could ride and shoot—just like Bud Shirley and Jim Reed. In 1880 Myra Shirley Reed changed her life dramatically. She married Sam Starr in the Cherokee Nation, lopped five years off her age, and renamed herself Belle Starr.

The old ambivalence remained, however. Part of Belle longed for domesticity and anonymity. Either she did not know how to achieve her goals or the part of her that craved public attention and excitement overpowered her. Sam Starr would prove to be another of Belle's poor choices of a male companion. Like daughters of alcoholic men who marry, divorce, and remarry alcoholic husbands, Belle had her own addiction: she seemed hooked on winsome but weak men.

At first, however, the Starr marriage went well. Sam claimed an allotment of communally held land in the Cherokee Nation. He and Belle moved from their tiny house to a cedar cabin on the allotment, where they grew corn and raised livestock. As Sam's wife, Belle was also a citizen of the Cherokee Nation and, in the case of Sam's death, would own any improvements on the allotment (but not the land itself). Situated near the town of Eufaula, yet tucked into hills lying in a curve called Youngers' Bend along the South Canadian River, the Starr place was nearly invisible. Following the Cherokee custom, Belle set about covering the interior walls of the cabin with flowered calico. John and Eliza Shirley's influence also manifested itself when Belle added a shelf of books and later, according to neighbors, paid to have a piano transported through the nearly impassable canyon that shut off the cabin from the outside world. Meanwhile, Belle named the canyon and a nearby creek after herself and changed daughter Rosie Lee's name to Pearl Starr.

Belle Starr exhibited all the characteristics of a woman determined to start a new life. She later wrote to a reporter with the *Fort Smith Elevator* that she "hoped to pass the remainder" of her life "in peace." She added, "So long had I been estranged from the society of women (whom I thoroughly detest) that I thought I would find it irksome to live in their midst." Evidently, Belle felt the sting of rejection from other women, whom she perhaps "detested" because she was outside their circle. Belle claimed that she also abandoned communication with "the boys who were friends of mine." Yet, according to Belle, slanderous gossip subverted her exertions: "It soon became noised around that I was a woman of some notoriety from Texas, and from that time on my home and actions have been severely criticized."

Even though Belle did not say so, she played a direct part in contributing to her own troubles. When such wanted criminals as Jesse James learned of Belle's whereabouts and found the Starr cabin, she allowed Jesse to remain in her home for three weeks. Belle may not have harbored scores of criminals or used Robbers Cave as a stolen-horse relay station, but she did not cut herself off entirely from the company of miscreants either. It is possible that Belle was lonely for people she had known for a long time, as well as nostalgic for the old days. But, by giving in to such whims, Belle endangered not only herself, but Pearl and especially Sam. As a Starr, Sam already was under suspicion; as a Cherokee, he was a convenient scapegoat for whites.

Despite Belle's indiscretions and Sam's tenuous position, she and Sam stayed clear of trouble until July 31, 1882, when the U.S. Commissioner's Court in Fort Smith put out an arrest order for the pair, charging that they had stolen an $80 horse belonging to a white man. Fannie Blythe Marks later described her deputy husband's difficulties in apprehending the Starrs, who reportedly bolted north toward Catoosa. According to Fannie Marks, after an extended hunt her husband finally ran down the Starrs, first arresting and disarming Sam. When Belle appeared, the marshals wanted to avoid using violence on a woman so "they hid behind trees on opposite sides of the path and stepped out as she passed, each catching an arm." Although Belle fought "like a tiger and threatened to kill the officers," she was captured. Her overskirt yielded a sixgun and they found two derringers in the bosom of her dress.

On the trip back to Fort Smith, Belle proved an "exasperating prisoner." Fannie Marks maintained that Belle's "one object . . . seemed to be to irritate and annoy those having her in charge." Belle cast such items as cutlery and bedding out of the wagon and seized a gun from a guard, whom she pursued with "a smoking revolver" in her hand. What happened, one may wonder, to the well-behaved woman of the Galena–Bruce Younger days? Did the horse-stealing charge and intense pursuit finally push Belle over the edge?

Subsequent testimony in a Fort Smith courtroom revealed not a woman suddenly grown felonious, but one turned belligerent and stubborn. A series of misunderstandings and miscommunications unfolded in which Belle had comported herself poorly. She had broken promises, shrieked and swore at those trying to locate the missing horse, and, by traveling in the company of another man, she had given Sam cause for suspicion regarding her fidelity to him. Perhaps worst of all, she had insisted on taking a horse out of the area that she knew belonged to Andrew Crane. When told of Crane's ownership, Belle reportedly replied, "God-damn the horse"—she did not want "to steal him," only to borrow him for a short period.

Sam's role was less clear. He had led the horse, as well as another that he and Belle did not own. He then penned them in a neighbor's corral and generally abetted Belle. Although Sam pleaded illness and the purchase of at least one of the horses, witnesses disputed Sam's claims. The court, however, released him from responsibility for the second horse, which another Cherokee owned. The court had no jurisdiction in a matter between two Indians.

Belle and Sam employed additional lawyers. Their case came before Judge Isaac Charles Parker, known as a "hanging judge," and lasted four days. Local newspapers made much of the event, saying that although Belle "could not be considered even a good-looking woman, her appearance is of that kind as would be sure to attract the attention of wild and desperate characters." Obviously, Belle had finally overstepped the bounds of female propriety to an unacceptable degree. According to the *New Era,* "the very idea of a woman being charged with an offense of this kind and that she was the leader of a band of horse thieves and wielding a power over them as their queen and guiding spirit, was sufficient to fill the courtroom with spectators."

In court, Belle created yet another spectacle. She sent frequent notes to her attorneys' table, tried to stare down Judge Parker, and let her fury show when the district attorney ridiculed Sam for "illiteracy." Even though the court found Belle guilty of taking two horses and Sam one, Judge Parker proved merciful. Rather than assigning long terms in a harsh prison, Parker took into account the fact that Belle was a woman and that it was a first offense for both Belle and Sam. As a result, Parker sentenced Belle to two six-month terms and Sam to one year in the House of Correction in Detroit, Michigan. Notably, Sam, a man and an Indian, received a greater sentence for a lesser offense, while Belle, a woman and an Anglo, received shorter sentences for two worse infractions.

Before the Starrs' departure for the Detroit House of Correction, Belle sent Pearl to live with a friend and decided to protect her whereabouts by addressing her, inexplicably, as Pearl Younger. On March 18, 1883, Belle wrote Pearl that "never again will I be placed in such humiliating circumstances." She assured Pearl that the time would pass rapidly and they would be "as gay and happy as the birds." On March 19 Belle boarded a railroad prison car bound for Detroit. She was the only woman among five guards and nineteen prisoners, including Sam.

The Starrs, especially Belle, were fortunate. The House of Correction was a model institution dedicated to education and rehabilitation. Apparently, Belle took full advantage of the programs offered. Unlike most women in nineteenth-century prisons who suffered abuse and degradation, Belle appeared to have spent her time at light labor. Sam, however, rejected the white-style education offered him and was assigned to heavy manual labor. After nine months, both gained release for good behavior.

Even though Belle had little to say about her prison experience and it appears to have been uneventful, her time in prison changed her physically. For one thing, it added weight to her hips but pared down her face. Her newly thinned cheeks were pale and her brunette hair showed signs of graying. Never a beautiful woman, Belle could no longer even be called attractive. Almost wizened-looking, Belle was anxious to return to the cabin on the Canadian with Sam, Pearl, and Pearl's orphan friend Mabel Harrison. She headed straight for Missouri to spend the Christmas holidays with the Reeds and to pick up Pearl and Mabel. Again, Belle hoped to live a quiet life of seclusion.

Her dreams were not to be. As historian Anne M. Butler so aptly asserted in *Gendered Justice in the American West* (1997), nineteenth-century women who served prison terms seldom escaped the ignominy of their status as former convicts. In Belle Starr's case, rumors flew across Indian Territory and beyond. Belle's "gang" grew beyond believable proportions and her supposed exploits exceeded the capability of one person.

Gradually, Belle seemed to accept her image and even to play to it. She wore gold earrings, affected a man's sombrero decorated with feathers, donned a black velvet riding habit for special occasions, and referred to her Colt .45 pistol as "my baby." Belle also preferred to ride a black mare named Venus, on whom she used a tooled sidesaddle, which became known as the Belle Starr saddle.

Despite the volatility of her situation, Belle evidently remained within the law during 1884, helping Sam with farm chores and Pearl and Mabel with the cooking. No mention of Belle appears in police registers or court records. Yet she could shake off neither her past nor her growing reputation as a bandit and a desperado. Early in 1885 former acquaintance and alleged murderer John Middleton sought out Belle. Handsome, daring, and skilled with weapons, the twenty-nine-year-old Middleton was Belle's kind of man. She did not disappoint him; she supplied the haven he sought.

In his nearly four months with the Starrs, Middleton established a friendship with Sam Starr. On more than one occasion, Sam secreted Middleton along the Canadian River. Finally, however, it was clear that Middleton could only evade law officers by leaving the Starr place. In an abortive escape attempt, Middleton lost his life when he attempted to swim a half-blind mare across the rain-swollen Poteau River south of Fort Smith.

Next it was Sam Starr's turn to run from the law. Implicated in several robberies, Sam eluded his would-be captors by disappearing into the river bottoms and canyons surrounding his and Belle's cabin. In the meantime, Belle defended Sam's actions, saying that his enemies had trumped up the charges and would falsely testify if the matter went to court.

By January 1886, however, Belle had her own troubles. After being charged with stealing the one-eyed mare on which Middleton had fled, Belle gave herself over to the U.S. marshal in Fort Smith. She pleaded not guilty to the charge of larceny and requested witnesses, especially her daughter Pearl, who had been with her continuously during the Middleton escape attempt.

In the meantime, Sam continued to flee, especially from Frank West, an unusually persistent Indian police officer. On March 11 the *Muskogee Indian Journal* reported that Sam had jumped his horse "off a bluff over twenty feet high" and swam the river to safety. The newspaper also claimed that Belle had since gone to Eufaula, where she "bought 100 rounds of cartridges." The account concluded that "it is advisable for every merchant likely to be visited by" the Starr gang "to be on his guard." Once again, newspaper coverage forced Belle into public notice, this time exaggerating her actions and the threat she posed to the community.

In late April 1886 a warrant served to Belle charged her with being a "gang leader" in a recent robbery. She assented to go with arresting officers to Fort Smith, where she retained attorneys, pleaded not guilty, and requested witnesses. Belle then posted bond, after which she visited friends in Fort Smith. She appeared to have accepted her fate; in many people's eyes she would never be anything more than a female outlaw.

In fact, Belle seemed to enjoy her dubious celebrity in Fort Smith. On May 23 she agreed to have her photograph taken for the St. Louis *Globe Democrat*. With Deputy Tyner Hughes by her side, Belle sat on a horse sidesaddle and held a rawhide riding whip and a borrowed pistol. The next day she stood next to Blue Duck, a Cherokee convicted of murder, and posed for what would become one of the most widely circulated photographs of Belle Starr. Belle looked commonplace, more like Blue Duck's mother than a criminal colleague. Her bright eyes, modest clothing, and simple jewelry gave little insight into her complicated personality.

Before she left Fort Smith, Belle went shopping. She purchased two Colt .45 pistols to replace the pair confiscated by the arresting officers. She also took time to give an interview to an unnamed journalist. When the story appeared on June 7 in the *Dallas Morning News,* its embellishment of Belle's life irritated and angered her. According to a Fort Smith historian, Belle later seized the reporter and beat him with her riding whip as she entered the courtroom for her robbery trial.

Belle's indictments for robbery and horse theft came to nothing. The court found that no witnesses remembered her; those who thought they did were soon discredited. On June 29 a jury exonerated Belle of the robbery charge. On September 30 the jury pronounced Belle not guilty of stealing the mare that carried John Middleton into the river and toward death. Belle no doubt felt vindicated as she headed toward the cabin on the Canadian River.

What she found there wiped any sense of elation out of her mind. Deputy Frank West had shot Belle's favorite horse, Venus, out from under Sam, wounding Sam in the process. Even though the Little Rock *Arkansas Gazette* reported that "fifty shots had been exchanged in the fight," the figure was improbable because Sam had leapt to his feet, seized a pistol, and escaped. Belle found Sam, hiding and hurt, at his brother's house.

Because Belle believed that a Fort Smith court would treat Sam better than a Cherokee tribunal, she begged Sam to give himself up to the U.S. marshal. In order to escape death or scourging at the hands of Cherokee officials, Sam agreed; on October 7 he surrendered in Fort Smith. Then, temporarily free on bond, Sam took Belle to Fort Smith's Seventh Annual Fair. Belle intended to enter several horseback-riding contests, but instead she allowed herself to be the central attraction in a hastily arranged "Wild West" show. Since May 1883, when William F. "Buffalo Bill" Cody introduced his first Wild West "exhibition" in Omaha, interest in the "Old" and "Wild" West had intensified across the United States and in Europe. When shooter Annie Oakley joined Cody in 1885, she added a female dimension to people's perceptions of the West. Perhaps Cody's and Oakley's popularity helped Belle Starr embrace her outlaw image. At any rate, one journalist noted that, à la shooting star Annie Oakley, Belle shot down clay pigeons and glass balls. At least on the surface Belle had become what the public wanted: a fearless woman of the Old Wild West.

As Belle and Sam waited for Sam's hearing to be scheduled, they learned that Judge Parker's court had convicted Sam's father for liquor and stock violations. Parker sentenced the aging Tom Starr to the Southern Illinois Penitentiary at Menard. Sam cursed Cherokee deputy Frank West for his father's and his own troubles and vowed to seek revenge, but Belle suggested that they put the matter out of their minds and attend, along with Pearl and Eddie, a Christmas party at the Surratt home. When they arrived, Belle took a seat at the pedal organ to accompany the fiddler. As a crowd of dancers swirled around Sam, he sat, morose and bitter, near the front door. On December 22, 1886, the *Muskogee Indian Journal* offered the following account of the party-stopping event that occurred after the arrival of Frank West:

> *A few hot words ensued, when Starr pulled his revolver, and West drew his as soon after as he could, but not until he had received a mortal wound, from which he staggered; but, recovering, he sent a ball through Starr, and then fell dead. Starr staggered for about ten feet and then he, too, fell a corpse.*

Some observers recalled that Belle cried; others maintained that she took Sam's death stoically. In any event, she was again on her own, without a man to help support her. To her dismay, Belle also discovered that she was no longer part of the Cherokee Nation. Although Cherokee officials wanted Belle to leave the Nation immediately, federal authorities took a more lenient stance. Before anyone could act on the matter, however, Belle invited a Cherokee named Bill July to live with her as her de facto husband, a long-standing Cherokee practice accepted by the Bureau of Indian Affairs. True to form, Belle had settled on a young, dashing, devil-may-care fellow, who had long since endeared himself to old Tom Starr by running liquor and horses with him. Also in her usual fashion, Belle gave Bill July a new name—July Starr.

Like her own birth family, Belle now lived in a family of disparate ages, backgrounds, and ambitions. According to age, July was in the middle—fifteen years younger than Belle, and five and seven years older than Pearl and Eddie. Eddie, who looked and behaved like his natural father, Jim Reed, acted out his resentment of the situation. After participating in several local fracases, Eddie received severe whippings at Belle's hands, which only infuriated him further. Nor could Belle control Pearl. After Belle tricked the young man Pearl loved into marrying another woman, Pearl became pregnant by the man. Upon discovering her daughter's disobedience, Belle banned her from the Starr home.

As her family fell into shambles, Belle made one more attempt to reform her image. She declared the Starr cabin out of bounds for fugitives. Belle also nursed and otherwise assisted neighboring women in need. But once again Belle's own husband undermined her actions. In early summer 1887 none other than Frank West's elder brother, John, served July Starr with a warrant for horse theft. Disgusted, Belle left July to his own devices. She refused to sanction his actions or help defend him in court. By the end of the summer she saw her young husband committed to a Fort Smith prison, his bail set at $500. Meanwhile, Eddie allegedly helped steal a horse and got shot while resisting arrest. Belle's list of woes seemed never-ending. She called Pearl to her side, but without Pearl's child, Flossie.

Pearl remained in Indian Territory for a while, appearing publicly with her mother. She also shielded Eddie from Belle's growing wrath. Despite the outward semblance of family unity, the Starr family remained conflicted in private. Belle hounded Pearl, who absented herself for a while to spend time with her baby, to give up the child for adoption. On one occasion, Belle brought teenage Eddie to his knees with a beating from a bullwhip; on another, she caused him to flee the cabin after a similar attack. Evidently, Belle felt out of control and resorted to the mechanisms that she had observed over the years: force and violence. Belle's actions served only to estrange her further from her own kin.

In the meantime, Belle made a public show of herself. When Belle and Pearl attended the International Indian Fair in Muskogee in September 1888, they amused the crowd with their riding skills. The *Vinita Indian Chieftain* of October 4 remarked that because "the 'wild Indians,' so extensively advertised, did not show up, Belle was substituted as the leading attraction." If Belle hoped to sanitize her reputation, she chose a poor way to do it. Nor was Pearl and Belle's attendance at parties and dances, along with the youthful July, who tied snake rattles into the ends of his long, black braids for the occasions, designed to make Belle appear "respectable."

Beneath her bravado, however, Belle was running scared. When she discovered that a white tenant on her farmland was a wanted man in his previous home of Florida, she remembered that Cherokee officials had vowed to banish her from the Nation if she ever again helped a criminal. Typically, Belle ended the contract with her tenant, Edgar A. Watson, in the worst possible way, cursing him and threatening disclosure of his crime. She had made yet another enemy.

On February 2, 1889, Belle rode with July into Fort Smith to answer a long-pending federal allegation of horse theft. After spending the night at a friend's place, Belle headed home. As Belle Starr rode toward her cabin on Sunday, February 3, 1889, an unknown assailant gunned her down. Although the primary suspect was Edgar Watson, insufficient evidence existed to indict him. Others surmised that the seething and vengeful Eddie murdered his mother, or that July Starr, reportedly involved with another woman, had freed himself of a wife he no longer wanted. In the end, no one was accused of shooting and killing Belle Starr.

With her favorite revolver in her hands, Belle was buried on February 6, one day after what would have been her forty-first birthday. In a sense, Belle's sudden end was a blessing. She was spared seeing July die in prison, Pearl turn to prostitution, and Eddie killed by an outlaw's bullet. From the perspective of the Belle Starr legend, her violent death also served a purpose—it led to almost instant notoriety. Belle Starr would never be forgotten. She would probably have been pleased that her many troubles were not in vain.

Who, then, was Belle Starr? Was she a gunslinger? No. Belle never killed anyone and, despite embellished tales, only drew her pistol on a few people. Was she an outlaw leader, directing and controlling a wild band of desperadoes? Not according to court records, which indicate that Belle was convicted of only one transgression and charged with few others. As far as controlling anyone, Belle never even learned how to control her own husbands and children.

Rather, Belle was a misfit in her own era. Coming from an unstable family background and living in chaotic times, Myra Maybelle Shirley Reed Starr July never found her niche, but she was not alone. Such women as the Rose of Cimarron, Calamity Jane, Cattle Annie, and Little Breeches also deviated from women's proper roles. But Belle Starr seemed especially enmeshed in a struggle against the world of women. She resented its boundaries, cloying restrictions, and its expectation that women had to depend on men for their opinions and economic support. Yet Belle Starr could not operate effectively in a world of men. She spent her time and energy attempting to reform men who resisted redemption and trying to right unsalvageable situations.

An illustration of the assassination of Belle Starr, which appeared in the National Police Gazette, *February 23, 1889. Courtesy of Glenda Riley.*

Belle also had difficulty living within the boundaries of the law. Although she clearly opposed lawlessness and criminality, she seemed drawn to the lawless and criminal types. One might argue that she was little more than a victim of unfortunate circumstances and evil people. Yet she was a strong woman who exhibited stubbornness, spunk, and sometimes even generosity toward others. Belle Starr was not one to let life shape her. Consequently, driven perhaps by her own psychological makeup, she chose her associates unwisely. And she colluded in her own victimization.

The gravestone of Belle Starr. Courtesy of Glenda Riley.

Even Belle's escape from the Anglo world into the Cherokee Nation proved unsatisfactory. She found herself in the middle of a hotbed of fugitive Anglo criminals, some of whom sought sanctuary in her home and, surrounded by countless Starrs, engaged in liquor trading and horse stealing. Moreover, misinformation, rumor, and prejudice, especially against people like Belle Starr, were rampant in Indian Territory. At the same time, many Indian and Anglo residents hoped to "clean up" the area, especially by eliminating much of its criminal element, including the Starrs. To complicate matters further, despite Belle's status as an intermarried citizen, she was a white woman living in an Indian world. With two sets of laws and customs governing her life, Belle never learned to operate successfully in either culture.

Moreover, Belle's own personality hampered her. Part of her craved adventure and attention. Another part wanted control over situations and people. Still another part hungered for retreat and asylum. Belle found it impossible to reconcile these conflicting desires. When Belle belatedly tried to enter women's society by befriending female neighbors, they ended up preparing her body for burial. Her personal history was inconsistent because her goals were incompatible.

Despite her checkered life, or perhaps because of it, Belle Starr provided excellent fodder for the growing myth of the Wild West. Only a year after her death in 1889, the U.S. Census Bureau declared the American frontier "closed" by virtue of its growing population density. In 1893, near the halls of the Columbian Exposition, historian Frederick Jackson Turner analyzed the meaning of the vanished frontier, while Buffalo Bill Cody's Wild West Exposition played to a huge crowd outside the fair's gates.

During the 1890s and early 1900s numerous other Americans lamented the passing of the Old Wild West. Open spaces seemed to be disappearing, while such ills as robber barons, labor union riots, a soaring divorce rate, and world war convinced many that the vanishing frontier represented a unique and important era in the nation's history—one marked by fierce independence, opportunity, and excitement. Even lawlessness and banditry appeared to be part of the West's mystique.

Although Belle Starr may have been an outcast in her own lifetime, she was a perfect subject for people anxious to idealize and romanticize the disappearing American West. With glee, such people seized on Belle Starr's story and turned her into the West's most daring and glamorous female gunslinger, known as the "queen of the bandits."

9

Jesse James

Borderman

Elliott West

He was one of "the boldest bandits to ever plague the world," dazzling and "dashing and skillful" in his bravery and nerve. He was "the worst man, without exception, in America," coldhearted and vicious. He was a friend of the poor, an enemy to tyrants. Compared to him, "Claude Duval, Robin Hood and Brennan-on-the-moor were effeminate, sunflowered aesthetes." Yet there "was nothing chivalrous in his nature," for "he lived for himself alone" and preyed on those closest to him, "a serpent sending his poisonous venom into the bosom that warmed it to life." Some have said he was "cut off in his prime of strength and beauty." Others have jibed that his baptizing preacher should have drowned him when he had the chance.

Jesse James always got mixed reviews. Successful criminals usually do, but the range of opinions on this Missouri bandit is far greater than usual. One word, however, is scattered often throughout the range of voices: "border." In book titles, Jesse and friends were *The Border Outlaws* and *The Border Bandits* and their deeds were the *During Exploits . . . of Border Train Robbers*. The term is sprinkled liberally among the dozens of potboilers and dime novels in which Jesse steals, murders, gives to penniless widows, and rescues swooning maids. Enemies held him high as glaring proof of the chaos waiting when society marked too poorly the border of rightful law. And after years of angry exchanges, scholars like Frederick Jackson Turner would complain about all the attention given to men like Jesse, "that line of scum [on] the waves of advancing civilization" who were consumed by "border warfare and the chase."

"Border" turns out to be a useful term in describing Jesse James's life, reputation, and place in our popular culture. At the time, it described the country where Jesse, Frank, and their gang operated—western Missouri,

eastern Kansas, northwestern Arkansas, and eastern Indian Territory, the far western border of the American South. As we look back, however, the term takes on other meanings. The Jesse James of fact committed his crimes along the historical boundary between two American eras, the age of sectional war and the age of industry. His myth took its shape from those same years, and as the flesh-and-blood outlaw met his bloody end, the mythic Jesse James was approaching another kind of border. He evolved neatly from a contentious legend of the first era into a national hero for the second. The western legend who emerged, and who continues to ride through American dreams, was a borderman who had skirted the lines among many parts of American history and our understanding of who we are.

In 1841 Robert and Zarelda Cole James moved from Kentucky to Clay County in western Missouri, a neighborhood of farms and woodlands that would remain the center of the family's bloody story for the next half century. Jesse Woodson James was born in September 1847, four years after his brother, Alexander Franklin. Their father, a minister, died in 1850 while prospecting in California. Five years later, their mother married Reuben Samuel, a medical doctor and farmer. Four children followed: Archie, John, Sallie, and Fannie.

"The border" in these years referred to a stretch of country from Council Bluffs on the north, down Missouri's western boundary, and through the land between Arkansas and Indian Territory. This region of new farms attracted a mixed population of tens of thousands during Jesse's first fifteen years and was a launching place for many people's journeys to the Pacific Coast. Life was unsettled and the general mood of the area was competitive. The border drew a lot of hard cases.

Although the word was usually not applied to it, there was another border in these years—the one between North and South. Values and lifeways in the two sections were increasingly in conflict in the 1850s, and where they merged along this line, they were chafed and raw. Emigrants heading westward moved in two broad streams, from north and south of the Ohio River Valley, converging in middle Missouri River ports, such as Kansas City and Atchison, and in the surrounding countryside that included Clay County. Factions from North and South were tossed together along the turbulent border where East met West. As national tensions were reaching their peak, Jesse and Frank grew up at this intersection—at the crosshairs of these two American dividing lines.

Virtually nothing outside of folklore is known about the brothers' childhoods. They developed their own personalities. By tradition, Jesse was mercurial and inventive, while Frank was more solid but persistent and dogged. As they grew older, their personalities were usually complementary, but there are hints as well that the brothers clashed. They presumably worked hard at the usual chores of farm life. Their stepfather did rather well, and the family probably wanted for little. Considering their mother's prominent role in their later lives, a clearer look at Zarelda would be useful, but, except that her personality was formidable, there is not much to learn. Nothing, in fact, suggests anything for Jesse and Frank except a normal upbringing—or as normal as possible in the most troubled part of America.

The Civil War exaggerated the worst of border life, and it proved to be the shaping event of Jesse's adolescent years. Frank volunteered immediately for the South, favored by their high-tempered mother, but Jesse, only fourteen years old, stayed behind. Formal Confederate forces in the state were soon defeated. Missouri, however, remained at war, and, except for Virginia, more engagements were fought there than in any other state. Southern opposition came from guerrilla forces led by men whose names would inspire remarkable hatred and loyalty: William Quantrill, William "Bloody Bill" Anderson, George Tate, and others. Frank fought on and off with these irregulars throughout the war. The guerrillas harassed troops and Unionist civilians in Missouri and Kansas and found refuge among clusters of sympathizers, like the "Cracker Neck" neighborhood east of Kansas City. Frustrated Union regulars and militia fought back as best they could.

It was a very nasty business. All sides were guilty of atrocities and innumerable petty cruelties. The lunacy reached its height in the late summer of 1863, when the Union commander, Brigadier General Thomas Ewing, tried to slow the guerrillas by arresting the wives, mothers, and sisters of some of their leaders. The maneuver failed tragically when the Kansas City Hotel, where they were confined, collapsed, killing five, including "Bloody Bill" Anderson's sister, and injuring several more. A week later, Quantrill led his infamous attack on Lawrence, Kansas. Frank James rode with him. More than 150 civilian men were murdered, some in front of their families, and the town was leveled before the guerrillas returned to their Missouri strongholds. Ewing responded on August 25 with his General Order Number Eleven. All persons in Jackson, Cass, and Bates Counties living more than a mile from a principal town were forced to abandon their homes. Anyone who could prove his or her loyalty could stay at a military post. The rest had to leave the area within fifteen days. As usual, even those in command were not in control. Troops and militia killed some of the twenty thousand evacuees and looted and destroyed the property of many more.

Around this time, according to tradition, the war's viciousness came home to the Samuel farm. According to a well-rooted story, a clutch of Union militiamen came in search of Frank. They abused and insulted a pregnant Zarelda Samuel. With a rope they hoisted Dr. Samuel by his neck several times from a tree limb, choking him to unconsciousness. When neither told the militia what they needed, the men chased and ruthlessly lashed young Jesse, again with nothing gained. Perhaps this really happened, or it might be a distillation of common experience in what had become a brutal theater of the war. In any case, according to local lore, this attack turned Jesse toward a life of violence. Sometime between the fall of 1863 and the following spring, he joined the guerrillas.

A rare photograph from this time shows an open-faced, reasonably handsome boy. Writers would make a lot of his clear blues eyes that were said to bore into whatever was in front of them, and, in fact, this Jesse has a direct and confident look remarkable for a sixteen-year-old. Perhaps he earned it. He rode with Anderson, now the guerrillas' prime leader, in a withering campaign against Union troops and militia. He helped in the slaughter of twenty-five unarmed soldiers in the "Centralia massacre" and in the killing of a hundred more in a battle the same day. He was shot twice. A bad chest wound left a large scar. Another bullet, either taken in battle or fired accidentally by Jesse himself, took off the end of the middle finger on his left hand. He was nicknamed "Dingus." By one account this came from his Baptist-pure exclamation after he shot off his fingertip: "That's the doddingus pistol I ever saw."

Sometime in the late spring of 1865 Jesse was shot again, an injury that became entwined in his life and legend. It was another bad chest wound, and his slow recovery took place partly at the home of relatives outside Kansas City, where he was nursed by Zarelda Mimms (who went by Zee), a pretty cousin named for his mother. His attraction toward her would grow into something more serious. As for the wound itself, no evidence shows how he got it, but a persistent story claims that soon after Appomattox, he and a few friends tried to surrender at Lexington, Missouri, only to be attacked by soldiers. Friends would say later that this incident set the conviction in Jesse that he and his fellows would never be allowed to lay down arms and live peaceably.

The war did provide one sure and vital bridge between Frank and Jesse and their outlaw days. In 1862 or 1863 Frank met another Quantrill irregular, Thomas Coleman (Cole) Younger, and his brother, James. All three hailed from the same area. Like Jesse, Cole claimed to have joined the guerrillas after family, in this case his father (ironically a Unionist), was abused and finally killed by militia. He became one of Quantrill's chief subordinates and was prominent in the Lawrence raid. By the time Jesse joined, Cole had left for California, but he returned to Missouri after 1865. Cole and James Younger and two other brothers too young to fight in the war, Robert and John, would join Frank and Jesse in their rush to notoriety.

Jesse Woodson James at age seventeen, already seasoned to border warfare as a Confederate guerrilla. Courtesy of the Western History Collections, University of Oklahoma.

Whatever happened in those closing days of the conflict, Jesse and Frank were back on the Samuel place by late 1865. Little is known about the next few years except that the brothers were at the farm, helping run a reasonably successful operation. That is of some importance. If, as later claimed, they were being pressed and hounded by wartime enemies, their open presence and easy movements seem a little odd. Jesse healed up and was baptized in nearby Kearney. He developed an eye for horses and a reputation for finding, raising, and racing fine animals. A passing visitor would have seen one of many scarred veterans presumably settling in for an ordinary life. This, however, was about to change.

In 1865 there was no doubt where Jesse James stood along the borders of American regions. He was a southerner in sympathy and action. Neighbors and acquaintances would have known him as one survivor among hundreds who had ridden under the black flag of Quantrill and Anderson. That was the association made when he and Frank embarked on what would become the most widely known criminal career of the day.

Not surprisingly, border violence never stopped after Lee's surrender. There were reprisals by both sides. A minority of guerrillas also reapplied their hit-and-run skills to new purposes. Wartime raiding became peacetime robbery. One target was especially popular—a bank. Not only were banks the most obvious concentration of money; they also represented to many an outside authority and an invasive northern institution. These border thefts were the birth of modern bank robbery.

Historians later would speculate that Jesse and Frank were present when several banks were robbed in Missouri and Kentucky between 1866 and 1868, but no good evidence connects them to any crime before December 7, 1869. On that day, two men took $700 from a bank in Gallatin, Missouri, shooting and killing an unarmed cashier before heading for Clay County.

The fleeing men abandoned a horse that was soon traced to the Samuel farm, and when lawmen approached the house Jesse and Frank burst from the barn on horseback, jumped a fence, and escaped in a hot exchange of pistol fire.

The Kansas City *Times* described the pair as "very desperate and determined men" experienced in "horse and revolver work," but the search cooled after family offered alibis and locals vouched for the brothers' characters. In June 1871 four robbers hit a bank barely over the Iowa line. Descriptions fit the James brothers, Cole Younger, and a man who would be an associate over the next several years, Clell Miller. Ten months later, five men grabbed $600 from a Columbia, Kentucky, bank and shot to death a clerk who raised an alarm. A furious posse pursued, but once more the thieves slipped away. The crime was more than five hundred miles from Clay County, but investigators concluded that Frank, Jesse, and Younger had been posing as horse traders in the area for weeks, and authorities charged the crime to what now was considered the James-Younger gang. Over the next year, the gang was accused of two more brazen robberies: one at the Kansas City fair and the other at a bank in Ste. Genevieve, Missouri, where the bandits shouted hurrahs for Confederate guerrillas as they galloped out of town with $4,000 and the teller's watch.

These early events set a pattern for the next decade. The James brothers (if they were the culprits) chose an especially brazen crime—the daylight robbery of a bank, a town's most prominent public target. They were not reluctant to kill people; in three robberies they murdered two men, one without resistance or provocation. They had a talent for evading pursuit; outside Gallatin they kidnapped a farmer as a guide, and in Kentucky they doubled back and around the posse. They protested their innocence publicly, but from a distance—in published letters claiming they were falsely accused by wartime enemies. Back home they were protected by family and probably by some friends, but both Frank and Jesse also showed a remarkable gift for social camouflage. They almost never identified themselves to strangers, showed no interest in notoriety, and had rather forgettable faces. Long after their names were familiar throughout the nation, this pair could walk unrecognized down any street in the country, even in nearby Kansas City.

The well-worn pattern of bank robberies was broken in July 1873, when the gang pulled a rail from the tracks outside Council Bluffs, Iowa, and derailed an engine of the Chicago, Rock Island, and Pacific Railroad. After looting the train's safe and stripping passengers of all valuables, the bandits, wearing Ku Klux Klan hoods, ran for the Missouri border. This theft claimed another life—the engineer, who was crushed trying to protect the passengers by slowing the engine as it leaned and toppled.

Like bank holdups, train robberies were a new phenomenon that garnered much public attention. The first one had occurred a few years earlier in Indiana, but the James-Younger gang would quickly seize the title of the nation's leading train thieves. The audacious next theft, a half year later at Gads Hill in eastern Missouri, made a special splash. Bandits seized the local depot just before the train pulled in, jumped aboard, and left with cash and loot from the express safe and from the pockets and purses of travelers. The bandits had a theatrical flair. Victims were selected from soft-handed males—the bandits swore they would take nothing from workingmen—and as the leader left, he presented a train worker with a carefully worded account of the incident. In effect, the thieves issued a press release; a blank spot was left where the amount stolen could be filled in.

Ten months after this bit of bravado, the gang was suspected of another criminal flamboyance—back-to-back robberies of a bank in Tishomingo, Mississippi, on December 7, 1874, and of a train not far from Kansas City the next day. Supposedly, the James-Younger gang divided forces and coordinated the thefts, which totaled nearly $40,000. The following September they were accused of striking far to the east to rob a bank in Huntington, West Virginia, of $10,000. One of the bandits in this robbery, killed while fleeing westward, was a Missourian previously thought to be a cohort of the James brothers. The dramatic, wide ranging crimes fed a growing popular fascination with the James-Younger gang. Newspapers from Boston to San Francisco kept readers apprised of particulars of what seemed a bold and stylish banditry. Curious readers now knew that Jesse was a family man, for word was published of his marriage in April 1874 to his cousin Zarelda (Zee). Not long afterward, Frank eloped with another Missouri girl, Annie Ralston. Most stories agreed that the brothers would be devoted husbands and fathers. The bold bandits' image took on a somewhat more human face.

Authorities, on the other hand, were not amused. Lawmen seemed incapable of finding the handful of men accused of crimes in six states, despite a consensus of opinion about who they were and the general neighborhood where they hid. The heat was increasing, however. Bankers earlier had offered rewards for the brothers' capture, but banks were, after all, local businesses with limited resources. Railroads were a different matter. When the outlaws began robbing trains in 1873, they assaulted some of the nation's largest and wealthiest corporations with interests spanning the continent. Railroads and express companies quickly began to use their unmatched power to intensify the search for the men who had taken their money, destroyed their property, killed and injured their employees, fleeced their customers, and stung their pride. To trace down Jesse and Frank, railway officials hired the Pinkerton Detective Agency, famous as much for its tenacity and ruthlessness as for its success.

These efforts made it all the easier for the gang's admirers to celebrate their boldness and evasive skills. The outlaws "only laugh at authorities," a journalist wrote, "and seemingly invite their sleepy enterprise." Using the Pinkerton Agency also fed the belief, encouraged by Jesse and Frank, that they were simple farm lads harassed by looming outside institutions, in this case a northern firm employed by those symbols of distant, uncaring power: the railroads. The Pinkerton Agency's failures—in a backroads firefight, two agents (and John Younger) were killed, and another was found murdered after trying to infiltrate the Samuel household—brought derisive hoots and loud applause.

A single episode at this point did more than any other to solidify the brothers' image as the victimized underdogs. Frustrated detectives, convinced that Jesse and Frank were hiding at their mother's home, made an aggressive move. Near midnight on January 26, 1875, a flaming fabric ball was thrown through a window of the Samuel home. As Zarelda and Reuben Samuel kicked it into the fireplace, a blazing metal missile followed it, and when it too was shoved into the fire, it exploded. Shrapnel tore into the side of Archie Samuel, the young half brother to Jesse and Frank, and Zarelda's hand was horribly mutilated. Archie died at dawn; his mother's hand and part of her arm had to be amputated. If Jesse and Frank were there, they soon fled. Pinkerton later claimed that agents only tossed an "illuminating device" into the darkened house after its residents had refused to come out. Whatever the facts, bloody reality now meshed with evolving myth. Anyone so inclined could easily see abusive authority assaulting a central symbol of traditional good—the home. A weapon at once cowardly and impersonal had killed an innocent boy and maimed an older woman. An explosion in the night seemed to confirm, not in fact but emotionally, the myth forming around the James boys.

Much of the Missouri press howled in outrage and contempt against the Pinkerton Agency and, indirectly, its employers. The brouhaha tended to drown out the mounting evidence that the James and Younger gang continued committing crimes along the border. Just where the gang was at any time, of course, was a matter of contemporary conjecture and future folklore. Between the more publicized bank and train robberies from Iowa to West Virginia, the outlaws probably moved between their home ground in Missouri and northern Texas, where they had friends and family roots. Stories floated around of small-scale banditry near Denison, Texas, and of a lucrative stage robbery far south near San Antonio. In January 1874 another stage robbery near Hot Springs, Arkansas, added a mythic dash when one of the bandits returned a watch to a veteran of the Confederate army out of loyalty to the stars and bars. Almost surely there were many smaller thefts from merchants and individuals never connected with any gang members.

Who took part in any particular crime was just as hazy. By 1875 it was widely argued that the gang had a core group of eight men: Frank and Jesse James; Cole, Bob, and Jim Younger; Clell Miller, Charlie Pitts, and Bill Chadwell. In addition, they often took on young men from the neighborhood to hold their horses and for the criminal equivalents of grunt labor. Only part of the group might be present even at the major robberies, however, and in cases like the Mississippi and Kansas thefts their forces might be divided.

So the remarkable contradiction persisted. At the time of the Pinkerton attack on the Samuel home, the James brothers were the most famous outlaws in the nation. Yet the gang's shifting makeup, as well as their talent for invisibility, made it possible to argue without a smirk that Jesse, Frank, the Youngers, and others were law-abiding citizens framed by malicious enemies. In early July 1876 a train was stopped in Cooper County, Missouri, and was robbed of $15,000. The practiced style of the thieves and the location, only three counties away from the Samuel farm, made the gang the obvious suspects, and when Missourian Hobbs Kerry was arrested after flashing large wads of money, he confessed and named Jesse, Frank, and the others as his fellow culprits. "Liar," Zarelda Samuel answered, and the *Times* published yet another letter, reputedly from Jesse, denying everything and promising an alibi. The editors tacitly agreed and turned their scorn on the paid "thief-catchers" who "kill twelve-year-old boys [and] blow off the arms of old women."

This situation made the news from Northfield, Minnesota, all the more stunning. On September 7, 1876, eight bandits tried to rob the Northfield bank. It quickly became a bloody botch. Two outlaws wounded a fleeing employee and shot to death a balky cashier after slitting his throat. On the street a premature alarm turned into a chaotic gun battle. Local shopkeepers blazed away with rifles, killing two of the bandit lookouts and wounding another. A Swedish immigrant, baffled by shouts in a foreign tongue, died under the robbers' fire. In a thorough scouring of the area, another outlaw was killed and three more were captured. The last two escaped.

Identification of the dead and apprehended seemed to confirm all charges against the gang. Clell Miller, Bill Chadwell, and Charlie Pitts were killed. Cole, Jim, and Bob Younger were wounded and subsequently captured. Somehow, the last two evaded several hundred pursuers in a southward flight through Iowa and Nebraska, and informers soon reported that the James boys were back in their home territory after a long, grueling journey. The

Youngers were jailed but treated well. While in captivity, Cole proved as adept at cultivating sympathy as he was at denying guilt when he was free. He chatted with curious visitors, gave public apologies, cited scripture, and spoke fondly of Sunday school. The three corpses were turned over to medical students for dissection.

The debacle began a critical time in the brothers' lives and in the shaping of their myth. Jesse and Frank were on a desperate run without seasoned companions. With six of eight names confirmed of the gang's personnel, many who had honest doubts concluded that all along the James boys had been at the center of the remarkable string of crimes. In his criminal career and in how he faced the public, Jesse was about to move in another direction.

Cole, Bob, and Jim Younger pleaded guilty in the Northfield killings and were sentenced to life in the Minnesota state prison. Suddenly gangless, Jesse and Frank fled to Tennessee, where they lived with their families near Nashville as J. D. Howard and B. J. Woodson. Evidence later suggested they had moved their families there in late 1875, shaken perhaps by the Pinkerton raid. Until about 1879 Frank worked at various enterprises while Jesse farmed, did some trading, speculated in commodities, and wagered at horse racing. Their lives were inconspicuous, highly domestic, and, in one way, quite productive. Zee gave birth to her first child, Jesse Edwards, several months before Northfield, and to a daughter, Mary, in July 1879. Robert Franklin, the only child of Frank and Annie, also was born during this time. It would be years before the children would learn their true last name. Jesse took the masquerade a step further, always calling his son and namesake "Tim."

This three-year hiatus offers a chance for a more probing look at the legend growing up around Jesse and the James gang. It was well entrenched by the time of Northfield, and during the following months, speculation about their whereabouts deliciously deepened the mystery surrounding them. Some said that they had run to Mexico to start a new life. Others claimed that Frank and Jesse were in the far-western mining camps, digging honestly for gold and silver. Because they were nowhere to be seen, they seemed to be everywhere. Front-porch whittlers and pickle-barrel detectives were free to stretch the limits of the absurd. By one story, Jesse the scamp was posing as a Republican and supporting Grant. By another, the ever-devout borderman had turned to preaching and was spreading the gospel from Baptist pulpits throughout the South.

The last two rumors were reminders of the setting and situation that created the legend. Years later Jesse would be called "western," but while he was alive and robbing his myth was unabashedly southern. This myth was born out of the hatred and resentment between North and South. Its context was Reconstruction, one of the most revealing and contentious times in American history. The first robbery charged to them, that of the Gallatin bank, came soon after congressional rule was firmly set and operating in the former Confederacy. The Northfield rout occurred shortly before the contested presidential election of 1876, the traditional marker for Reconstruction's end.

Missouri took no direct part in that troubled postwar process, but its many Confederate sympathizers identified with states that did. In fact, with so many citizens on either side of the issues, Missouri probably was more passionately torn over Reconstruction than states that knew it firsthand. The myth of Jesse James found its first shape in this charged atmosphere along the border between the Union and defeated Confederacy.

Most directly, the James-Younger gang was said to have been forced into anonymity by false charges from carpetbaggers and enemies from the war, some of whom, it was claimed, were the true perpetrators of the crimes. Soon after the first charges against him, Jesse wrote the Kansas City *Times* to say that he had lived by the law since leaving the guerrillas, but he would never hand himself over to his accusers, the "bloodthirsty poltroons" who meant him harm. Those admirers who thought the boys were the culprits believed the brothers were striking a few final blows for the mistreated South. The cashier killed in cold blood in the Gallatin bank supposedly had been mistaken for S. P. Cox, the federal officer responsible for "Bloody Bill" Anderson's death. In an especially laughable stretch, Cole Younger later claimed that the gang chose the Northfield bank because they thought it held some funds of Benjamin Butler, hated by southerners for his administration during the Union occupation of New Orleans.

Another southern postwar theme emerged from the gang's early crimes. After the fourth robbery attributed to them, a local journalist wrote: "we are bound to admire it and revere its perpetrators." These men and others like them, he added, were poetry personified, chivalrous souls who might have supped with Arthur at the Round Table. The journalist's admiration is puzzling, given the specifics of the crime—snatching a tin money box at the Kansas City fair, firing at the cashier and missing, wounding a young girl in the leg. Like much of the boys' career, however, this sordid business was cut and retrimmed to fit the South's changing perception of itself. Defeated and humiliated southerners were engaged in their own reconstruction. They were reflexively reshaping the remembered South into an idyllic land of heroic grace, honor, gallantry, and beauty. The James brothers were tailored to match this reimagined past. Men like the James brothers were criminals, it was claimed, because the "social soil" of the new America starved their kind of heroism. They were "bad because they live out of their time."

The journalist who praised the gang for its tin-box heroics would play as great a role as Jesse or Frank in creating the James myth. He was John Newman Edwards. A Virginian, he had come with the human tide to Missouri in 1850, fought with the Confederate General Joseph O. ("Jo") Shelby, followed Shelby briefly into Mexico after the war, and returned to Kansas City to help found and edit the *Times* in 1868. Few ex-Confederates were less repentant. None had been caught up more completely in the southern cause as romance. Edwards compared Quantrill and the border guerrillas to errant knights and to gladiators who fought beside Spartacus. Jesse was innocent, he said, but he agreed that former guerrillas had committed the crimes. He praised their spirit and élan. They struck their blows "in the teeth of the multitudes." They stole not for money but for "the wild drama of adventure." They had far less in common with ordinary thieves than they did with the Old South beaux ideals of Lancelot and Ivanhoe.

The specific mood of the time colored the universal elements of the legend. Jesse James was portrayed as an American Robin Hood for giving to the weak and impoverished what he stole from the rich and powerful. The most famous story has Jesse and Frank stopping at a widow's door to buy a meal. When they learn a banker is on his way to foreclose on her house, Jesse gives her money for the mortgage and makes sure she will demand a receipt. Then he waits down the road for the banker and takes the money back. There is nothing in the record to support this story, which fits a folk pattern in many cultures. The tale of the widow's mortgage is likely an invention to testify that Jesse, similar to bandit heroes throughout history, had a tender heart and openhandedness. The particulars here are what seem significant: the victim represented a symbol of economic Yankeedom, the banks that Jesse also robbed openly, and in many versions the banker is a carpetbagger to boot.

Just as vital to the James brothers' image was their deep love for—and their intense loyalty to—family and kin. Jesse supposedly had been brought into the war by the bullying mistreatment of Dr. and Mrs. Samuel. Devotion between mother and sons ran especially deep. Zarelda Samuel defended her boys on every charge and called them affectionate and dutiful. Jesse doted on Zarelda, and without getting too Freudian, something might be made of his marrying a woman named for his mother.

It's also important not to miss the obvious: America's two most famous bandits were brothers—and partners with Cole, Jim, and Bob Younger. A decade after the gang's demise, the Dalton brothers were robbing trains and banks in the same area of the country. Family crime has always been an inherent part of American culture, but this series of prominent brotherly felons was unique.

Near the height of his career, the man on horseback (purported to be Jesse James in this photograph) mimics his dangerous, dashing reputation among family and friends. Courtesy of the Amon Carter Museum, Fort Worth, Texas.

This fraternal theme had a special appeal in the Reconstruction South. The family, like the new myth of a chivalrous South, took on an inflated significance. With the collapse of authority and occupation by a widely distrusted government, people relied far more than usual on kinfolk and the most trusted nearby friends. This innermost circle seemed the only thing they could depend on, and, for years after surrender, these bonds remained important for everyone, including thieves. This pragmatic reliance on family became another part of the ideal of the lost South. Family and neighborhood loyalty was elevated as a cardinal virtue of a vanishing world.

Every nuance of this southern myth was contrasted to the North and its people. If southerners were said to have fought with an individual flair and lived by a chivalrous code, the North was plodding ahead, machine-like, toward a future of factories and dollar chasers. Southern dedication to family and a close radius of neighbors was giving way to a faceless mass culture. The James brothers, as southern heroes, were created as exemplars of the good side of these paired opposites. The Jameses and Youngers were not thieving killers but gallant banditti, striking out against powerful alien institutions—railroads and banks. They embodied a doomed romance, fierce localism, and familial loyalty thought to be under siege from corrupt and soulless authority. And their enemies helped. The Pinkerton raid could not have been better designed to show this new American order—faceless, mechanistic, unfeeling—brutally assaulting an older decency and innocence.

Of course, not all Missourians saw things that way. The James myth had an enormous visceral appeal. It was like a shouted taunt across a bitter divide. Opinions on the other side were just as passionate. To Union veterans and supporters of Reconstruction, Confederate guerrillas were not Arthurian knights but traitorous bushwhackers and cowardly renegades. Farmers who resisted development were deadweights on a nation straining toward greatness. Close-knit and clannish settlers were scorned as lazy rubes and inbred, ignorant sluggards.

In the North a minor genre of books and articles blended comedy with a withering critique of the southern border. In 1867, riding through northwest Arkansas just south of the Missouri line, a northern tourist met a man in a collapsing cabin, who was flabbergasted to learn that Lincoln had been dead two years. "I asked him if the Arkansas Legislature had met during the winter," the visitor recalled. "He did not know, but was certain they had not met in his neighborhood." The experience led the Yankee to comment on the typical "sallow-faced, stoop-shouldered, lank, long-haired, angular and awkward" southerner in the backwoods borderland:

> *What does the "native" before-mentioned care for education, so long as he can get along without it? Nature has saved him the trouble of brain or hand labor. . . . There are places where men do not live in any true or exalted sense; they simply vegetate as do the beets and carrots, lifting their heads it is true into the air and light of heaven, but rooted all the while to the sordid earth.*

The northern press mocked the crime wave blamed on the gang. The *Chicago Tribune* thought that the thefts and murders "are a disgrace to [Missouri], and argue a degree of inefficiency or cowardice upon the part of the state authorities." A Pittsburgh paper dubbed Missouri "the bandit state," where "notorious robbers and cut-throats" operated virtually at will. Boosters warned that Missouri would never move ahead if weighed down by this reputation. When the prominent reformer Carl Schurz ran for reelection to the U.S. Senate in 1874, he argued that until the criminals were caught, ambitious immigrants would avoid Missouri, capital would flow elsewhere, and property values would drop steadily. The future would sour. All this, of course, echoed the gibes of easterners. Incompetent government and killers running loose—what else could one expect from snoozing primitives in the land of the Beet People?

Originally, the James myth found its power in the crackling tension between these sets of views. In the waning months of Reconstruction, the gang suddenly moved to the center of this impassioned conflict over current politics and the past and future meanings of the South. In March 1875 the Missouri legislature considered a joint resolution that would have granted the James and Younger brothers full amnesty and pardon for anything done during the war and guaranteed special protection and fair trials on all postwar accusations. As guerrillas, the brothers had "gallantly periled their lives and their all in defense of their principles." They had tried to put war behind them, but government accusations had driven them from honest toil into hiding. The resolution hinted darkly that robberies and murders might have been done by the very officials who leveled the charges at the gang and then "arm[ed] foreign mercenaries [Pinkerton detectives] with power to capture and kill." Jesse and Frank, in any case, were models of southern manhood: "too brave to be mean, too generous to be revengeful, and too gallant and honorable to betray a friend or break a promise." Missouri should pursue the true culprits and return these wronged citizens to the bosom of family and neighbors.

The resolution would have made the James legend a legislative dictate. Within its overripe rhetoric we can see Americans still looking across the deep divide of North and South. It reveals plenty about both Reconstruction America and the popular culture of banditry. And it almost passed. A strong majority of fifty-eight to thirty-nine supported it, but a joint resolution required a two-thirds vote, so it remained a historical footnote.

The first stage of the James myth had reached its high point. At this moment, Jesse's image was of a gallant cavalier—chivalrous and bold, southern virtue saddled up and ready to ride. It had no appeal outside the region and, in fact, drew whistles and applause by flicking its chin at anyone outside the Confederacy. But that would soon change. Americans were leaving the Reconstruction era for an age of new divisions. New tensions were felt and new heroes were needed to act them out. The mythic Jesse James would ride out of the South, across boundaries of history and myth, and find his place as a national legend.

Jesse resumed his criminal career on October 8, 1879, more than three years after the Northfield raid, with the robbery of a Chicago and Alton train at Glendale, Missouri. The method and style of the robbery—locals taken and held at a station, the train stopped by an agent's signal, the express safe looted—were so familiar that the boys were immediately suspected. Sometime during the previous months Jesse apparently had decided to return to his earlier enterprise, although Frank decided to stay in Tennessee. The gang at Glendale included a collection of new faces: Tucker Bassham, James A. "Dick" Liddl, William Ryan, Robert Woodson "Wood" Hite, and Ed Miller, whose brother Clell had died at Northfield.

The James saga ran its rapid final course over the next two and a half years. Something important yet diffuse happened with Jesse during the break in the action after Northfield, as the pattern of crimes after 1879 differed in a few crucial ways. Previous robberies had been scattered from Minnesota to West Virginia, but now they were concentrated in a small radius close to the gang's home turf. Although the gang had not shied from violence before, these crimes were especially brutal and reckless. The focus and tone suggested a conscious carelessness, a "catch-me" fatalism. Perhaps the bloodbath at Northfield turned Jesse and Frank into harder men. Maybe they spent the next years recognizing what they were and where they were headed.

The brothers also may have sensed the changing times. With the first easing of postwar passions, their supportive climate of opinion began to dissipate. The claim that thefts and murders were somehow defenses against Yankee persecution was wearing thin. Republicans kept ridiculing the Democratic administration for failing to catch the culprits and "for permitting a Republican state [Minnesota] to perform that duty." Especially after the nasty depression of 1877 the repeated charge that this ineptitude "prevented immigration . . . , the introduction of capital and the growth and development of industries" bothered Missourians who hoped to join the march toward industry and progress. These included Governor Thomas T. Crittenden, a Unionist Democrat with close ties to railroads and business leaders. Except for a few editors and, of course, John Edwards, press support for the James brothers cooled. Many journalists now demanded the crimes be stopped.

In this shifting mood, the next robbery had an especially wrenching effect. On the night of July 15, 1881, several bandits bought tickets on a Chicago, Rock Island, and Pacific train that was heading east from Kansas City. Not far outside the small town of Winston, one of them, dressed in a duster, rose from his seat, pulled a revolver, and shot the conductor in the back, then fired again as the dying man fell out the door. A couple of others joined the killer in firing around the car, fatally wounding an aging railroad employee named Frank McMillan. After throttling an agent, the men rifled the express safe and fled. Missourians in general were not easily shocked, but the viciousness of this crime aroused a widespread outrage, and although Zarelda Samuel and Edwards made the usual denials, the James brothers were widely accused. Frank probably was along this time, as well as Dick Liddl, Wood Hite, and his brother, Clarence.

In the national uproar, with papers such as the *Chicago Tribune* calling Missouri "The Outlaw's Paradise," Governor Crittenden persuaded railroad and express officials to offer substantial rewards for information on the James brothers. The local press admitted the criminals were an embarrassment, and old-line Democrats, who had looked benignly on earlier crimes (like "a medieval saint upon the sins of his devotees," Crittenden later wrote), were quiet and cowed. The general response in the weeks after the bloody robbery was startlingly different from the mood a few years earlier.

Then, astonishingly, the gang struck again. On September 7, five years to the day after Northfield, bandits stopped a train at Blue Cut, just east of Independence. After pistol-whipping an agent, they terrorized and robbed almost one hundred passengers. As wallets and watches were taken, the tall, dark-bearded leader of the thieves, who fit closely the description of the killer in the previous robbery, strode down the aisles. He was Jesse James, he bellowed, and he was taking vengeance on the railroad for its offer of a bounty. After a bit of familiar flamboyance—the leader threatened to kill the engineer, but in the end called him brave and gave him $2 to buy a drink—the bandits took their leave.

Crittenden deplored this "foul stain" on the state's reputation and called on all honest Missourians to lend a hand in catching or exterminating the culprits. More and more of the public agreed. Even the Missouri convention of Confederate veterans commended the governor and called for a return of law and order to the state. In fact, supporters much closer to Jesse and Frank were starting to fall away. Shortly after the last crime, William Ryan, a gang member arrested several months earlier, went on trial for helping with the Glendale train robbery. His prime accuser was Tucker Bassham, who had pleaded guilty to the same crime the previous year. Now, pardoned by Crittenden and pressed by the aggressive Jackson County prosecutor, William Wallace, Bassham told the court a detailed account of the robbery he swore was led by Jesse James. The jury sent Ryan to the penitentiary for twenty-five years.

Other, even wider cracks were appearing within the group. Ed Miller vanished, and it was generally suspected that Jesse had killed him, fearing Miller would follow Bassham in trading a confession for freedom. Three local farm boys, who were lesser lights of the gang, were arrested for the Winston robbery. Greater trouble was brewing much closer to the circle's center. The revived gang included another set of brothers, Wood and Clarence Hite, who were also cousins of Jesse and Frank. Wood and another gang member, Dick Liddl, apparently were rivals for the same woman's affections, and in the fall of 1881 Liddl and a companion beat and shot Wood Hite to death in the woman's house. Here was a touchy situation. In one act Liddl had killed a criminal compatriot and, much worse, had violated the sacred sanctum of border culture—the family. It was time for another line of work.

Liddl secretly surrendered in late January 1882, and authorities quickly put to use the information he spilled. When Clarence Hite was arrested soon afterward and confronted with the mounting evidence, he pleaded guilty and took a twenty-five-year sentence. The web of complicity was rapidly unraveling, and before long, the authorities followed the strands to the central characters in the drama. The end came at the hands of yet another insider who was lured by advantage and by fear for his own life. When Liddl had murdered Jesse's cousin, Wood Hite, he had had help. His accomplice was a fresh-faced new addition to the gang named Robert Ford.

Ford and his brother, Charlie, had taken part in the last train robbery, although Ford himself did little more than watch the horses. Sometime in early 1882 they had made contact with authorities. Turning on Jesse had a triple appeal: they would escape his wrath; they could win pardon for their crimes; and they might walk away with the $10,000 offered for Jesse's capture or death. Jesse was living with Zee and their children in a cottage in St. Joseph, invisible as always even in this city close to his home base. As the gang was dying of internal hemorrhaging, Charlie and Bob were living with Jesse. Either they had won his confidence or he distrusted them and wanted to keep them close. With a few remaining cohorts scattered around the vicinity, the three were planning a bank robbery in nearby Platte City.

The final moment of Jesse's life would become one of the most familiar in American folklore. On the morning of April 3, 1882, the day before the scheduled robbery, Jesse, Bob, and Charlie rose from the breakfast table and entered the living room. The day was warm and Jesse removed his coat, then his gunbelt with two revolvers, and laid them on a bed. He noted that a favorite picture on the wall—by later tellings it was a likeness of his mother, but in fact it was a racehorse—had gathered dust. Standing on a chair, he reached to straighten and clean the picture, turning his back on the Fords. Bob and Charlie edged between Jesse and his guns, drew their own, and fired. Bob was faster, and his bullet tore into the back of his target's head. Without a cry, Jesse James fell to the floor in a pool of blood. Within seconds he was dead. Zee ran to his side, screaming in fury and grief, as the Fords bolted from the house to spread the boast that they had killed America's most famous outlaw. The story moved with them, widening by its own power and being retold as Americans needed to hear it.

The James brothers had remained so anonymous that it was several days before authorities could say for sure that the corpse on the floor was Jesse's. Doubts continued, in keeping with heroic tradition, and stories still circulate about the "real Jesse" living to a ripe age and obscure death in this hollow or on that farm. The murdered body of 1882, well verified by its chest wounds and cropped middle finger, was buried on the Samuel place.

Frank surrendered the following October. His only trial was for the murder of Frank McMillan, the elderly employee shot during the Winston robbery. The only direct word against him was from Liddl, a highly compromised witness, and the jury quickly set Frank free. All other charges were dismissed or dropped. For the next thirty years Frank flitted from job to job. He came up short in the Democratic caucus vote for doorkeeper in Missouri's lower house, but he did work as doorman of a St. Louis burlesque house. He dropped the starting flag for horse races at dozens of county fairs. He died in 1915 at age seventy-two on the Samuel family farm. Frank had kept his distance from the myth, condemning the dime novels and curtain-chewing stage productions about the gang, but he did spend the 1903 season with the James-Younger Wild West Show. Before riding in the final parade of each performance, he would play a silent role in vignette, sitting in a stagecoach as it was robbed.

April 3, 1882: Jesse James the bandit lies dead, but the mythic outlaw will ride on in the national consciousness. Courtesy of the Western History Collections, University of Oklahoma.

Convicted of murder, Bob Ford was immediately pardoned and given an undisclosed reward by Crittenden. Bob toured in a melodrama built around Jesse's demise, although, by some accounts, audiences came mainly to jeer and throw food. As his moment of fame faded, Bob turned enthusiastically to drink. He was shot to death in his Creede, Colorado, saloon in 1892, six years after Charlie committed suicide. Bob Younger died in prison of tuberculosis, but Jim and Cole were paroled in 1901. Jim killed himself soon afterward, asserting in his suicide note that he died a socialist and advocate of women's rights. Cole sold tombstones, traveled with a Wild West show described by one editor as "the poorest ever seen in our city," wrote an autobiography, gained considerable weight, endorsed Prohibition, and frequently delivered a canned lecture titled "Crime Does Not Pay." He died in 1916.

Zee James lived quietly with her children until her death in 1900. She never acknowledged any crime on the part of her husband. Mary grew up to live inconspicuously with her farmer husband near her father's resting place. Jesse Edwards James eventually turned to lawyering after writing *Jesse James, My Father* and being acquitted of train robbery in 1898. His grandmother, Zarelda, provided his alibi. Since Jesse's death, Zarelda had been charging twenty-five cents for a tour of the farm and her son's gravesite, complete with her tearful memories, assurances of her boys' innocence, and rages against the family's tormentors. Stones from the grave were available for a fee. The supply seemed limitless. In 1902, nine years before her death, Zarelda reburied Jesse's remains in nearby Kearney beneath an eight-foot marble monument. Thirty years later the shaft had vanished, chipped and carried away, shard by shard, by admirers and relic collectors.

By then a long shelf of books had appeared. The earliest, such as John Newman Edwards's *Noted Guerillas* (1877), defended Jesse and Frank as noble and persecuted Confederates driven from honorable lives. A spate of new titles hit the market with the gang's return to crime. Most were admiring, but all recognized that Jesse and Frank were the men behind some or all of the robberies and killings. News of Jesse's assassination brought more publications, these with titles referring to his "tragic" and "treacherous" death. One company alone produced nine titles. Dozens of dime novels fed a hungry national audience.

Not everyone was happy with this attention. Stage dramas with lurid versions of the gang's exploits were especially criticized. Twenty years after Jesse's killing, one critic went so far as to seek a court order to stop performances of *The James Boys of Missouri.* It was a question of morality, he said:

> *The dad-binged play glorifies these outlaws and makes heroes of them. That's the main thing I object to. It's injurious to the youth of the country. . . . What will be the effect upon these young men to see the acts of a train robber and outlaw glorified?*

The critic was Frank James.

Frank was asking an excellent question and implying another: why have Americans given such attention to a man who was, by any fair reading, a persistent and unrepentant criminal? In the famous folk song about Jesse's death, Bob Ford is scorned as "that dirty little coward that shot Mr. Howard." The man he killed, who hid behind the Howard alias, had a hand in murdering at least four unarmed persons, shooting one in the back and slitting another's throat. "Jesse stole from the rich and gave to the poor," the song continues, but when he was killed he was wearing a watch taken from a middling stage passenger. A search of the premises found horses, saddles, and a cache of items lifted in petty thefts from farmers and clerks. He never admitted the slightest crime, although a mountain of evidence made him a liar. He would not come in, he said, because political authorities would deny him a fair trial—this in a state whose legislative majority formally declared that they thought him innocent. Jesse is soberly described as unconcerned with mere money, an openhanded, straight-talking man who asked only the same from others. Yet while living under a false name in Kentucky, accused of nearly a dozen major robberies, he sued a neighbor for $56, indignantly claiming the man had made deceitful statements and "acted to injure my credit."

The reason for the continuing fascination, of course, is that Americans have not admired the Jesse James of fact—a lying, murderous, thieving hypocrite. They have invented and celebrated a character who fits the peculiar needs of their time. Jesse certainly helped create his own legend. His gifts at evading capture were impressive, and his criminal theatrics bordered on the brilliant. Flagging down trains, piling rocks on the tracks, seizing stations, galloping boldly out of towns as bank clerks stood with their eyes wide and their pockets empty—the gang's style seemed scripted for dime novels and movies. As thieves go, he was pretty successful. His total take came to about $100,000, or roughly $1,275,000 by 1990 currency standards—about $90,000 per crime. Personally, based on what can be said for sure, Jesse apparently had that mix of likability and menace found in other outlaw heroes.

And he was very, very lucky. Countless times he slipped free from pursuers by turns of fortune. He was helped by his enemies' bungles and by supportive writers who knew how to touch a public nerve. Luck's greatest gift, mythically speaking, was Jesse's death. Just as he was facing capture and the ignominy of prison, just as he was about to become ordinary, he was shot in the back by a turncoat friend. The story of the powerful hero undone through betrayal has fed mythic traditions for millennia. Americans needed their own Caesar and Brutus (or Christ and Judas). Jesse and Bob Ford answered the call.

Jesse James died as he lived: with perfect timing. The James brothers rose to prominence when southerners, stinging from defeat, needed heroes who spoke for their lingering resistance and shaken pride. The gang's image of honor, dash, and adventurous independence fit the emerging cavalier tradition of the Old South, and their victims and enemies, the banks, the railroads, and the Pinkerton Agency, were perfect foils in those angry years of Reconstruction. That appeal, however, could never reach beyond the former Confederacy, and when Jesse and Frank resurfaced after the Northfield fiasco, the climate feeding the early legend was fading badly.

But just then another possibility was opening. America's transformation to a modern industrial state—increasingly urbanized, knit together by new technologies, and dominated by corporate power—generated terrible tensions. As they passed from an era of sectional hatred to an age of harsh class division, Americans looked again for popular figures to act out their anxieties.

Once again Jesse's timing and luck held. Most themes of his first incarnation transferred nicely to the present. Was there resentment throughout the nation toward powerful distant forces controlling everyday lives? The gang's prime targets, railroads and banks, became to many the villainous manipulators of the new America. Pinkerton detectives, seen earlier as Yankee goons, now were pictured as corporate shock troops sent against honest workers in every region. The boys' devotion to mother and home jibed nicely with the late Victorian worship of the hearth as a sacred refuge in a corrupt world. Class divisions were deepening, and the gap was widening between rich and poor—the perfect setting for Jesse's Robin Hood image. It looked like the James gang could be retooled easily for a national constituency of discontent.

But there was a problem. The original mythic Jesse had fought to destroy the sacred Union. Before he could claim to be a national hero, that part of his image had to be obscured. This turned out to be fairly easy. The James brothers, after all, had always lived on the border, with frequent forays into Kansas, Indian Territory, and Texas. The James legend could survive the crossing of the chronological boundary into modern, class-ridden America by stepping over another border, that of regional identity. By shifting the angle of vision only slightly, Jesse the Confederate raider emerged as someone else. He became a westerner.

This transformation could move ahead smoothly once Jesse James was dead and no longer confusing matters by hurting actual people. Frank Triplett's *The Life, Times, and Treacherous Death of Jesse James* (1882) was in the shops only a few weeks after the assassination. Triplett spent barely twenty pages on the war, and even there he wrote that Jesse and the guerrillas combined "the infinite physical endurance of the Western Indian and the indomitable soul and mental qualities of the Anglo-Norman." Elsewhere, he called the gang "Anglo-Norman Comanches." Jesse the Confederate was blurring away. Coming into focus was a character made from the most familiar formula in our national mythology. The best of blue-eyed Europe (the "Anglo-Norman") was joined with the finest savage traits (the Indian's prowess and nobility) to produce a unique and superior blend—the American. From Daniel Boone and Deerslayer through countless characters in movies and novels, this fusion of civilized and primitive virtues has stood tall in the American pantheon. In one sense these heroes are regional, but in another they are national. They might live in the West, but to many they are ideal composites, the best of a common American soul.

At the same time, Jesse brought with him selected virtues from his southern past. As Americans pulled further away from the war, they looked back and saw a lot to like in the Old South, especially its newly romanticized version. Several traits would be grafted onto the traditional western hero, most obviously in Owen Wister's *The Virginian,* the prototype of the modern western novel. The title character took the southern gentleman's civility and sense of honor and dressed them in chaps and boots. His famous showdown with Trampas is a deep South duel migrated to a dusty western street.

Jesse James was the earliest instance of this southern intrusion into the western myth. From then on, what were considered the best characteristics of an idealized South—an easier pace of life, an inner-directedness, an insistence on respect (the Virginian's "When you call me that, smile"), and a code that placed loyalty and principle over profit and practicality—were woven into the western hero's character. Even his speech changed. The rambling monologues of Leatherstocking and other backwoods blabbermouths gave way to the slow drawl, the "Yup," and the "Howdy, ma'am." All this stood in defiance of what many feared in the new America: a driven, regimented, colorless culture of wage slaves and indebted farmers who labored under the yoke of distant money-grubbers and paid-for politicians.

Jesse has played one variation of the western myth, the dashing but doomed outlaw who refuses to kneel to autocrats and bullies. Cut loose from the Confederacy, he has roamed the American nation and consciousness. In dime novels it was not only *Jesse James in New York; or, A Plot to Kidnap Jay Gould* (1890), but also *The James Boys in Deadwood; or The Game Pair of Dakota* (1891) and *Jesse James at Coney Island; or the The Wall Street Banker's Secret* (1898). On the silver screen Henry King's *Jesse James* (1939) was a depression-era morality tale that anticipated *The Grapes of Wrath* (1940), with Frank and Jesse driven to crime when callous railroad officials force the honest farmers off their land. During the anti-establishment mood of the 1960s and 1970s, the Frank and Jesse of such movies as *The Great Northfield Minnesota Raid* (1972) do not specifically go to war against moneyed power. As in *Butch Cassidy and the Sundance Kid* (1969), the bandits are likable misfits finally crushed by a stifling social order.

Westerner and southerner, victim and avenger, ruthless killer and defender of the weak, Confederate raider and Robin Hood, the bandit king has negotiated artfully many boundaries of the American experience. Like so many mythic heroes who seem to know when to die, Jesse James is a survivor, and he shows no sign of going away.

10

Pearl Hart

Desperate Woman or Desperado?

Shelley Armitage

In October 1899 *Cosmopolitan* magazine ran a story about Pearl Hart, a female bandit convicted of robbing one of the last stagecoach lines in Arizona. Written in first person, the article chronicled the circumstances that led the five-foot, one-inch Canadian native to the single criminal act that characterized her life in popular histories, periodicals, and newspapers as a "bandit queen." Aside from the robbery, Pearl Hart broke no other major laws, yet as the photographs that accompanied the magazine piece demonstrate, her interviewers and the public preferred to glamorize her outlaw status. Posed with a Winchester rifle and bandoliers, seated casually in men's pants and suspenders, a cigarette pinched between her fingers, Pearl presented the image of a tough young woman. As she said in the *Cosmopolitan* article: "I was good-looking, desperate, discouraged, and ready for anything that might come." In fact, once Hart realized she could act as accomplice to her own image-making, gaining a measure of status with the public while seeking the ideal of her personal freedom as a female in early-twentieth-century America, she frequently cultivated an ambiguous nature that played to and challenged the expectations of womanhood during her times.

If Hart's self-depiction as "desperate" yet "ready for anything" typified her upon being arrested in 1899, some forty years later she remained just as mysterious and multifaceted. Clara Woody, an Arizona census-taker and amateur historian who met Pearl Hart three times—initially as a witness for a marriage by civil ceremony and subsequently in 1940 and 1949 as a census-taker—indicated some of the mystery surrounding Hart. In the 1940s, when the notoriety of Hart had slipped into folk memory, Woody and other Arizona historians persisted in their search for more details about the western woman's life. Little was known about Hart's childhood, though, during her early western years; not until her release from prison in 1903

were they fairly well documented. Then, after 1903 contradictory accounts about her whereabouts appeared, but by 1910 she seemingly had disappeared. Summing up the ambiguity of Pearl Hart's life and personality in *Globe, Arizona* (1977), Woody wrote:

> *Perhaps the strangest feature of this extraordinary chapter in frontier folk history is the fact that public opinion is split down the middle just as it was in 1899. People are still discovering Pearl Hart, researching Pearl Hart, writing Pearl Hart up for magazines, trying to understand Pearl Hart. Outlaws held an intense fascination for Americans—a fact which social historians are still trying to understand. One possible explanation is that these people do as they please and walk over anybody who gets in their way—something which becomes increasingly impossible for us in these regimented times. We identify with the outlaw and idealize him, ignoring his obvious drawbacks. A female outlaw is rarer and even more interesting than her male counterpart. So you can call Pearl Hart "this pitiful woman," or you can go along with those who think she was "a lovely girl with a heart of gold who wanted to help the sick and needy."*

For these reasons, Pearl Hart remains to this day an intriguing example of the woman outlaw. Late-twentieth-century curiosity about Hart has resulted in a novel, a radio play, and a website. Numerous popular accounts of her life also exist in western magazines. Yet the mysteries of Pearl Hart's desperateness persist. Only by reexamining the facts of her life as well as the conflicting attitudes about who she was can we hope to discover the woman behind the actions.

Historians and popularizers of Pearl Hart do agree upon the details of her early life, the 1899 robbery, and her subsequent conviction. Born in 1871 in the town of Lindsay in Ontario, Canada, Pearl Taylor was reared by a widowed mother and sent to a girls' boarding school in her teens. There, at age seventeen, she met Sam Hart (also called Frank), a "charming" man with whom she eloped. Most researchers believe that Pearl's name and her husband's were aliases. The couple initially drifted around Ontario. Sam was a small-time gambler, a racing tout, and a bartender, occupations that made for a feast-or-famine existence.

Because of these economic straits, Pearl returned to her mother. However, in 1893 Hart won Pearl back for a time through his ever-present charm. He also promised to take her to the World's Columbian Exposition in Chicago. His plan was to work at the exposition in some capacity, but he failed to provide well for her there too. On the other hand, Pearl

Pearl Hart posing for Cosmopolitan *magazine, October 1899. Courtesy of the Arizona Historical Society, Tucson.*

soon was enraptured with the accomplishments of other men—the Indian fighters, sharpshooters, range riders, and alleged outlaws performing in the Buffalo Bill Wild West show.

Pearl may even have become romantically involved with one of these performers. In any event, her husband's lack of success and her own romanticism about western life led her again to leave Hart, and she took a train to Trinidad, Colorado. There she gave birth to her first child, a boy, the father unknown. If she had romanticized the West and western men as compared to her background and marriage, she quickly found single motherhood in the West sobering. Although she tried to support herself and her son working as a domestic, hotel maid, and cook, she was not successful and had to send her son to her mother in Ontario for care.

By 1895, after moving from town to town, Pearl had found work in Phoenix, where she met up with her estranged husband. Sam renewed his pledge of supporting her, insisting that he would get a real job. Having barely survived the intervening years as a camp follower, Pearl consented and the couple settled down for three years as Hart worked as a bartender and hotel manager. This period was the most stable time in their marriage. A second child was born, a girl named Pearl. However, Bert Fireman, historian and journalist in Arizona, later reported what many investigators of Pearl's life speculated: "Pearl had drifted to Arizona in the company of a dance-hall musician and tin-horn gambler.... He was handsome but amoral. He taught Pearl to smoke, drink, and some say even to use morphine. For several years they lived on the tawdry side of Washington Street."

As a husband, Hart not only was an unreliable breadwinner, but perhaps introduced her to the less savory aspects of frontier existence. He also was given to wild swings and extremes in personality. More than once he abused Pearl, and in Phoenix, during an argument, he slapped her unconscious. Fundamentally a rover, Hart went to serve in the Spanish-American War. Tired of his abuse and his unwillingness to put down roots, Pearl was glad to be rid of him. After he left to serve in the war, however, she again was left as a single provider with no consistent or lucrative means of support. She briefly returned to the East, working for two years in New York as a maid. But Hart appeared once again, enticing her back. Pearl then sent her daughter back to her mother, who by now had moved to Ohio and was running a boardinghouse.

The marriage did not last, with Pearl dismissing Sam for the last time. In the spring of 1899 she found a job as a cook at the Mammoth Mining Camp in Arizona just east of Tucson. There she struck up a friendship with a man she called Joe Boot. A miner by trade, Boot first helped the hapless Pearl when the camp closed down, and she was again out of work. The two tried working a claim that Boot had nearby. At this point Pearl began dressing, for practical reasons, in men's clothes. Soon, both partners were completely out of money, for the claim was useless. When she received a letter from her brother in Ohio indicating her mother had heart trouble and that she was needed at home, Pearl was desperate for money even beyond her already dire conditions.

A rifle-toting Pearl Hart strikes a less mannerly pose, again for Cosmopolitan *magazine, October 1899. Courtesy of the Arizona Historical Society, Tucson.*

Apparently, Boot suggested robbing the Florence to Globe stagecoach line, a suggestion that Pearl initially rejected. But after resolving to do no physical harm to the passengers, they proceeded with their plans of the heist, which they thought would be simple in both execution and escape. Pearl and Boot went so far as to check at the stage office in Florence about the scheduled passengers to make sure their efforts would yield some cash.

On May 29, 1899, Joe Boot and Pearl Hart prepared for the event that would catapult these two indigent individuals into the public eye. Utterly unseasoned, either by experience or any real inclination to break the law and successfully get away with it, they situated themselves at a bend in the road of the stage route where the driver would brake.

Well along in his sixty-mile Globe to Florence route, driver Henry Bacon sat alone in the driver's seat. Although he carried a Colt .45 revolver, he hardly expected to use it, because the days of stage holdups had all but passed in Arizona. In fact, the Globe-Florence line was one of the few remaining stage lines in the territory. Three passengers were aboard, suffering the bumps and bounces of the stage on its rugged mountain road: a traveling salesman, a "tenderfoot," and a Chinese man. As the stage approached Cane Springs, a sharp turn demanded that the driver slow down. When he did, two robbers suddenly appeared with pistols drawn, demanding that Bacon halt and the passengers get out with their hands up. One robber kept his .45 on them. The smaller of the two thieves, dressed in boots, overalls, and a white sombrero, searched each passenger, discovering that the salesman carried $380 in cash, the tenderfoot $36, and the Chinese man $5. The bandit, whose generous bosom identified her as a woman, took all the money, plus the salesman's watch, but returned $1 to each so they would have enough for food. The robbers also took the driver's Colt .45, and then rode to the south, threatening the lives of any who dared to follow.

Quickly, the driver unhitched one of the team horses and rode to Florence. Pinal County sheriff W. E. Truman immediately formed a posse, and they found the robbers' trail easy to follow. Amateur in every way, the fugitives seemed merely to lose themselves in the forest off the main road, drifting past the small towns of Riverside and Mammoth, apparently in an effort to use the railroad in nearby Benson as a means of escape. They slept in the brush by day and traveled by night, but the horses became exhausted, and food and tobacco were scarce. Only twenty miles from Benson, they were trapped. The posse had spotted the robbers and decided to wait out the night to surround them.

The following morning, when the officers shouted to awake and arrest the fugitives, Pearl exhibited the wildcat nature that captured the imagination of later celebrity-drumming reporters and photographers. Joe Boot meekly complied, but Pearl sprang up fighting, reproaching her partner with profanity. "One would think," Sheriff Truman told reporters two days after the arrest, "that she is a very tiger cat for nerve and for endurance. She looks feminine enough now, in the women's clothes I got for her, and one can see the touch of a tasteful woman's hand in the way she has brightened her cell. Yet only a couple of days ago, I had a struggle with her for my life. She would have killed me in my tracks could she had got to her pistol. Surely women are curious creatures."

From this point in Pearl Hart's life, public curiosity swirled around the female bandit. Fascination developed, fueled by the local and even national press, when she appeared in jail in the respectable dress of Victorian womanhood, yet posed also in boots, men's pants, shirt, and suspenders, with guns and cigarettes. Rumors also spread about a possible opium habit and her foul language. Still, some observers sympathized with Pearl, justifying

The Yuma Territorial Prison with the prison cells built into its natural wall, circa 1890. Courtesy of the Arizona Historical Society, Tucson.

her behavior because of her family obligations, her impoverishment, or her lack of male support.

These contradictions in female behavior continued to evoke either sympathy or titillation. Then, in November 1899, after two attempted jailbreaks in Florence and Tucson, Pearl was convicted of stealing driver Bacon's handgun. She was sentenced to five years in the Yuma Territorial Prison, a formidable enclave where she would be the first female prisoner.

In 1903, however, Pearl Hart was granted a pardon, perhaps for good behavior and possibly because some argued that women prisoners could not be housed successfully at Yuma. Little is known about Pearl's life after her release. There were reports that she lived initially with her sister's family in Kansas City, Missouri. She seems to have suffered from economic problems there and succumbed to unlawful ways of making money. Then, threatened by local police with a return to Yuma to serve out her term, Pearl all but disappeared from public record after 1910. In his book *Boots and Bullets* (1969), Jesse Hayes gives Pearl's death as December 30, 1955. Other accounts range from individual recollections of seeing Pearl Hart in the area to Clara Woody's research that establishes Pearl as the wife of Calvin Bywater.

Given such limited information and that Pearl Hart committed only one "desperate" act as a woman bandit, why does she continue to intrigue so many writers and readers? Perhaps not only because many of her activities and a consummate identity remain unknown, but because she illustrates the unfathomable lives of most women of her times. Like many women of the late nineteenth and early twentieth centuries, Pearl had to speak through others to speak for herself. That is, her behavior, attitudes, and feelings were described through the words and perceptions of male interviewers, reporters, and local authorities. And even more as a woman criminal, Pearl suffered from yet another layer of established social expectations and attitudes. Consequently, her own "quoted" comments and the reports of her behavior and motivations were largely encouraged by social prescriptions.

Still, any substantive interpretation of Hart's life must come from these subjective sources outside herself. By pairing the documented details of her life with the readings of them by others, we begin to see that Pearl Hart, like many women of her time, worked within as well as against existing social constructions. In her actions and comments, then, are the imbedded psychological and emotional elements that illuminate her personal struggles, desires, and conflicting actions.

One of the earliest examples of the relationship between public opinion and Pearl's nature survives in a recollection of Hart as a girl in Ontario. In 1954 William B. Davy of Joplin, Missouri, wrote to the head of the Arizona Historical Society, Eleanor Sloan, about his childhood acquaintance with Pearl Hart. Davy praised Pearl's natural talents and abilities, saying "she was very pretty and had a wonderful figure and voice, and could imitate a croaking frog, an owl, and a hawk. She was lithesome, blithe, and witty, gushing with fun and jollity, also a wonderful dancer." However, Davy went on to admit that Pearl Hart had one fault: "She was too amorous, accepted too many dates with handsome young men, which finally caused her undoing."

Davy was undoubtedly alluding to Pearl's elopement and consequent relationship with her first husband as being shaped by her earliest encounters with other men. Pearl admitted in the 1899 *Cosmopolitan* article that she naïvely ran off and got married, which unfortunately resulted in "abuse," her infatuation with other men, and her roaming throughout Colorado and Arizona. If these romantic notions motivated Pearl to abandon school and her mother for male charm, they also led her to stay too long in an abusive relationship. Pearl's first love and her marriage involved both physical and economic abuse. Only once in their marriage, during the stable three years in Phoenix, did Sam Hart provide consistently for his wife and daughter.

Pearl's other romance was with the West and its characters. Her late teenage and early young adult years, from age seventeen, when she eloped, to age twenty-two, were shaped and motivated by charming adventuresome males and her own romantic notions of the West. In Trinidad, however, Pearl found herself alone, a single mother and only able to support herself and her son through the odd jobs a woman of her circumstances could find. The "catch-as-catch-can," hand-to-mouth existence that made her a camp follower and forced her to send her son to her mother to raise dashed her immature ideas of a romantic life. Whereas this experience did not prevent Pearl from seeking the companionship and support of other men throughout her life, including that of her husband, this early failure was a reminder that male power was to be reckoned with. It was necessarily a part of every woman's life, in a time when women lacked education and economic independence. This period also signaled Pearl's maturation, a determination to manipulate men in order to realize some of her own desires.

Although badly disappointed, Pearl had a practical sense of survival. During the ensuing years from 1893 to 1898, when Pearl attempted to salvage her marriage, she learned through association with Hart the value of aliases. Shifting identities or reconstructing oneself according to prevailing circumstances marked their marriage from the beginning, as Hart regularly used bogus names. According to historian Bert Fireman, Sam Hart was known as Dan Bandman when he moved to Phoenix in the mid-1890s. As a gambler and ne'er-do-well, he tried to evade the law through such aliases. For example, in Phoenix he and Pearl were accused of breaking a number of city ordinances, with Pearl herself using at least two aliases. Later, after release from prison, she adopted a married name, Mrs. Keeler, hoping to disguise her previous "criminal" associations in Arizona as Pearl Hart. After Pearl's apparent disappearance from about 1910 through 1940, she reappeared, in Clara Woody's opinion, as Mrs. Calvin Bywater. When the two women first met during the civil marriage service where Woody was a witness, the bride had used the name "Pearl." But afterward she never admitted to that first name and insisted on being called Mrs. Calvin Bywater. Thus, early, Pearl learned the benefits of chosen personas and used this ploy of renaming herself throughout her life.

Whether because of emotional attachments or survival techniques, Pearl recognized the shelter and sanctions of the married state. But her boldest and most individualized behavior came during the years she was known solely by her own name. During these years Pearl was separated from her husband or was known as a convicted criminal on her own. During this time, she also had cultivated a complexity for the identity of Pearl Hart. She played on the public fascination with female outlawry and the subsequent, if brief, personal power and freedom such notoriety accorded her. During these middle years of her life, beginning with the robbery in 1899, Pearl also displayed outward signs of the respectable femininity of her times. From dress to behavior, language to stated opinions, Pearl Hart constructed a persona that surprisingly mixed criminal with feminine elements.

Perhaps Pearl Hart resorted to attention-getting tactics and alternating displays of feminine and masculine behavior because, by social standards of her day, she already was a "fallen woman" previous to committing the robbery with Joe Boot. The social prescription for proper and respectful female behavior in the nineteenth century—the "Cult of True Womanhood"—held that middle- and upper-class women should be pious, subservient to men, domestically engaged, and quiet. But since her girlhood, Pearl had relinquished whatever opportunities proper education and traditional marriage would have given her. Pearl's fallen condition also made her a candidate for a redeemed femininity; her victim status paradoxically could be appealing.

Therefore, when she and Joe Boot robbed the Globe stage, journalists first clamored to pass judgment on her male accomplice to explain the circumstances that drove Pearl to such aberrant behavior and to debate the consequences her activity had for the image of the state of Arizona. When Pearl and Boot were captured, one reporter contrasted Pearl's "rosebud mouth" and "baby-like eyes" with Joe Boot, "a weak, morphine depraved specimen of male mortality, without spirit, and lacking intelligence and activity." Sheriff W. E. Truman also recalled that Pearl told him she had robbed the stage to get money to travel to see her sick mother. Newspaperman Paul Hull, editorializing in the *Arizona Graphic,* worried about these mixed messages of sympathy for Pearl. Instead, he thought she was not only "a fallen human" in need of lifting "out of the mire," but one of the worst women in Arizona. He also challenged stories in the eastern press that Pearl was "a highly educated woman of eminent family who had been wronged and shunned by society into becoming a social outcast." For Hull, the most disturbing element of public curiosity about this "fallen human" was the propensity of the "yellow" press to glamorize and thus excuse her despicable state. His damning comments not only reveal a distrust of Pearl's underclass status, but his fear that eastern presses would scoop local reporting and sensationalize the conditions in Arizona, whose citizens wanted to be known as civilized rather than as "wild and wooly."

When Pearl retained her male dress in the Florence jail and complained that Joe Boot had botched the robbery and escape, she confounded the social judgment of her jailers, journalists, and the general public. She also taunted her captors by remarking that if she were a man held up by a woman, she would not say much about it. In addition, she appealed to the vanity and the curiosity of her jailers, posing for local and eastern presses in photographs, once with Sheriff Truman in the background. From the time of her capture to her trial, Pearl capitalized on the public's perception of her uniqueness—smoking cigarettes, speaking in western slang, and talking tough about the heist. A powerless, poor, and desperate if resilient woman before the robbery, she now had access to status, power, and attention.

If male authorities debated the justifications for Pearl's deed and her consequent actions, they also underestimated her as a woman. Pearl clearly manipulated the situation, attempting two escapes yet playing to her vulnerability as a woman in a mock suicide. In Florence she attempted a jailbreak. When that attempt failed, she feigned suicide by swallowing a white powder, claiming to "end it all" as she fell into a swoon. The jailer called the doctor, who chastised her for swallowing talcum powder. Sensing Pearl was more than he wanted to handle, Sheriff Truman had her transferred to the Pima County Jail in Tucson, where, he argued, officials could take better care of a woman prisoner.

But in Tucson, Sheriff Wakefield also underestimated his woman prisoner. Pearl was put in a makeshift cell, and though policed more carefully, her relationship with other trusted prisoners was overlooked. Pearl befriended Ed Hogan, who was sent up for drunken and disorderly conduct. As a trustee, he had free rein in the jail. Professing to have fallen in love with Pearl, he arranged for their double escape, breaking through the lath-and-plaster partition in the ceiling to her upper-story cell. After the escape, one local journalist made fun of the fact that Pearl could squirm out of a mere fifteen-inch hole in the ceiling. She had used a chair on a table below to hoist herself up to the waiting hands of her second male accomplice. The couple fled to New Mexico.

By this time, Pearl Hart clearly knew how to use the full range of her feminine wiles to appeal to public curiosity and sympathy. By doing so, she achieved unprecedented power and control for herself. Her willingness to create any persona to free herself suggests that she was anything but the compliant and contrite female some expected. It was during her escape from Tucson that local presses in Arizona and New Mexico began to tout Pearl as the "bandit queen" and speculated that she was heading up a nest of robbers around Lordsburg, New Mexico. But even as Pearl basked in the unprecedented attentions she received as a cigarette-smoking, foul-mouthed woman robber, she never relinquished her feminine side, as evidenced in her flirty behavior, her occasional womanly dress, and her devotion to family responsibility. On the morning after her escape in Tucson, the Phoenix *Herald* printed a letter received from her brother-in-law in Ohio, pleading for mercy in her case. Along with the news of a sick mother, he particularly mentioned Pearl's opium habit, suggesting yet another explanation for her behavior.

The Arizona Star also reported that Pearl had argued for her release on the grounds of her unequal treatment as a woman. She was quoted as saying she would never consent to being tried by a law under which she or other women had no voice in making or to which women had no power to consent. This was Pearl's most compelling and interesting argument for her freedom. The sympathetic editor for the *Star* concurred with her, humorously concluding: "To carry out what she deemed her right under the principles of our government, she struck out for liberty and at this writing she seems free as the birds in the air."

Yet this writer also hinted that such boldness on Pearl's part ironically argued for even more protection by men. He reasoned that "the intelligence of the escape appeared to create a sentiment favorable to the prisoner. Every true frontiersman hallows the thought that his mother was a woman, and he owes respect and protection to her sex, no matter where she may be nor what her misfortunes may have been."

By this time, Pearl had managed to call up opposing opinions about herself. Her notoriousness encouraged some to want to rescue her, others to condemn her. Still others feared her bad influence, particularly as a poor model for young, impressionable women. Because photographs in the *Cosmopolitan* article so clearly identified her, and because the essay circulated widely in Arizona and New Mexico, western lawman George Scarborough, an assistant U.S. marshal based in El Paso, spotted Pearl and arrested her in Deming, New Mexico. When he returned her to Tucson, he was reported to have worried about the request by two adult women that they get Pearl's autograph for a girl accompanying them on a trip from the East. But Pearl was reported by the *Lordsburg Liberal* to have held her tongue and given a quite "respectable" interview.

In October 1899 Pearl finally came to trial in Florence. The trial illustrated Pearl's apt manipulation of attitudes about women and her own utmost desire to escape them. This woman had posed for photographs, escaped from jail, flirted with inmates, claimed full responsibility for planning the robbery even as she reached through the bars of her jail cell toward Joe Boot, claiming she could never be separated from him. She also pleaded not guilty to the holdup charges. The jury returned a guilty verdict for Joe Boot, with a prison sentence of thirty years, but for Pearl Hart they returned a verdict of not guilty. Although Pearl seemed free for the moment, the judge, furious that the jury could let their personal fascination or sympathies mold their decision, promptly had Pearl rearrested for the theft of Bacon's handgun. On this count and after serious upbraiding by the judge, the jury returned a verdict of guilty, sentencing Pearl to five years in the Yuma Territorial Prison.

Despite her past multiple inventions of herself, Pearl, now convicted of her crime, went to Yuma a hardened woman and a criminal. Whereas Pearl's escapades as an accused woman bandit helped fuel the curiosity and romanticizing usually associated with western desperadoes, declaration of her guilt invited another imposed identity. When Pearl left Florence by train to travel to Yuma to prison, she passed through Mariposa, Arizona, where she drew one of her largest crowds. The reporter in the area described her as smoking cigars, the smoke of which rivaled that of the locomotive. Now viewed as a convict, she entered an all-male world of guards, prisoners, and wardens, where she would face an unprecedented concentration of male power.

When Pearl arrived at the Yuma Territorial Prison in 1899, she was admitted as the only female inmate. Records include a one-page admittance, revealing that she was five feet tall, one hundred pounds in weight, and literate. Awaiting Pearl were physical and social conditions that defined her next four years as well as the remainder of her life.

The Yuma facility was typical of turn-of-the-century prison conditions in the West. Not only was it an all-male facility, but the administration, methods of punishment, work, and general governing attitudes of such institutions were masculine, with no provisions for special physical, psychological, or social needs of women. In addition, the location of the Yuma prison was especially formidable. A desert installation, with portions of the cellblock literally carved out of the desert's sand walls, the prison registered summer temperatures of more than 110 degrees. If an inmate escaped, there was little hope of surviving in the surrounding desert. Included in Pearl's records at Yuma was a newspaper report: "During most of Pearl Hart's incarceration, she was the sole female prisoner. Her cell was enclosed within thick walls located on Prison Hill, a granite bluff on the bank of the Colorado River. Conditions were horrifying. The average span of life of prisoners was about five years."

In prison Pearl quickly moved, in the public eye, from a glamorized freedom-seeking female outlaw to a woman criminal. Like many other women criminals, Pearl suffered from her failure to meet the cultural expectations of womanhood and experienced societal judgment about her "fallen state." In the psychology of early criminology, assumptions about a woman's nature, intelligence, and propensity for deviant behavior shaped already existing social constructions of womanhood.

Because of the standards for female respectability, once a woman becomes a criminal, she disappears into another identity as "moron," "whore," or "villianess." As influential British penal authority Frederick William Robinson opined, "male prisoners exhibit some amount of reason and forethought," whereas a woman behaved more like a "madwoman than a rational, reflecting human being." Thus, according to these standards, a woman prisoner not only was subordinate or inferior as a woman but because of her crime doubly so.

Not surprisingly, Pearl's Yuma files contain the same disparate opinions of her that surfaced because of assumptions about her character as a woman even before her crime. From the beginning, Pearl seemed to recognize

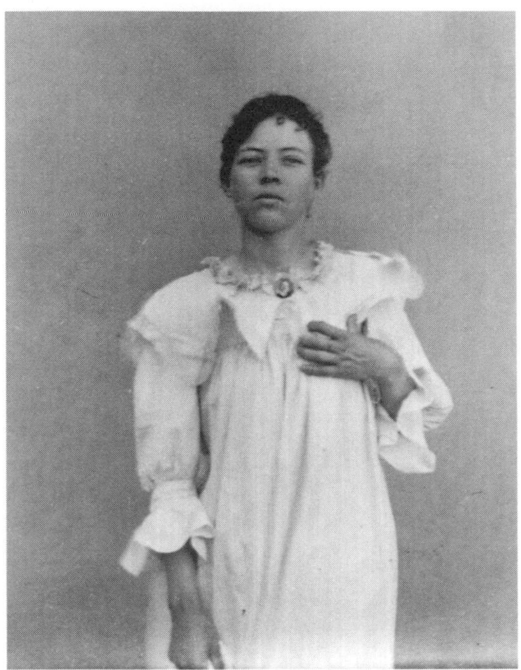

Pearl Hart in the Yuma Territorial Prison, 1899. Courtesy of the Arizona Historical Society, Tucson.

that compliance rather than arrogance or teasing her captors was essential in the prison setting. She also learned lacework to pass the time and sold her handiwork to visitors. At one point she professed a new religious fervor, apparently stumping for reform within prison through religious enlightenment, thus seeking forgiveness. She also recommended the Christian life as a preventative to crime.

Still, visitors—in particular journalists—speculated that Pearl received special treatment *because* she was a woman. In a January 27, 1900, article based on his visit with Pearl, one reporter wrote that "she has a house yard in which to take her constitutional whenever she is minded. She is evidently living off the fat of the prison, as there was a pound of butter on the table of her cell in the morning I called on her." The same reporter seemed to delight in emphasizing Pearl's depraved, privileged state. Her records also reveal that she was "cured" of her opium habit. But the writer added: "Several weeks of prison life had freed the physical system of its load of opium, for Pearl was a 'hop fiend' of insatiable appetite, but her wicked face is sallow for she has not been deprived of her cigarettes." Although other accounts indicate that Pearl was the mastermind behind the robbery for which she and Boot were sentenced, this reporter notes that her cigarette habit "led to her capture, for her male companion was arrested while trying to purchase cigarettes for her." If Pearl was a convict, still she "delighted to tell the story of her stage robbery."

This newspaper account and the blame it contains reveal other social attitudes about women criminals. Rehabilitation was believed fundamentally improbable for such women. One writer snipped: "She is in reality a dried-up dope fiend, needing only the guidance of some good woman to bring her to repentance." Yet for others, Pearl was "enjoying prison life, basking in a flood of public sympathy and Yuma sunshine."

Embedded in these very critical, trivializing, sarcastic descriptions of her situation are indications of Pearl's actual condition. A writer from the *Arizona Graphic* noted: "Pearl is lonesome, and she wants Ira Smith to let her have pups in her prison yard. Mr. Smith declines. He says Judie [the mother dog] is a lady and her pups are well bred, and he doesn't propose to have their morals contaminated by association with Pearl." Another viewer was more sympathetic. Walter T. Gregory, whose letter is in Pearl's Yuma prison file, recalled Pearl as having an excellent record and was inclined to being "polite and timid." Such contrasting opinions add to the obvious conclusion that preconceived notions about gender and class often colored these so-called factual records. Reading between the lines, we must conclude that Pearl's prison years were similar to her earlier notorious period after the robbery. Her own needs, opinions, and feelings appear more in her response to existing power bases than in any direct way. The way she negotiated or subverted authority is the key to understanding her interior life.

In her book *Gendered Justice in the American West* (1997), historian Anne M. Butler documents how women survived in a situation in which, even more than in normal society, the dynamics of male behavior dominated daily life. Composed of male convicts, guards, and wardens engaged in routines solely involving men's labor, occupations, and vocabulary, nineteenth-century prison systems stigmatized as well as ignored women. Already invisible or silenced in normal social situations wherein male prescriptions of acceptable female behavior predominated, women prisoners had to develop strategies of compliance and resistance to counter such pronounced conditions. Their efforts arched across the entire masculine power structure, from guards to governors. Despite these large challenges, women inmates succeeded in varying degrees, finding agency in small ways. Two ways women often responded to a lack of control of their environment were direct or indirect participation in legal procedures and their personal actions inside the prison.

Pearl Hart's actions exemplify some of these strategies. Like most female prisoners, Pearl participated in alternatives to men's hard physical labor by sewing or mending. She also attempted as much as possible to develop the persona of the "good" woman. She dressed again in female clothing, for example. Similar to the strategies of other women prisoners, she also cultivated alliances with key people—the warden, the guards, or the governor. These individuals could be very important for gaining justice and, possibly, parole.

Most women also depended extensively on their families outside the prison for contact with influential people who might expedite their early release or even gain special treatment for them. Often, relationships with lawyers, types of advocacy, and the financial support needed to facilitate such assistance depended on such outside family connections. Freedom, a cleared name, or mere survival in often filthy or potentially violent conditions might be alleviated by letter-writing campaigns, for example. Parole petitions often took months or even years, because of the number of petitions and sluggish bureaucracies. Even with family pressure or persistence from the outside, an inmate could wait months or years to hear whether such pleas had even been considered. Given the complexity of gender bias against women, "good time" or good behavior could be a factor but was dependent on the opinion of male guards and wardens.

In a variety of ways, Pearl Hart attempted to work the system. In addition to her religious reform, her domestication as exemplified in her handiwork, and her general cooperation, Pearl attempted to utilize her limited family support. A sister, Mrs. C. P. Frizzle from Silver City, New Mexico, visited Pearl, bringing with her a proposal that Pearl be released early in order to star in Mrs. Frizzle's play *The Arizona Bandit.* This proposal may appear to be a rather bizarre solution for Pearl, given that earlier citizens of Arizona had worried about the perpetuation of the image of Arizona as the "Wild West." In the new script, Pearl apparently would reenact the criminal deed with a new twist: she would turn the event into a moralistic melodrama, thereby dramatizing her own reform.

But Pearl Hart was not released for one of these reasons. Instead, on December 15, 1902, she was mysteriously granted early parole. The reason the warden gave was "good behavior" and the ever-prevalent excuse that prisons could not successfully accommodate women prisoners. Pearl and one other woman prisoner, who had become Pearl's cellmate, were released, supposedly because even more women criminals needed to be admitted.

Just how cleverly Pearl again had manipulated male power and feigned romantic attachments surfaced fifty-two years later when the real reason for her parole was disclosed. George Smalley, secretary to Governor Alexander O. Brodie of Arizona at the time, had pledged silence on the issue. Toward the end of his life, he privately contacted Bert Fireman to reveal the secret. In turn, Fireman did not reveal the truth of Pearl's release until after Smalley's death at age eighty-four in 1956.

According to Smalley, the warden of the Yuma Territorial Prison came to Governor Brodie's office in Phoenix, fearing a scandal might undermine the territorial administration. The prison doctor had notified the warden that Pearl Hart was pregnant. If she should have a baby while in prison, a member of the staff would be implicated. The matter was particularly sticky because the only men alone with Pearl in her cell had been the warden, the governor, and a trustee. The warden and even the governor might lose their jobs. More practically, a baby could not be cared for within the prison walls. Although Governor Brodie wrote "Good Behavior" on Pearl's papers, there is speculation that the simultaneous release of Pearl's female cellmate may have been because she knew too much.

Even though the identity of the "father" of the child was never discovered, Smalley believed that Billy Stiles, bank robber and also a member of the Arizona Rangers, might be to blame. As a trustee, he had the run of the prison. He had visited Pearl but was killed in Nevada in 1908, so his relationship with Pearl never was made clear. In fact, no record of the birth of a baby after Pearl left the prison was discovered. Apparently, a feigned pregnancy, possible under her circumstances, ultimately may have been Pearl's most successful manipulation of the power structure to gain her freedom.

Contrary to earlier romanticizing of Pearl's behavior and appearance, journalists noted a difference in the ex-convict's womanly aspects. Although Pearl was released to her sister, and went directly from Yuma to Kansas City to live, the promise of a vaudeville act and even rumor that she would be performing with the Zeigfield Follies was reported in a mocking tone by the press. A part of this disparaging attitude was no doubt the firm belief that women criminals rarely reformed. Also, journalists seemed to have lost infatuation with Pearl when her physical appearance changed while in prison. Once described as lithe and witty, Pearl was now described as "sallow." Another reporter also slammed her acting talent, her sincerity, and her looks by saying: "Pearl has quit the real thing and decided to reform. She will try to elevate the stage instead of robbing it. Pearl is a pretty name, but if those features of hers do not cause a stampede of the audiences when she appears before the footlights, it will be because of her reputation as a dead shot." Contrary to these opinions, Pearl was not a greenhorn. She was an expert horsewoman and a respectable "shot." Apparently, at this stage in her life, good looks and a clean moral slate took precedence over her abilities as a western woman.

The play was never performed. Pearl's only artistic expression came in the form of a poem, published in 1904 in Yuma's *Weekly Sun*. In the poem, rather than take the robbery to another level, even as a reform or melodramatic vehicle, Pearl seemed stuck in the endless recounting of the deed that briefly made her visible:

The sun was brightly shining on a pleasant afternoon
My partner speaking lightly said, "The stage will be here soon."
We saw it coming around the bend and called to them to halt
And to their pockets we attended, if they hurt it was their fault.

While the birds were sweetly singing, and the men stood up in line
And the silver softly ringing as it touched the palm of mine.
There we took their money, but left them enough to eat
And the men looked so funny as they vaulted to their seats.

Then up the road we galloped, quickly through a canyon we did pass
Over the mountains we went swiftly, trying to find our horses grass,
Past the station we boldly went, now along the riverside,
And our horses being spent, of course we had to hide.

In the night we would travel, in the daytime try and rest
And throw ourselves on the gravel, to sleep we would try our best.
Around us our horses were stamping, looking for some hay or grain
On the road the Posse was tramping, looking for us all in vain.

One more day they would not have got us, but my horse got sore and thin
And my partner was a mean cuss, so Billy Truman rapped us in.
Thirty years my partner got, I was given five
He seemed content with his lot, and I am still alive.

Pearl's history was treated in more than self-immortalized minor doggerel verse, however. A stipulation of her early release from Yuma ordered that she not set foot in Arizona until the term of her original sentence had passed. Regrettably, like some other female ex-cons, neither family connections nor the attempt to start a new life were enough. Shortly after Pearl rejoined her family in Kansas City, authorities apprehended her as part of a pickpocket gang of local thugs. Although Pearl identified herself as a "Mrs. Keeler," the police recognized her as Pearl Hart and threatened to return her to Arizona to complete her sentence. When interviewed by the *Yuma Examiner* for an article in its May 5, 1910, issue, county attorney James Durham recalled talking to Pearl in Kansas City. Although the newspaper reported she was then "leading a degraded life in the city slums," Durham explained more reasonably that Pearl's family fared poorly during that time. Although Pearl's mother had left property to her daughters, all income had been lost because of her brother-in-law's conviction for horse theft. A consequent divorce by his wife left her destitute, and Durham says she fell into a "dissolute life" like her sister, Pearl. There is also evidence that the family earlier attempted to cash in on Pearl's fame, as well as to borrow money from her when she went out west. Continued hard times and marginal activities further challenged any new start Pearl may have attempted.

After this *Yuma Examiner* article, little appeared about Pearl Hart. The woman who sought romance, glamour, personal freedom, and escape appeared to find an ultimate way to release herself. She disappeared. When historian James D. Horan prepared to write his book *Desperate Women* in the 1950s, he searched intensively in Kansas City for records on Pearl Hart and found nothing except a story that Pearl had run a cigar store in the city and had "moved West ten years ago."

Other records suggest, however, that Pearl Hart moved back to her old Arizona haunts as Mrs. Calvin Bywater, living a quiet life on a ranch near Globe. Apparently, the Bywaters had married previously in Mexico but had been advised to get a U.S. certificate as well. Clara Woody noted that the wife initially called herself "Pearl" Bywater, but in later years denied that name, preferring only "Mrs." Calvin Bywater. Witnesses in the old courthouse at Tucson also claim that Pearl paid a visit to the building asking to see the room where she was jailed and from which she escaped. That stop supposedly was part of a sentimental journey that included the Yuma prison as well.

According to the sources, the Calvin Bywaters lived on the Dripping Springs Ranch on the edge of a wash of that name just under the old Christmas Mine in the mountains southeast of Globe, a few miles from Cane Springs, where Pearl's outlaw career began. Seeking to discover in the 1970s whether anyone else could confirm Pearl's identity, Woody interviewed separately three elderly men in the area who claimed to know Hart. Each reported seeing Pearl. Dan Williamson said he had seen her in a restaurant in Globe. He remembered her eyes as still black and keen. Johnny Crampton of Phoenix said Pearl attended a funeral in Phoenix in 1941. Another local man claimed to have had dinner with Pearl and her husband and mentioned that she had lived an exemplary later life on a ranch near where the holdup occurred.

Even if these later persons physically identified Pearl, she always called herself Mrs. Calvin Bywater. When Clara Woody saw this woman, once in 1940 as a census-taker and again in 1949 as part of an agricultural census, she tried to find out more about Pearl. Recalling their meeting in 1940, Woody described Mrs. Bywater as stout and dressed in well-worn jeans, as one might expect of a woman living on a working ranch. The room the two women were in was reportedly littered with cigar butts. Woody also inquired about the birthplace of Mrs. Bywater. The woman, described as having the tell-tale dark eyes of Pearl Hart, replied: "I wasn't born anywhere."

Another twentieth-century historian also attempted to solve the mysteries of Pearl Hart's latter years. In his book *Boots and Bullets,* Jesse Hayes states that Pearl died on December 30, 1955, and that both she and Calvin

Bywater are buried in the cemetery in Hayden, Arizona. According to Hayes, Mrs. Bywater had three children, grandchildren, and great grandchildren by that time, but apparently none of them was ever told anything about "Pearl Hart." Thus, the woman of many aliases, adopted personas, and secret personal struggles ultimately carried many of the mysteries of her life to the grave.

So, was Pearl Hart a desperate woman or a desperado? Popular notions of her character rest on her sensational leading role in the stage robbery of 1899 and on her subsequent resistance of the law through her attempted escapes from jail and, most notably, her supposed pregnancy. But beneath public curiosity and fascination with women bandits of her time, and the tendency to think romantically about them as a kind of "western" woman, more compelling issues of failed romance and marriage, abuse, single parenthood, family expectations, economic straits, and social realities exist.

Although Pearl Hart seems unique for her time in that she assisted in the last stagecoach robbery in Arizona and was the only known woman to rob a stage in that territory, she nevertheless is representative of larger issues shared by many women whose stories remain unknown. The social construction of respectable womanhood, connected to class as well as individual behavior, the power men possessed in American culture of this era, the particular attitudes about convicted women and female criminals—all of these themes circumscribed the ways in which Pearl Hart's life was shaped. The particular responses Pearl had to social and cultural structures—marriage, relationships, family, business, and institutions such as the Yuma Territorial Prison—indicate that women of her era, in order to express and act on their own desires, constantly negotiated and manipulated these structures, using female "wiles" or even bolder behaviors to achieve a measure of personal freedom. Although Pearl Hart was no heroine—especially of the type identified as an underdog, a wronged criminal, or a "western" hero—she was a persistent survivor. At the very least, she was a psychological outlaw, challenging the laws and codes that prescribed women's values and behavior. She became a self-constructed "desperado" whose theatrical deeds were closely connected to a private desperateness.

SOURCES & FURTHER READING

CHAPTER 1: WYATT EARP

The literature on Wyatt Earp is voluminous, but until the publication of Casey Tefertiller's *Wyatt Earp: The Life Behind the Legend* (New York: John Wiley & Sons, 1997), no truly satisfactory biography of Wyatt Earp existed. William B. Shillingberg's *Tombstone, A. T.: A History of Early Mining, Milling, and Mayhem* (Spokane, WA: Arthur H. Clark, 1999) is a major work that treats the most important phase of the Earp story in context. Richard Maxwell Brown's *No Duty to Retreat: Violence in American History and Society* (New York: Oxford University Press, 1991), though flawed by too great a dependence upon uncritical sources, provides a broad interpretive framework for the Earp story. Allan Barra's *Inventing Wyatt Earp: His Life and Many Legends* (New York: Carroll & Graf, 1998) examines Earp's life within the context of the growing legends about him. Together, these works provide a gateway to the literature.

Virtually all of the standard works that preceded these studies have been marked by a tampering with the historical record. Walter Noble Burns's *Tombstone: An Illiad of the Southwest* (Garden City, NY: Doubleday, Page & Co., 1927) was the first book to provide a reasonably accurate chronology for the Tombstone period, but Burns could not resist the temptation to romanticize the story. William M. Breakenridge's *Helldorado: Bring the Law to the Mesquite* (Boston, MA: Houghton Mifflin, 1928) presented the story from the perspective of one of Sheriff John Behan's deputies who portrayed Earp as a killer and badman. Stuart N. Lake's *Wyatt Earp: Frontier Marshal* (Boston, MA: Houghton Mifflin, 1931), written after a brief collaboration with Earp himself, became the touchstone biography of Wyatt Earp, but Lake would later admit that he embellished the story and attributed many of his own conclusions to Earp himself.

For the next thirty years, most of the writings about Wyatt Earp were derivative in nature, either accepting uncritically Stuart Lake's hero or assailing Earp as a killer, con man, and thief after Breakenridge. Then, Frank Waters's *The Earp Brothers of Tombstone* (New York: Clarkson N. Potter, 1960) appeared, alleging to be the memoirs of Virgil Earp's widow, Allie. It was a bitter, wholesale debunking of Stuart Lake, that, like Lake, was later criticized for tampering with the principal narrator's memoirs. Waters was followed by a two-volume diatribe against Earp in Ed Bartholomew's *Wyatt Earp: The Untold Story* and *Wyatt Earp: The Man and the Myth* (Toyahvale, TX: Frontier Book Co., 1963, 1964), which was so poorly organized and so one-sided as to be virtually worthless.

Glenn G. Boyer's *The Suppressed Murder of Wyatt Earp* (San Antonio, TX: Naylor Book Co., 1967), despite the unfortunate title, appeared to introduce a fresh and welcome balance to the Earp story. The same author's "edited" work, *I Married Wyatt Earp: The Recollections of Josephine Sarah Marcus Earp* (Tucson: University of Arizona Press, 1976), was hailed as a major contribution, but his *Wyatt Earp's Tombstone Vendetta* (Honolulu, HI: Takei Publishing, 1993), billed as a "nonfiction novel," raised questions about Boyer's work that eventually discredited *I Married Wyatt Earp* as the memoir of Mrs. Earp.

Other works, including Steve Gatto's *Wyatt Earp: A Biography of a Western Lawman* (Tucson, AZ: San Simon Publishing, 1997), Paula Mitchell Marks's *And Die in the West: The Story of the O.K. Corral Gunfight* (New York: William Morrow and Co., 1989), Richard A. Erwin's *The Truth About Wyatt Earp* (Carpenteria, CA: O.K. Press, 1992), and Don Chaput's *Virgil Earp: Western Peace Officer* (Encampment, WY: Affiliated Writers of America, 1994) are good-faith efforts that made contributions. Alford E. Turner, editor, *The O.K. Corral Inquest* (College Station, TX: Creative Publishing, 1982) and *The Earps Talk* (College Station, TX: Creative Publishing, 1982); and Don Chaput, editor, *The Earp Papers* (Encampment, WY: Affiliated Writers of America, 1994) are edited works that present documents and reminiscences important to the Earp story.

The periodical literature is vast, but it must be consulted because some of the most useful contributions to the Earp story are to be found there. These can be found by reference to the bibliographies of the books listed here and by consulting James A. Browning, editor, *The Western Reader's Guide: A Selected Bibliography of Nonfiction Magazines, 1953–1991* (Stillwater, OK: Barbed Wire Press, 1997). A substantial literature also exists on other individuals involved in the Earp story, providing insight into the character of Wyatt Earp.

CHAPTER 2: WILD BILL HICKOK

There is a wealth of material on the life and times of James Butler Hickok, much of which is fictional and which ranges from dime novels to pseudobiographies and other so-called "factual accounts." Having spent more than forty years researching the subject and examining a great deal of the available materials, I would caution the student or history buff to beware of unsourced materials and to treat them on merit, either as obvious fiction or inspired romanticism.

For this essay, I have relied to some extent on my four books on Hickok: *They Called Him Wild Bill: The Life and Adventures of James Butler Hickok* (Norman: University of Oklahoma Press, 1964, revised 1974), *The West of Wild Bill Hickok* (Norman: University of Oklahoma Press, 1982), *Wild Bill Hickok: The Man and His Myth* (Lawrence: University Press of Kansas, 1996), and *Alias Jack McCall* (Kansas City, MO: The Kansas City Posse of the Westerners, 1967).

Discerning students should also examine local court and civil records, newspapers, and government archives. The National Archives in Washington, D.C., are boosted by regional centers. The one in Kansas City, Missouri, for example, houses the Jack McCall trial papers and a lot of material relevant to Hickok's period as a deputy U.S. marshal (see also Joseph G. Rosa, "J. B. Hickok, Deputy U.S. Marshal," *Kansas History* [Winter 1979]). Other primary sources are the Kansas State Historical Society and the Nebraska State Historical Society, both of which have a great deal of information on Hickok. Members of the Hickok family have also contributed important information, in particular his grand-niece Edith Harmon, whose two books *Another Man Named Hickok* (focusing on Wild Bill's great-grandfather Aaron and his descendants) and *Pioneer Settlers of Troy Grove, Illinois* cover the family history from 1635 to the present day (both were privately published in Mendota, Illinois, in 1973).

Also of importance are the works of the late Ramon Adams, whose *Six-Guns and Saddle Leather: A Bibliography of Books and Pamphlets on Western Outlaws and Gunmen* (Norman: University of Oklahoma Press, revised edition, 1969) and *Burs Under the Saddle* (Norman: University of Oklahoma Press, 1964) contain informed opinion on the factual or fictional content of the books listed. For a general coverage of gunfighters based upon official court, census, and newspaper accounts, Nyle H. Miller and Joseph W. Snell's *Great Gunfighters of the Kansas Cowtowns, 1867–1886* (Lincoln: University of Nebraska Press, 1966) is highly recommended.

There are a number of books devoted to Hickok, many of which contain much fiction. Among these are Wilbert Eisele's *The Real Wild Bill Hickok: Famous Scout and Knight Chivalric of the Plains—A True Story of Pioneer Life in the Far West* (Denver, CO: William H. Andre, 1931), Frank J. Wilstach's *Wild Bill Hickok: The Prince of Pistoleers* (Garden City, NY: Doubleday, Page & Co., 1926), and William E. Connelley's *Wild Bill and His Era: The Life and Adventures of James Butler Hickok* (New York: The Press of the Pioneers, 1933). Eisele's book relies a great deal upon J. W. Buel's *Heroes of the Plains* (New York: N. D. Thompson & Co., 1882), whereas Wilstach's contribution showcases the discovery of Sarah Shull. Connelley's book was purported, at the time of its publication, to be the most important book on Hickok's life. Published three years after the author's death in 1930, it was edited for publication by Connelley's daughter, who discarded most of the citations and deleted parts of the manuscript, which made the book historically worthless. Fortunately, many of Connelley's original notes and materials are now in the Western History Department of the Denver Public Library.

General George A. Custer's *My Life on the Plains* (New York: Sheldon & Co., 1874, 1876) contains a valuable description of Hickok, as does Elizabeth Bacon Custer's *Following the Guidon* (New York: Harper & Bros., 1890). For a semifictional account that hints at a factual origin, J. W. Buel's *Heroes of the Plains* is worth reading. Similarly, every student of Wild Bill should read Colonel George Ward Nichols's "Wild Bill" published in *Harper's New Monthly Magazine* (February 1867), the text of which is reproduced as an appendix in *Wild Bill Hickok: The Man and His Myth*. Despite fictional aspects, the article contains a lot of fact. Soon thereafter, Henry M. Stanley published his interview with Hickok in the St. Louis *Weekly Missouri Democrat* on April 16, 1867. Clearly, Stanley much admired Hickok and did not realize that Hickok was pulling his leg. W. E. Webb's *Buffalo Land: An Authentic Narrative of the Adventures and Misadventures of a Late Scientific and Sporting Party upon the Great Plains of the West* (Chicago, IL: E. Hannaford & Co., 1872) contains some interesting comments on Hickok, and Richard B. Hughes's *Pioneer Years in the Black Hills,* edited by Agnes Wright Spring (Glendale, CA: Arthur H. Clark, 1957), describes Hickok's last days and McCall's trial in Deadwood.

CHAPTER 3: PATRICK FLOYD GARRETT

This article is based on documents from the Center for Southwest Research, Zimmerman Library, University of New Mexico. Most useful were the Marshall Bond, John William Poe, and Miguel Otero manuscript collections. In addition, some of these individuals wrote books that depict New Mexico during the time Garrett lived. These include Miguel A. Otero's

The Real Billy the Kid: With New Light on the Lincoln County War (1936; New York: Rufus Rockwell Wilson, 1959), John W. Poe's *The Death of Billy the Kid* (Boston, MA: Houghton Mifflin, 1933), and *Buckboard Days* (1936; Albuquerque: University of New Mexico Press, 1981) by Sophie A. Poe, John Poe's wife. Period newspaper articles can be found in *Billy the Kid: Las Vegas Newspaper Accounts of His Career, 1880–1881* (Waco, TX: W. W. Morrison, 1958).

By far the most valuable secondary source, which remains the best study of the New Mexico lawman to date, is Leon C. Metz's *Pat Garrett: The Story of a Western Lawman* (Norman: University of Oklahoma Press, 1973). Metz has also produced a series of articles, including "Pat Garrett: El Paso Customs Collector," *Arizona and the West* 11 (Winter 1969); "*True West* Legends: Pat Garrett," *True West* 44 (July 1997); and "Strange Death of Pat Garrett," *Wild West* 45 (February 1998).

Other useful biographies on Garrett include John M. Scanland's *The Life of Pat Garrett and the Taming of the Border Outlaw* (1908; El Paso, TX: J. J. Lipsey, 1952); Richard O'Connor's *Pat Garrett: A Biography of the Famous Marshal and the Killer of Billy the Kid* (Garden City, NY: Doubleday, 1960); Colin Rickards's *Sheriff Pat Garrett's Last Days* (Santa Fe, NM: Sunstone Press, 1986); and Jack DeMattos's *Garrett and Roosevelt* (College Station, TX: Creative Publishing, 1988), which details the final years of Garrett's life and career. Rickards also wrote "Pat Garrett Tells 'How I Killed Billy the Kid,'" *Real West* 12 (Summer 1972).

Despite its inaccuracies, Pat F. Garrett's book *The Authentic Life of Billy the Kid* . . . is a must. Published in 1882, it has been reprinted several times over the past fifty years, most recently in 1978 by University of Oklahoma Press. Unfortunately, it is fanciful at best and generally reads like a dime novel. Walter Noble Burns's *The Saga of Billy the Kid* (Garden City, NY: Doubleday, Page, 1926) has deep ties to the Garrett book, but also establishes Billy as hero in the Lincoln County War, thus changing pre-1926 attitudes.

Several other sources proved useful as well, especially Charles A. Siringo's *A Texas Cowboy, or Fifteen Years on the Hurricane Deck of a Spanish Pony* (1885; Lincoln: University of Nebraska Press, 1979) and *Riata and Spurs* (Boston, MA: Houghton Mifflin, 1927); Emerson Hough's *The Story of the Outlaw* (New York: Outing, 1907); William A. Keleher's "Patrick Floyd Garrett," in *The Fabulous Frontier: Twelve New Mexico Items* (1945; Albuquerque: University of New Mexico Press, 1962); and W. H. Hutchinson's *Another Verdict for Oliver Lee* (Clarendon, TX: Clarendon Press, 1965). A few shorter works are "The Short Life of Tom O'Folliard," *Potomac Westerners' Corral Dust* 6 (May 1961) and "Garrett's Favorite Deputy [Barney Mason]," *Potomac Westerners' Corral Dust* 9 (Fall 1964), both by Philip J. Rasch; Jack DeMattos's "Gunfighters of the Real West: Pat Garrett," *Real West* 25 (August 1982); Harold L. Edwards's "Barney Mason: In the Shadow of Pat Garrett and Billy the Kid," *Old West* 26 (Summer 1990).

A number of well-researched works provided good background material. A few of the best are Larry D. Ball's *Desert Lawmen: The High Sheriffs of New Mexico and Arizona, 1846–1912* (Albuquerque: University of New Mexico Press, 1992), which contains general observations about lawmen in territorial New Mexico; *George Curry, 1861–1947: An Autobiography,* edited by H. B. Henning (1958; Albuquerque: University of New Mexico Press, 1986); W. H. Hutchinson's *A Bar Cross Man: The Life and Personal Writings of Eugene Manlove Rhodes* (Norman: University of Oklahoma Press, 1956); Ruth K. Hunt's *A Place of Her Own: The Story of Elizabeth Garrett* (Santa Fe, NM: Sunstone, 1983); and Glenn Shirley's *Shotgun for Hire: The Story of "Deacon" Jim Miller, Killer of Pat Garrett* (Norman: University of Oklahoma Press, 1970).

Of course, interested readers must consider general histories of the Lincoln County War, even though Garrett is conspicuously absent in most of them. In particular, see Maurice

G. Fulton's classic *History of the Lincoln County War,* edited by Robert N. Mullin (Tucson: University of Arizona Press, 1968); Frederick Nolan's *The Lincoln County War: A Documentary History* (Norman: University of Oklahoma Press, 1992); Robert M. Utley's *High Noon in Lincoln: Violence on the Western Frontier* (Albuquerque: University of New Mexico Press, 1987) and *Billy the Kid: A Short and Violent Life* (Lincoln: University of Nebraska Press, 1989); William A. Keleher's *Violence in Lincoln County, 1869–1881* (1957; Albuquerque: University of New Mexico Press, 1982); Jon Tuska's *Billy the Kid: His Life and Legend* (1994; Albuquerque: University of New Mexico Press, 1997); John P. Wilson's *Merchants, Guns, and Money: The Story of Lincoln County and Its Wars* (Santa Fe, NM: Museum of New Mexico Press, 1987); and Joel Jacobsen's *Such Men as Billy the Kid: The Lincoln County War Reconsidered* (Lincoln: University of Nebraska Press, 1994). These works detail the events that made Billy an outlaw in the first place.

Published accounts about Billy the Kid and Pat Garrett in legend and film include Joseph G. Rosa's *The Gunfighter: Man or Myth?* (Norman: University of Oklahoma Press, 1969), Stephen Tatum's *Inventing Billy the Kid: Visions of the Outlaw in America, 1881–1981* (Albuquerque: University of New Mexico Press, 1982), and Terence Butler's *Crucified Heroes: The Films of Sam Peckinpah* (London, England: Gordon Fraser, 1979). Garrett is the subject of one documentary film, *Sheriff Pat Garrett: Killer of Billy the Kid* (Albuquerque, NM: Video Enterprises, 1991). Readers might also check out the various interpretations in feature films such as *The Outlaw* (United Artists, 1943), *The Left-Handed Gun* (Warner Brothers, 1958), *Chisum* (Warner Brothers, 1970), *Pat Garrett and Billy the Kid* (MGM, 1973), Gore Vidal's *Billy the Kid* (Turner Home Entertainment, 1989), and *Young Guns II* (Twentieth-Century Fox, 1990).

CHAPTER 4: TOM HORN

Any study of Tom Horn must begin with his autobiography, *The Life of Tom Horn: Government Scout and Interpreter, A Vindication* (Denver, CO: Louthan Book Co., 1904). Horn devotes most of the book to the Apache Wars and makes wild claims as to his role in the conflict, but he also presents a coherent and lively story. Because Horn says nothing about the last decade of his life, we must regard his services in the Apache Wars as a "vindication" of his subsequent life. Unfortunately, we do not know how much Horn's friend and employer, John C. Coble, edited the manuscript as he prepared it for publication. Nor do we know the role of a third party, Hattie Louthan, who, presumably as a member of the publisher's family, claimed to have ghostwritten the book. Surviving letters by Horn indicate that he was capable of writing this book, but Hattie Louthan may have had some role in editing the work for John Coble. *The Life of Tom Horn* has been reprinted at least four times: (Norman: University of Oklahoma Press, 1964), (Glorieta, NM: Rio Grande Press, 1976), (New York: Jingle Bob/Crown Publishing, 1977), and (Chicago, IL: Lakeside Press, R. R. Donnelley, 1987). The Lakeside edition, edited and annotated by Doyce Nunis Jr., is the best of these reprints.

A flurry of interest in frontier personalities in the 1920s and 1930s included new attention to Tom Horn. Most of the writings published in these decades depended almost solely on *The Life of Tom Horn.* In *Fighting Men of the West* (New York: E. P. Dutton, 1932), Dane Coolidge devoted a chapter to Tom Horn. In another piece, a wildly exaggerated article titled "Talking Boy," Owen P. White sparked a debate about Horn's role in the surrender of Geronimo (*Collier's,* February 18, 1933). Several retired army officers, including Britton Davis in *The Truth About Geronimo,* edited by Milo M. Quaife (1929; Lincoln: University of

Nebraska Press, 1963), and Thomas Cruse in *Apache Days and After* (Caldwell, ID: Caxton Press, 1941), were especially critical of Horn, although both admit that he was present in the last Geronimo episode. Charles H. Coe, who became a livestock detective in Wyoming after Horn's death, offered a lengthy defense of the frontiersman in *Juggling a Rope: Lariat Roping and Spinning, Knots and Splices; Also the Truth About Tom Horn* (Pendleton, OR: Hamley & Co., 1927).

The most balanced treatment of Tom Horn, although somewhat dated, is Jay Monaghan's *Tom Horn: Last of the Badmen* (Indianapolis, IN: Bobbs-Merrill, 1946). This volume is available in a convenient reprint (Lincoln: University of Nebraska Press, 1997), with a new introduction by Larry D. Ball. An early resident of western Colorado, Monaghan interviewed persons who knew Horn and collected pertinent manuscript material as well. Unfortunately, Lauran Paine's *Tom Horn: Man of the West* (Barre, MS: Barre Publishing Co., 1963) adds little that is new to Horn's life and contains many errors. Although confined to Horn's last years, Dean F. Krakel's *The Saga of Tom Horn: The Story of a Cattlemen's War* (Laramie, WY: Laramie Printers, 1953) remains a valuable documentary treatment and includes a transcript of Horn's trial. Doyce Nunis Jr.'s *The Life of Tom Horn Revisited* (San Marino, CA: Los Angeles Westerners, 1992) presents the most up-to-date assessment of Horn's life. This is an expanded version of his introduction to the Lakeside Press edition of *The Life of Tom Horn.* Chip Carlson, a Wyoming writer, presents new material in *Tom Horn: "Killing Men Is My Specialty . . ."* (Cheyenne, WY: Beartooth Corral, 1991). Carlson's *Joe LeFors: "I Slickered Tom Horn . . ."* (Cheyenne, WY: Beartooth Corral, 1995) is a new edition of LeFors's recollections with additional material. However, the earlier edition of Joe LeFors's autobiography, *Wyoming Peace Officer* (Laramie, WY: Laramie Printers, 1953), prepared with the assistance of Agnes Spring Wright, a knowledgeable Wyoming author, should not be ignored. Novelist Will Henry, using the technique of the discovery of a lost fragment of Tom Horn's autobiography, presented a fictionalized treatment of Horn's life in *I, Tom Horn* (Philadelphia, PA: J. B. Lippincott, 1975).

Another work that fills a gap in Horn's life is Wilson Rockwell, editor, *Memoirs of a Lawman* (Denver, CO: Sage Books, 1962), which are the recollections of Cyrus Shores, the Colorado sheriff who introduced Tom Horn to the Pinkerton Detective Agency. In addition, Mark Dugan's *Tales Never Told Around the Campfire: True Stories of Frontier America* (Athens, OH: Swallow Press, 1992) and Dugan's *The Making of Legends: More True Stories of Frontier America* (Athens, OH: Swallow Press, 1997) examine Horn's activities as a livestock detective in Wyoming from 1893 to 1895. For a defense of persons whom Horn arrested in 1893, see Dever Babb Langhoff's *Tom Horn and the "Langhoff Gang" of Wyoming* (Albuquerque, NM: Alphagraphics, 1993). The author is the youngest son of Fred Langhoff. For Horn's participation in the Cattlemen's Invasion of Wyoming in 1892, see Daisy F. Baber, as told by Bill Walker, in *The Longest Rope: The Truth About the Johnson County Cattle War* (Caldwell, ID: Caxton Printers, 1940). Even though Walker makes some ridiculous claims in this book, his recollection about meeting Tom Horn in the Cattlemen's Invasion appears to be firsthand. The most recent research that confirms Horn's presence in Wyoming in 1892 is contained in Robert K. DeArment's *Alias Frank Canton* (Norman: University of Oklahoma Press, 1996).

A fully researched biography of Tom Horn's life has yet to be written and would be a most welcome addition to the available literature. A thorough study of Horn would require an examination of the records of the Military Department of Arizona in the National Archives, as well as the Arizona Historical Society and the Special Collections Department of the University of Arizona, both in Tucson. For the robbery trial in Reno, Nevada, see *Territory of Nevada v. Thomas H. Horn,* Special Collections Department, University of Nevada, Reno. Other files are housed in the western history collection at the Denver Public Library, the Wyoming State Museum in Cheyenne, and the American Heritage Center at the University of Wyoming in Laramie.

CHAPTER 5: DOC HOLLIDAY

Unless the reputedly massive collection of Doc Holliday letters to his cloistered cousin, Sr. Mattie Holliday, a close friend of his youth who became a member of the Sisters of Charity, turns up someday, there are virtually no sources from Holliday's own hand. Apparently completely unconcerned with others' opinions of him, he submitted to an interview only once, late in life, by a Denver reporter. Otherwise, he accounted for himself only under court subpoena or with gun and knife. Almost all of what we know of him therefore comes from news stories, court records, and recollections of his friends and enemies.

The contentious and contradictory literature on the Earp brothers is correspondingly contentious and contradictory on Doc Holliday, from the early canonizations of Wyatt by Walter Noble Burns and Stuart N. Lake to Frank Waters's gullible reporting of the jealous revisionary rebuttals of Virgil's widow, Allie. Casey Tefertiller's *Wyatt Earp: The Life Behind the Legend* (New York: John Wiley & Sons, 1997) is a judicious and exemplary new biography based in part on recently discovered sources, but offers no similar reappraisal of Doc Holliday. Glen G. Boyer's edited reminiscences of Wyatt Earp's widow, *I Married Wyatt Earp: The Recollections of Josephine Sarah Marcus Earp* (Tucson: University of Arizona Press, 1976), must be used with caution as a firsthand corrective to Allie Earp's sour appraisal of Holliday as reported by Waters. But she knew Holliday only briefly in Tombstone. An even more important primary source for Holliday's Tombstone years is Douglas D. Martin's *Tombstone's Epitaph: The History of a Frontier Town as Chronicled in Its Newspaper* (Albuquerque: University of New Mexico Press, 1951; revised edition, Norman: University of Oklahoma Press, 1997). Although the *Epitaph* was heavily biased toward the Earps, and the files of the opposition paper, *The Nugget,* were destroyed in the last of Tombstone's fires (so we have no corrective from the other side), the *Epitaph* is nevertheless invaluable, not the least for its verbatim reportage of the trial following the OK Corral shootout.

Two older Holliday biographies, written almost simultaneously and apparently without the authors' awareness of each other, similarly take sides, though less polemically than the generally deplorable Earp literature. Pat Jahns's *The Frontier World of Doc Holliday* (New York: Hastings House, 1957) is well researched but biased against the Earps, sensational in tone, and padded with irrelevant background detail. John Myers's exceptionally well-written book *Doc Holliday* (Boston, MA: Little, Brown, 1955), although perhaps too willing to accept the Holliday legends at face value, deftly sketches the social milieu of frontier boomtowns, the traditions of gambling and violence, and other aspects of the environment in which Doc Holliday functioned. Both books, however, must be reappraised in the light of Karen Holliday Tanner's *Doc Holliday: A Family Portrait* (Norman: University of Oklahoma Press, 1998). Tanner, who is herself a Holliday, bases her study largely upon family traditions and documents hitherto unavailable to researchers and brings to light important new material on Doc's family environment and Georgia years. She is at some pains to refute Doc's legendary reputation for violence and gives us a much less trigger-happy Doc Holliday than any preceding books.

Myers's *The Last Chance: Tombstone's Early Years* (New York: E. P. Dutton, 1950) describes that town's factionalized society and politics around the time of the Earps and Doc Holliday. Charles Robinson III's *The Frontier World of Fort Griffin: The Life and Death of a Frontier Town* (Spokane, WA: Arthur H. Clark, 1992) does the same for the Texas community where Holliday gained much of his early notoriety, while Dodge City is similarly served in Robert R. Dykstra's classic study *The Cattle Towns* (New York: Alfred A. Knopf, 1968). Paula Mitchell Marks's *And Die in the West: The Story of the O.K. Corral Gunfight* (New York: William Morrow, 1989), is a thoroughly researched and judiciously interpreted reconstruction of that famous episode that marked the apogee of fame for both Doc Holliday and the Earps. Finally, Jack Burrows's *John Ringo: The Gunfighter Who Never Was* (Tucson: University of Arizona Press, 1987) offers a boldly revisionist look at one of Holliday's famous opponents and the world in which they lived.

The subject of frontier violence, to which Holliday made such a major contribution, has been the subject of several thoughtful studies. Its southern roots, which came out in the lives of the Earps and Doc Holliday, among others, are perceptively examined as part of W. J. Cash's classic study *The Mind of the South* (New York: Alfred A. Knopf, 1941). W. Eugene Hollon's *Frontier Violence: Another Look* (New York: Oxford University Press, 1974) minimizes its frequency and importance in western history, as does Robert R. Dykstra's "Field Notes: Overdosing on Dodge City," *Western Historical Quarterly* 27 (Winter 1996): 505–14. Robert M. Utley's *High Noon in Lincoln: Violence on the Western Frontier* (Albuquerque: University of New Mexico Press, 1987) offers a model of preconditions for violence based on circumstances in Lincoln County, New Mexico, in 1878—but those conditions were almost completely reversed in Tombstone, Arizona, in 1881. Finally, Richard Maxwell Brown, the most prominent current student of the subject, in "Western Violence: Structure, Values, Myth," *Western Historical Quarterly* 24 (February 1993): 5–20, suggests, without discussing it specifically, that the Earp-Clanton feud in Tombstone was an example of the "Western Civil War of Incorporation," in which a group of northern, conservative, Republican proponents of social order went to war with an anarchic group of southern, outlaw Democrats. Brown's thesis seems to fit Tombstone society and politics well enough, but Doc Holliday fits the thesis rather poorly: personally an almost perfect representative of the latter group, he nevertheless fought with the former.

CHAPTER 6: JOAQUÍN MURRIETA

For the earliest histories of Murrieta's legend, along with the facts about his life, see Theodore Hittell's *History of California,* vol. 4 (San Francisco, CA: Pacific Press, 1897) and Hubert Howe Bancroft's *History of California,* vol. 7 (San Francisco, CA: The History Book Company, 1890). To understand Murrieta and the times in which he lived during the gold rush, see Rodman Paul's classic *California Gold: The Beginning of Mining in the Far West* (Lincoln: University of Nebraska Press, 1947). A more recent synthesis is Malcolm Rohrbough's *Days of Gold: The California Gold Rush and the American Nation* (Berkeley: University of California Press, 1997).

For the twentieth century, the best historical source on Joaquín Murrieta remains Remi Nadeau's *The Real Joaquin Murieta: Robin Hood Hero or Gold Rush Gangster?* (Corona del Mar, CA: Trans-Anglo Books, 1974), a critical and thorough exposition of the primary and secondary literature. Kent L. Steckmesser's *Western Outlaws: The "Good Badman" in Fact, Film, and Folklore* (Claremont, CA: Regina Books, 1983) adds to the historiography on Murrieta by exploring how his story has been interpreted in literature, film, and television.

Frank F. Latta's *Joaquín Murrieta and His Horse Gangs* (Santa Cruz, CA: Bear State Books, 1980) is eclectic in its presentation, but full of details gathered from a lifetime of research. The best Mexican historical study is Manuel Rojas's *Joaquín Murrieta, "El Patrio"* (Blythe, CA: La Cuña Aztlan Publications, 1996), which is, in part, a translation of his longer study in Spanish by the same title (Mexicali, 1986).

Of the popular literature on Murrieta, one should start with John Rollin Ridge's (Yellow Bird) classic book, *The Life and Adventures of Joaquin Murieta: The Celebrated California Bandit* (San Francisco, CA: W. B. Cooke and Co., 1854). The poem by Joaquín Miller is "Joaquín Murieta," *Joaquín Miller's Poems* (San Francisco, CA: Whitaker & Ray Company, 1915). Walter Noble Burns's *The Robin Hood of El Dorado* (New York: Coward-McCann, 1932) is an imaginative interpretation, which adds lots of dialogue to the historical account. In addition, there are the Latin American versions of Murrieta: Ireneo Paz's *Vida y adventuras del mas célebre bandido sonorense, Joaquín Murrieta: Sus grandes proezas en California* (Mexico, 1904; English translation, *Life and Adventures of the Celebrated Bandit, Joaquín Murrieta: His Exploits in the State of California* (Chicago, IL: Charles T. Power Co., 1937) and Pablo Neruda's play *Fulgor y muerte de Joaquín Murieta: Bandido chileno injusticiado en California el 23 de Julio de 1853* (Buenos Aires, Argentina: Editorial Losada, 1974). The most recent historical work on Murrieta is James Varley's *The Legend of Joaquín Murrieta: California's Gold Rush Bandit* (Twin Falls, ID: Big Lost River Press, 1995). The latest fictionalized view is Don Gwaltney's lurid adventure book *The Bandit Joaquín: An Orphaned Mexican's Search for Revenge in the California Gold Rush* (Northbrook, IL: Apple Core Press, 1997).

CHAPTER 7: BILLY THE KID

As the rival of George Armstrong Custer, Buffalo Bill Cody, and Wyatt Earp for the most popular figure of the Old West, Billy the Kid has been the subject of thousands of essays and books. The most recent and best guide to roughly nine hundred of these books, essays, novels, films, and other sources about the Kid is Kathleen Chamberlain, compiler, *Billy the Kid and the Lincoln County War: A Bibliography,* Occasional Paper No. 13, Center for the American West (Albuquerque: University of New Mexico Press, 1997).

In addition to Chamberlain's very useful work, one should consult three other listings for major works treating Billy the Kid. J. C. Dykes provided commentaries on all the important nonfiction, fiction, and films appearing before 1950 in his book *Billy the Kid: The Bibliography of a Legend* (Albuquerque: University of New Mexico Press, 1952). More recently, Stephen Tatum's *Inventing Billy the Kid: Visions of the Outlaw in America, 1881–1981* (Albuquerque: University of New Mexico Press, 1982) furnishes the best analytical study of a full century of interpretations on the Kid. Jon Tuska's *Billy the Kid: His Life and Legend* (Albuquerque: University of New Mexico Press, 1994) devotes full chapters to the historical, fictional, and cinematic treatments of Billy and is perhaps the most opinionated of these bibliographies. Paul Andrew Hutton contributes a brief, lively overview of popular images of Billy the Kid in his "Dreamscape Desperado," *New Mexico Magazine* 68 (June 1990): 44–57.

Most of the premier books on Billy the Kid and the Lincoln County War have appeared in the last decade. Noted western historian Robert M. Utley's *Billy the Kid: A Short and Violent Life* (Lincoln: University of Nebraska Press, 1989) is the best biography. Utley's *Four Fighters of Lincoln County* (Albuquerque: University of New Mexico Press, 1986) and *High Noon in Lincoln: Violence on the Western Frontier* (Albuquerque: University of New Mexico Press, 1987), although utilizing information contained in the later biography, are also model examples of stirring writing and strong research. Even more extensive is the account in Frederick Nolan's *The Lincoln County War: A Documentary History* (Norman: University of Oklahoma Press, 1992). Running more than five hundred oversized pages in length and containing long sections from many important documents, Nolan's intriguing volume may be the definitive study on this important subject. Meanwhile, Joel Jacobsen's *Such Men as Billy the Kid: The Lincoln County War Reconsidered* (Lincoln: University of Nebraska Press, 1994) draws on the author's experience as a lawyer to expand on the importance of legal and court decisions in the Lincoln County story.

For many years, Maurice Garland Fulton, a professor at the New Mexico Military Institute, interviewed survivors of the Lincoln County War and collected a mountain of other sources. Although Fulton never completed his book, another lay historian, Robert N. Mullin, edited Fulton's fact-filled manuscript and readied it for publication as Fulton's *History of the Lincoln County War* (Tucson: University of Arizona Press, 1968). Another well-researched overview is John P. Wilson's *Merchants, Guns and Money: The Story of Lincoln County and Its Wars* (Santa Fe: Museum of New Mexico Press, 1987).

Several other books deserve mention, even if their interpretations or findings now seem dated. One year after Billy the Kid's death, Pat Garrett published *The Authentic Life of Billy the Kid* . . . (Santa Fe: New Mexican Printing and Publishing Co., 1882). This sensational biography, primarily ghostwritten by Garrett's journalist friend, Ash Upson, is particularly unreliable on Billy's first years, but the second half contains useful, firsthand information. Billy received little attention for the next forty years or so until journalist Walter Noble Burns's *The Saga of Billy the Kid* (Garden City, NY: Doubleday, 1926) became a Book-of-the-Month selection, a best-seller, and an electrifying account for hundreds of thousands of readers. This biography probably did more to immortalize Billy the Kid than any other book. Like Burns, Miguel Otero interviewed several survivors of the Lincoln County imbroglio. His volume *The Real Billy the Kid: With New Light on the Lincoln County War* (New York: Rufus Rockwell Wilson, 1936) comes as close as any book to capturing the Hispanic perspective on these topics. Another well-known New Mexican, lawyer William A. Keleher, furnished a solid study based on important primary documents in his *Violence in Lincoln County, 1869–1881: A New Mexico Item* (Albuquerque: University of New Mexico Press, 1957).

Especially helpful on the mysterious early years of Billy's life are Robert N. Mullin's *The Boyhood of Billy the Kid,* Southwestern Studies Monograph No. 17 (El Paso: Texas Western Press, 1967), and Jerry Weddle's *Antrim is My Stepfather's Name: The Boyhood of Billy the Kid* (Tucson: Arizona Historical Society, 1993). Several of the useful essays derived from the work of indefatigable researcher Philip J. Rasch have been collected in three recent volumes: *Trailing Billy the Kid* (Laramie, WY: NOLA, 1995), *Gunsmoke in Lincoln County* (Stillwater, OK: NOLA and Western Publications, 1997), and *Warriors of Lincoln County* (Laramie, WY, and Stillwater, OK: NOLA and the University of Wyoming, 1998).

Other studies just completed or currently under way should fill large gaps in the Billy the Kid–Lincoln County War story. Frederick Nolan has recently published an indispensable pictorial biography of Billy, *The West of Billy the Kid* (Norman: University of Oklahoma Press, 1998), and Kathleen Chamberlain is at work on a much-needed biography of Susan McSween. Biographical studies of John Chisum, Alexander McSween, L. G. Murphy, and J. J. Dolan are also sorely needed. A model for these life stories is Frederick Nolan's *The Life and Death of John Henry Tunstall* (Albuquerque: University of New Mexico Press, 1965). In addition, much more work on the ethnic dimensions of Lincoln County is needed because nearly seventy percent of the county residents were Hispanic during Billy's time there.

For students and scholars interested in further research on Billy the Kid, several important collections of manuscript materials are available. The Lincoln County Heritage Trust in Lincoln, New Mexico, holds the Philip Rasch and W. A. Carrell collections, as well as other pertinent documents. Housed at the Haley History Center in Midland, Texas, are the important interviews J. Evetts Haley conducted in the 1920s and 1930s for his projected, but never completed, biography of Billy the Kid. Much more extensive are the notable research collections of Robert N. Mullin, also on file at the Haley Center. Another major research collection is the Maurice G. Fulton Papers (available on microfilm) at the University of Arizona Library in Tucson, a repository that also contains the Walter Noble Burns and Taylor and Mary Ealy collections. The correspondence between Billy the Kid and Governor Lew Wallace is housed at the Indiana Historical Society in Indianapolis. The Chamberlain bibliography and the bibliographies in the Utley and Nolan volumes likewise include citations to the most important regional and federal documents. Finally, other important collections on Billy the Kid and the Lincoln County War are available at the libraries of the University of New Mexico–Albuquerque and New Mexico State University–Las Cruces, as well as at the New Mexico State Records Center and Archives in Santa Fe.

CHAPTER 8: BELLE STARR

The only Belle Starr biography worthy of the label is Glenn Shirley's *Belle Starr and Her Times: The Literature, the Facts, and the Legends* (Norman: University of Oklahoma Press, 1982). Since its publication, tenacious researchers have turned to it for factual material and documentation. Although Shirley's investigation is superb, his organization is difficult to follow, and his book lacks an interpretive framework that "explains" Belle Starr.

The legend of Belle, which Shirley debunked, has had a long development. The Belle Starr obituary that provided much grist for the pulp mill is reprinted as "The Weekly Elevator, Fort Smith, Arkansas, February 15, 1889," in Jerry J. Gaddy, compiler, *Obituaries of the Gunfighters: Dust to Dust* (San Rafael, CA: Presidio Press, 1977), 67–73. The accounts that set the pattern for inflated Belle Starr interpretations were Alton B. Meyers's *Bella Starr: The Bandit Queen, Or, The Female Jesse James* (New York: Richard K. Fox, 1889) and S. W. Harman's *Hell on the Border* (Fort Smith, AR: Phoenix Publishing Co., 1898). These bombastic narratives helped shape myths of both Belle Starr and the Wild West.

One of the first authors to question the customary Belle Starr stories was the Ozark folklorist Vance Randolph. Publishing under pseudonyms, Randolph released Anton S. Booker's *Wildcats in Petticoats* (Girard, KS: Little Blue Books, 1931) (see pp. 52–63) and William Yancey Shackleford's *Belle Starr: The Bandit Queen* (Girard, KS: Haldeman-Julius Publications, 1943). Another writer who combined Belle Starr stories with an occasional accurate date or unique theory was Burton Rascoe in his *Belle Starr: The Bandit Queen* (New York: Random House, 1941). James D. Horan's *Desperate Women* (New York: G. P. Putnam's Sons, 1952) also promised accuracy and offered one of the few compassionate treatments of Belle Starr, but was still generally unreliable.

During the 1970s Carl W. Breihan and Charles A. Rosamond, in their *The Bandit Belle* (Seattle, WA: Hangman Press, 1970), put the usual legends in a highly readable format for a general audience. Charles W. Mooney's *Doctor in Belle Starr Country* (Oklahoma City, OK: Century Press, 1975) claimed to relate his father's experiences with Belle Starr as her doctor, but actually repeated many of the local myths. The work of Robert G. Winn in *Two Starrs: Belle, the Bandit Queen, Pearl, River Front Madame* (Fayetteville, AR: Washington County Historical Society, 1979), which later appeared as *Who Killed Belle Starr?* (Fayetteville, AR: Washington County Historical Society, 1994), was error-ridden, but offered more information than usual regarding Pearl Starr and speculated on a list of possible murderers of Belle Starr.

More recently, William Watkins's *Was There a Real Belle Starr?* (N.p., 1986) presented a fifteen-page rehash of legends from "Belle Starr country," where Watkins grew up. Carl R. Green and William R. Sanford's *Belle Starr* (Hillside, NJ: Enslow Publishers, 1992) offered a readable version of Belle Starr's life for young adult readers. Phillip W. Steele's *Starr Tracks: Belle and Pearl Starr* (Gretna, LA: Pelican Publishing Co., 1992) added Pearl's story to that of Belle's, and included family letters.

An excellent resource for the many other essays on Belle Starr is James A. Browning, editor, *The Western Reader's Guide: A Selected Bibliography of Nonfiction Magazines, 1953–91* (Stillwater, OK: Barbed Wire Press, 1997) (see pp. 293–94).

CHAPTER 9: JESSE JAMES

Readers are lucky to have two excellent studies of Jesse James, man and myth. William A. Settle Jr.'s *Jesse James Was His Name* (Columbia: University of Missouri Press, 1966) has held up beautifully since it appeared more than thirty years ago, primarily because of the author's careful digging through contemporary newspapers and the few archival sources on Jesse, the James family, and the gang. Settle's work is at least as strong on the evolution of the James myth, especially during the first generation after Jesse fell to the floor of his St. Joseph living room. Marley Brant's recent *Jesse James: The Man and the Myth* (New York: Berkeley Books, 1998) complements Settle's book nicely. Her story differs on some points. She places Jesse and Frank at bank robberies before Gallatin; Settle is not at all sure the brothers took part. She pays much less attention to the evolution of the James myth. For the most part, however, she enriches the story by filling in Jesse's career, tracing his movements, and adding delicious detail to a fascinating story.

These historical treatments should be read alongside other books that make no bones about their sympathies. Homer Croy's *Jesse James Was My Neighbor* (New York: Duell, Sloan and Pearce, 1949) pulls us back into the stories and lore still told about the James boys in western Missouri and the Ozarks. In 1926 a Kansas City journalist, Robertus Love, published a wonderfully overwritten account titled *The Rise and Fall of Jesse James* (New York: G. P. Putnam's Sons, 1926), which was in many ways a more measured reprise of John Newman Edwards's paean to the brothers and their cohorts, *Noted Guerillas* (St. Louis, MO: Bryan, Brand and Co., 1877), which is worth reading both for color and a sense of the passions of the time. Love splices stories like those from Homer Croy into a historical narrative, with plenty of personal asides, that catches a sense of the loyalty that Jesse and Frank inspire even today. A few of the many overwrought treatments of the time have been reprinted, such as Frank Triplett's *The Life, Times, and Treacherous Death of Jesse James* (1882; Chicago, IL: Swallow Press, 1970).

Jesse and Frank have received more attention from popularizers than from professional historians, but there are a few exceptions. Paul Wellman has placed the James and Younger brothers in their regional context in *A Dynasty of Western Outlaws* (Garden City, NY: Doubleday, 1961). He writes of the borderland, especially eastern Oklahoma, as a breeding ground for bandits, and he takes the story well into the twentieth century with such criminals as Charlie "Pretty Boy" Floyd (who considered himself a disciple of Jesse James).

Richard White considers whether the James gang and the Dalton brothers were "social bandits," outlaws supported and protected by common folk who feared and resisted powerful forces of change ("Outlaw Gangs of the Middle Border: American Social Banditry," *Western Historical Quarterly* 12 [October 1981]: 387–408). In an essay in *The Oxford History of the American West* (Clyde Milner, Carol A. O'Connor, and Martha A. Sandweiss, editors, New York: Oxford University Press, 1994), another master western historian, Richard Maxwell Brown, uses the James brothers several times to illustrate his views on the social and economic currents that shaped western violence after the Civil War.

Finally, leading American novelist Ron Hansen's *The Assassination of Jesse James by the Coward Robert Ford* (New York: Knopf, 1983) is a fascinating fictional account of Jesse's outlaw career that captures the mystery surrounding both the man's life and the enduring appeal of his shrouded personality.

Chapter 10: Pearl Hart

Of the book-length studies of women outlaws that include an individual chapter on Pearl Hart, James D. Horan's *Desperate Women* (New York: Putnam, 1952) provides a lengthy chronicle of her life. Typical of some of the writers in the 1950s, Horan stylistically embroiders his factual material. His witty, ironic, or decorative commentary often calls more attention to the writer than to the subject. Still, Horan's discussion is a good place to begin reading about Pearl Hart.

Other book-length studies also refer to Pearl Hart as one of the memorable women bandits of the late-nineteenth- and early-twentieth-century West. An early work, Duncan Aikman's *Calamity Jane and the Lady Wildcats* (New York: Henry Holt & Co., 1927) treats the major events of Hart's life. Like Aikman, most authors who write about Pearl Hart focus almost exclusively on the stagecoach robbery itself, leaving much of the other periods of her life to speculation. However, Jesse G. Hayes's *Boots and Bullets: The Life and Times of John Wentworth* (Tucson: University of Arizona Press, 1969) contributes to the theories of Hart's later life, arguing that she lived her later years near Globe, Arizona.

Among other authors who devote a book chapter to Pearl Hart, Clara T. Woody and Milton L. Schwartz, in *Globe, Arizona* (Tucson: Arizona Historical Society, 1977), consider all aspects, especially the last years of Hart's life, more completely. In the chapter "Pearl Hart: The End of an Era," Woody, who served as secretary of the Arizona Historical Society, combines newspaper records, interviews, and other historical data to reconstruct Hart's Arizona years. Particularly insightful in this account is the information from eyewitness accounts and from people who knew Hart. Because Woody claimed to have met Hart three times, her account of Hart's later life is essential.

Two of the shorter newspaper articles by reliable researchers and historians of Arizona also warrant special attention. Bert Fireman's "For More than a Half Century George Smalley Kept a Woman's Secret," in *Arizona Days and Ways Magazine* (September 23, 1956): 38–39, and Nancy Sortore's "Pearl Hart: An End to the Story," in *Arizona Daily Star* (September 22, 1974), focus on the conditions of Hart's alleged prison pregnancy and her mysterious identity after leaving Yuma prison. Fireman broke the pregnancy story with this article. Sortore, who interviewed Woody and consulted her papers, concisely presents the most recent ideas of Hart's whereabouts after 1903.

Several manuscript collections also contain material on Pearl Hart. For example, the papers of Bert Fireman and Clara Woody at the Arizona Historical Society contain correspondence, newspaper accounts, interviews, and manuscripts that form the background and foundation for their published accounts of Pearl Hart. Other important records exist at the Yuma Territorial Prison Museum in Yuma, where the original prison records, newspaper accounts of this period, and photographs offer primary sources that are key to understanding Hart's prison years.

Not as reliable, but nonetheless fascinating, is the October 1899 *Cosmopolitan* article "The Return of Pearl Hart." Although told in a melodramatic manner likely recast by the interviewer himself, the article provides the only insight into Pearl Hart's description of her acts, feelings, and motivations after the robbery and before her sentencing. The article also is a quick study of the hunger eastern writers and readers had for western adventures and subjects. The photographs that accompany this article are particularly revealing. They show us Hart's practical masculine attire as well as the way in which her audience, as imagined by the interviewer and photographer, wished to see her. Posed with rifle, one booted foot upon a stump, Hart displays her outlaw self. When photographed in typical late-nineteenth-century female attire, Hart's gendered descriptions, as represented to the readers of *Cosmopolitan* in 1899, suggest her compliance with her popularizers' fascination. The text and photos in this popular article are an interesting example of the ways in which preconceived notions of a deviant female perpetuate the myths surrounding women outlaws and criminals. Furthermore, the text and photos also give insight into Hart's need to manipulate existing opportunities for power, attention, and personal freedom.

There are dozens of other popular treatments of Pearl Hart. They appear primarily in the publications *Golden West, True West, Real West, Pioneer West,* and *Frontier West.* These mass-audience pieces, often only two pages long, primarily repeat well-known facts about the holdup, Hart's early life, and her attempted escapes. Unfortunately, they are too repetitive to offer a more sophisticated understanding of Hart.

Other recent works on Hart indicate how, as subject and personality, she still engages the imagination. A play, *Waiting Woman* by Sylvia Gonzalez, based on the Yuma Territorial Prison records, dramatizes this particular period. "Pearl Hart—Bandit Queen" is a radio drama based on the screenplay by Donald Quan and directed by Lindsay Robinson. The only novel-length literary treatment is Jane Candia Coleman's *I Pearl Hart: A Western Story* (Unity, ME: Five Star, 1998). Attempting to tell the Hart story from Pearl's point of view, it is an interesting and important work because so many questions exist about Pearl's life. The attempt to locate Hart's voice also is significant because numerous articles and historical accounts attempt to speak for her. Although the novel works best when juxtaposed against other popular renderings of Hart's personality and happenstance, it is nevertheless a minor work of fiction in conception and style.

All attempts to understand the meaning of Pearl Hart's attitudes and actions need to consider larger, contextual studies of women and society in the West during her time. In particular, Anne M. Butler's *Gendered Justice in the American West: Women Prisoners in Men's Penitentiaries* (Urbana: University of Illinois Press, 1997) offers new, crucial, insightful, and interpretative material on the status and circumstances of women criminals and prisoners.

CONTRIBUTORS

SHELLEY ARMITAGE is professor of English and director of women's studies at the University of Texas–El Paso. She has published numerous books and scholarly articles on women artists, western women, and women writers. She has been a Fulbright scholar in Portugal, taught in Eritrea, and held grants from the National Endowment for the Arts and the Humanities as well as a Rockefeller grant. She is adjunct professor of American studies at the University of Hawaii–Manoa. She will hold the Distinguished Fulbright Chair in American Literature and Culture at the University of Warsaw in the spring of 2000.

LARRY D. BALL is professor of history at Arkansas State University with research interests in frontier law and order. Among his publications are *The United States Marshals of New Mexico and Arizona Territories, 1846–1912* (1978), *Desert Lawmen: The High Sheriffs of New Mexico and Arizona, 1846–1912* (1992), and *Elfego Baca in Life and Legend* (1992).

KATHLEEN P. CHAMBERLAIN completed her Ph.D. in 1998 at the University of New Mexico and is now assistant professor of history at Castleton State College in Vermont. She recently completed a study of the Navajo and oil and has begun a biography of Susan McSween Barber, a central figure in the Lincoln County War.

RICHARD W. ETULAIN is professor of history and director of the Center for the American West at the University of New Mexico. He specializes in the history and literature of the American West. His most recent book is *Telling Western Stories: From Buffalo Bill to Larry McMurtry* (1999). He served as president of the Western History Association in 1998–1999.

RICHARD GRISWOLD DEL CASTILLO is professor of Chicano and Chicana studies at San Diego State University. He has published a number of books, including

The Treaty of Guadalupe Hidalgo: A Legacy of Conflict (1990), *La Familia: Chicano Families in the Urban Southwest, 1848 to the Present* (1984), *César Chávez: A Triumph of Spirit* (with Richard Garcia) (1995), and *North to Aztlan: Mexican Americans in United States History* (with Arnoldo De Leon) (1996).

GLENDA RILEY is the Alexander M. Bracken Professor of History at Ball State University in Indiana as well as coeditor of the Notable Westerners series (Fulcrum Publishing), in which this book is the second volume. Riley is past president of the Western History Association and the recipient of two Fulbright awards as well as many other honors. She is the author of numerous books and articles about women in the American West. Her most recent book is *Women and Nature: Saving the "Wild" West* (1999).

GARY L. ROBERTS, professor of history at Abraham Baldwin College in Tifton, Georgia, has devoted his career to the study of western violence. The author of *Death Comes to the Chief Justice: The Slough-Reynerson Quarrel and Political Violence in New Mexico* (1990), Roberts has also had a longtime interest in Wyatt Earp, publishing his first article on Earp in 1960.

JOSEPH G. ROSA has had a lifelong interest in the American West. Inspired by childhood trips to watch old-time western films, he graduated to the factual West, and, following a lengthy "research by airmail," wrote his first book, *They Called Him Wild Bill* (1964). Besides his books on Wild Bill Hickok, he also has published a number of western books, including two studies of the western gunfighter, *The Gunfighter: Man or Myth?* (1969) and *Age of the Gunfighter* (1995). From 1992 to 1997 he was the first non-American president of Westerners International. He is the current president of the English Westerners Society.

GARY TOPPING teaches American history at Salt Lake Community College in Utah. A specialist in the intellectual and cultural history of the West and the history of the Colorado Plateau, his most recent publications include *Glen Canyon and the San Juan Country* (1997) and *Gila Monsters and Red-Eyed Rattlesnakes: Don Maguire's Arizona Trading Expeditions, 1876–1879* (1997).

ELLIOTT WEST, professor of history at the University of Arkansas–Fayetteville, is a specialist in western social history. Two of his five books have received the Western Heritage Award for nonfiction. His latest book is *The Contested Plains: Indians, Goldseekers, and the Rush to Colorado* (1998).

INDEX

(*Note:* Boldface numerals indicate an extended treatment of the subject.)

Wild Women of the Old West

ISBN 1-55591-295-8
60 B/W photos
6 x 9, 256 pages, PB $17.95

Chiefs & Generals
Nine Men Who Shaped the American West

ISBN 1-55591-462-4
35 B/W photos, maps
6 x 9, 256 pages, PB $17.95

By Grit & Grace
Eleven Women Who Shaped the American West

ISBN 1-55591-259-1
37 B/W photos, illustrations
6 x 9, 240 pages, PB $17.95

The Hollywood West
Lives of Film Legends Who Shaped It

ISBN 1-55591-434-9
14 B/W photos
6 x 9, 256 pages, PB $17.95

Fulcrum Publishing
16100 Table Mountain Parkway, Suite 300, Golden , CO 80403
To order call 800-992-2908 or visit www.fulcrum-books.com
Also available at your local bookstore.